MW00575426

Transforming Our World

President George H. W. Bush and American Foreign Policy

Edited by Andrew S. Natsios
and Andrew H. Card Jr.

ROWMAN & LITTLEFIELD
Lanham • Boulder • New York • London

Published by Rowman & Littlefield
An imprint of The Rowman & Littlefield Publishing Group, Inc.
4501 Forbes Boulevard, Suite 200, Lanham, Maryland 20706
www.rowman.com

6 Tinworth Street, London SE11 5AL, United Kingdom

Copyright © 2020 by The Rowman & Littlefield Publishing Group, Inc.

All rights reserved. No part of this book may be reproduced in any form or by any electronic or mechanical means, including information storage and retrieval systems, without written permission from the publisher, except by a reviewer who may quote passages in a review.

British Library Cataloguing in Publication Information Available

Library of Congress Cataloging-in-Publication Data

Names: Natsios, Andrew S., and Card, Andrew H. Jr., editors.
Title: Transforming our world : president George H.W. Bush and American
    foreign policy / edited by Andrew S. Natsios and Andrew H. Card Jr.
Other titles: Transforming our world (Rowman & Littlefield, Inc.)
Description: Lanham, Maryland : Rowman & Littlefield, 2020. | Includes
    bibliographical references and index. | Summary: "This book brings
    together a distinguished collection of foreign policy practitioners–
    career and political–who participated in the unfolding of
    international events as part the Bush administration to provide insider
    perspective by the people charged with carrying them out"—Provided by
    publisher.
Identifiers: LCCN 2020024781 (print) | LCCN 2020024782 (ebook) | ISBN
    9781538143445 (cloth) | ISBN 9781538143452 (epub)
Subjects: LCSH: Bush, George, 1924-2018. | United States—Foreign
    relations—1989–1993. | World politics—1989-
Classification: LCC E881 .T73 2020 (print) | LCC E881 (ebook) | DDC
    327.73009/0511—dc23
LC record available at https://lccn.loc.gov/2020024781
LC ebook record available at https://lccn.loc.gov/2020024782

♾™ The paper used in this publication meets the minimum requirements of American National Standard for Information Sciences—Permanence of Paper for Printed Library Materials, ANSI/NISO Z39.48-1992.

We dedicate this book to President George H. W. Bush and Lieutenant General Brent Scowcroft, who inspired the creation of the Bush School of Government and Public Service at Texas A&M University and institute and continue to shape the aspirations and values of students.

President Bush and National Security Advisor Brent Scowcroft take a walk on the White House grounds. George H. W. Bush Presidential Library and Museum.

Contents

Acknowledgments

This book would not have been possible without the help of Bush School students Katherine Carwile, Steven Weirich, Amanda Satterwhite, and Locky Catron; and Global Main Streets Associates, LLC, employees Katherine Mercer, research associate, and Frank Cerbo, archivist, who assisted the authors in searching the Bush Library archives, checking sources, and researching newspaper articles on the Bush presidency. From the start of the project we had the support and encouragement of the Bush School Dean, Mark Welsh (former chief of staff of the U.S. Air Force). Tyson Voelkel, president of the Texas A&M Foundation, provided important foundation funding for the project. Lauren Zajicek, administrative coordinator of the Scowcroft Institute of International Affairs at the Bush School, managed the various editions of the essays, made sure we all met deadlines, searched the Bush archives for photos, and kept in contact with the authors and their staffs. Nick Lawrence, associate professor of English at the University of South Carolina Lancaster, did yeoman's work getting the manuscript ready for publication. Nancy Bearg and Jean Becker provided sage advice and recommendations on the shape, potential authors, and political sensitivities of the project. My colleague at the Bush School, Dr. Raymond Robertson, read the introduction and made many helpful edits as did Jean Becker, Andy Card, and Nancy Bearg. Dr. Chuck Hermann, the founding director of the Bush School, helped in thinking through the structure of the book and proposed the title in recognition of George Bush and Brent Scowcroft's book *A World Transformed*.

Introduction

Andrew S. Natsios

The Cold War went on for more than forty years. The post–Cold War world that followed has lasted thirty years at most. The era of great power competition has begun, but it remains to be seen what its structure of power will be and how it will shape the threats facing the United States. This book is about the transition during the George H. W. Bush presidency from one international order to another. It is a collection of essays by the practitioners of foreign policy recruited (with one exception) by George H. W. Bush to manage the foreign policy apparatus of the U.S. government during that transition. All the essays are by Americans save one: Horst Teltschik, the national security advisor to German chancellor Helmut Kohl. We thought it important to consider his view of events in order to fully understand the impact of German reunification to the stabilization of the post–Cold War European power structure. Most, but not all, of the nineteen authors who contributed to this book have not written on their subjects before. Some of those chosen by Bush to carry out his foreign policy have since died.[1] Many others are advanced in years, and thus it is important that we capture their memories of events for the historical record before they are lost.

Because of space and time limitations, these essays do not cover all of the accomplishments of the Bush administration in foreign policy. For example, we have not fully covered Bush's successful efforts to end the civil conflicts in Central America or the successful Latin American debt reforms designed by Secretary of the Treasury Nicholas Brady. The Scowcroft Institute at the Bush School of Government at Texas A&M University will cover these in future publications.

Bush's successes were a function of the team of senior advisors and administrators he assembled to manage U.S. foreign affairs; it was arguably one of the most able in the twentieth century. The most important executive function of the president of the United States (other than making the final "big" decisions) is to appoint his own staff in the White House and twelve hundred Senate-confirmed executives to manage the federal government. Since the president's authority in foreign policy is so much greater than in domestic policy, selecting personnel to run the foreign policy apparatus is particularly important. Bush chose his foreign policy team deliberately and carefully, as described by Chase Untermeyer. Bush's national security team, which included Secretary of State James Baker, Deputy Chief of Staff Andy Card, Secretary of Defense Dick Cheney, Deputy National Security Advisor Robert Gates (who Bush later appointed as Director of the CIA), Chairman of the Joint Chiefs Colin Powell, National Security Advisor Brent Scowcroft, Chief of Staff John Sununu, and Vice President Dan Quayle was one of the strongest in the post-War World II period. Philip Zelikow and Condoleezza Rice write about the connection—a virtual mind meld—between Bush and James Baker that Washington heavyweights ignored at their peril. Bush had an equally strong, lasting friendship and professional relationship with Brent Scowcroft. Few of the senior foreign policy makers in the Bush administration either resigned or were fired in the four years he held office, a situation that provided stability and continuity in policy making and execution.[2]

Both Richard Haass and Chase Untermeyer in their essays describe how well prepared George H. W. Bush was for the presidency. He enlisted in the U.S. Navy on his eighteenth birthday, and his service in World War II as a fighter pilot informed his use of U.S. military power while he was president. When he was twenty years old, his plane was shot out of the air during a battle in the Pacific, and his two crewmen—William "Ted" White and John Delaney—died. He once said not one day went by when he did not think of his two crewmates. He wondered why he was spared, and he suffered from what we would now call survivor's remorse, but instead of becoming depressed and dysfunctional, he decided to use his life for a greater purpose. The family values of service and sacrifice—inherited from his parents and grandparents and woven into his personality and worldview—arguably helped him convert survivor's remorse into survivor's service.

George Bush moved to Texas after his service in the war, and his political career is properly associated with that great state. However, he was born, brought up, and educated in New England and is a product of its culture and history. He graduated from Philips Andover Academy, an elite private high school, and Yale University, at a time when Yale still represented the old order of American culture. His father, Prescott Bush, a two-term U.S. senator from Connecticut (1952–1963), was on a list of ten people compiled by President Eisenhower at the end of his term who would make his best successor.[3] So President Bush was not the first Bush to be considered presidential material, or the last. Bush's family history, upbringing, worldview, and values reflect the public service ethos of his family. This ethos held public service, including military service, to be a "noble calling," as Bush himself wrote. He believed it was possible in a country as diverse and complex as the United States to pursue the common good and the public interest; he held suspect violent, radical revolution; he embraced slow incremental change to address public policy problems; and he avoided utopian schemes to supposedly "perfect" human society.

As Chase Untermeyer writes in these pages, George Bush was the first president in 128 years with prior experience as a diplomat. He was also the only president with experience in U.S. intelligence agencies, the last veteran of World War II to serve as president, and the last president to have been injured in combat.

But translating Bush's impressive government experience into electoral success is no longer determinative of how viable a candidate is for the presidency in modern American politics. Under the century-and-a-half-old presidential nominating convention system (as opposed to the current presidential primary process), candidates were expected to have substantial elective or executive experience in government to be taken seriously. The old system was "reformed" away when the McGovern-Fraser Commission was established by the Democrats after their disastrous 1968 convention in Chicago. In its place, a system of binding presidential primaries was created. George H. W. Bush was a throwback to the old electoral system even though he was elected under the new system. Most successful candidates under the old system were former governors, vice presidents, cabinet members, congress members, or generals. Before the current era, two-thirds of the U.S. House of Representatives were former state legislators. A large proportion of the U.S. Senate was made up of former members of the House of Representatives. In my home state of Massachusetts, I once did an informal survey in the late 1970s of the members of the state legislature (where I served for twelve years), and two-thirds were former local officials. Thus we had in place for much of the American Republic's history a career ladder of sorts for public office, a system that produced a series of able leaders who managed the rise of America as a great power.[4] This old system taught policy makers in their early careers the risks of impetuous decisions, the downside of superficially attractive but ultimately imprudent policy options, and the importance of careful execution.

In the case of George Bush, all of his former appointive and elective positions— CIA director, UN ambassador, envoy to China, and vice president—gave him remarkable experience in foreign affairs positions to prepare him for a crucial moment in the remaking of the world order. His election to the presidency in 1988, however, was an aberration given the dysfunctional dynamics of the new presidential nominating process. As Horst Teltschik argues, it was a "stroke of luck" having George H. W. Bush with his diplomatic skills at the helm of the most powerful nation in the world during the process of the reunification of Germany and collapse of the Soviet Empire.

Bush's diplomatic successes are well established, but these essays add detail, nuances of policy, historical interpretation, and anecdotes that have not been recorded until now. We used the Bush archives in his presidential library that sits next to the Bush School of Government and Public Service at Texas A&M to confirm or correct the memories of the sequence of events, provide details of the discussions, and explain the final policy decisions. These essays also correct some misinterpretations by others of the Bush record. For example, Zelikow and Rice note that there was never really a so-called "pause" in 1989, as many historians have argued, while the administration developed policy on how to deal with the changes in the Soviet Union.

4 *Introduction*

Bush and Baker had already formulated the outlines of what the United States would do on Soviet policy and had begun to implement it, which the president publicly described in a speech at Texas A&M University in March 1989.

The very decisions Bush was attacked for at the time by liberal internationalists on the left and neoconservatives on the right have turned out to be the wisest and most prudent decisions. Bush's refusal to endorse Ukraine's independence movement—for which he was widely criticized—was a consequence of intelligence reports that a coup attempt against Gorbachev might be orchestrated by the old order in the Kremlin.[5] Had Bush pressed for Ukrainian (and other parts of the Soviet Union) independence, the coup attempt that eventually did take place later against Gorbachev might well have succeeded earlier and a reactionary cabal reasserted control in the Soviet Union, which would have ended Bush's efforts at remaking the international order.[6]

Bush was not a gifted public speaker and much better in one-to-one interactions than on television. He preferred action to rhetoric and thus followed Theodore Roosevelt's admonition (from a West African tribal chief) "Speak softly and carry a big stick," to which he added by his own action—the Bush corollary "and use it when necessary." While Ronald Reagan is credited with a muscular foreign policy, in fact Bush *successfully* initiated U.S. military intervention using ground forces more than any other president in decades, including Panama, Kuwait, Northern Iraq, and Somalia. Bush disliked speaking loudly and even less carrying an emaciated twig; he believed in a strong military and was prepared to use it with overwhelming force. Bush avoided making idle threats or drawing unenforceable red lines because it would have destroyed U.S. credibility. Jim Baker put it well years later when he said, "If you're not going to pull the trigger, don't point the gun."[7]

Woven through these essays is a fundamental insight about the interconnected nature of action in foreign relations. Bush knew from his experience that all important actions in diplomacy, particularly with globalized communications, are connected with each other. Major actions in international diplomacy often produce second-, third-, and fourth-order consequences that, if not considered very carefully ahead of a decision, can have unintended effects. In a world with nine countries with nuclear weapons, one mistake could be catastrophic. Bush, Baker, and Scowcroft were constantly calculating the effect of one move on all other moves on the diplomatic chessboard. All three of them understood that change was not always for the better. Scowcroft once said that some might see "light at the end of the tunnel," but he wasn't sure "if it was the sun or an incoming locomotive."[8] Jeffrey Engel, in his fine book *When the World Seemed New: George Bush and the End of the Cold War*, described Bush's approach to the crises cascading across the world as "Hippocratic Diplomacy" as he sought to avoid making any crises worse by imprudent actions.

Bush understood the value of international diplomacy. For example, he knew that as permanent members, China and Russia each had veto power over any resolution before the UN Security Council and that he might need their support in the future on a critical vote. Thus, he tried to keep communications open with them even during times of great tension, such as after the Tiananmen Square bloodshed. Douglas

Paal, in his essay on Bush and China, relates that Bush understood that China's relationship with the United States (and Russia) would indirectly affect the vote in the U.S. Congress on the liberation of Kuwait. Congressional approval would lower the domestic backlash to military action (even though we know from Bush's diaries that he intended to proceed or without congressional approval if necessary). As described by Robert Kimmitt in his essay, Bush knew getting UN Security Council approval to use military force to liberate Kuwait from Saddam Hussein would influence the U.S. Congress vote on the war resolution, at least for liberal internationalists. Bush also knew that Security Council approval would make it much easier to recruit other countries into the U.S.-led military coalition.

Bush's own temperament facilitated his style of diplomacy. He was a gentleman, which his critics mistakenly confused with being weak (the so-called "wimp" factor). His good manners, dignity, and polite demeanor were disarming and encouraged trust from those he was negotiating with. As Jean Becker reports, he cultivated personal relationships in good times with foreign leaders before, while, and after he was president, which proved very useful during difficult times. While countries usually act in their own interests, sometimes they do not know those interests, and having a respected American president they knew personally might help them in making decisions. Horst Teltschik writes that Gorbachev told him that had he not trusted George Bush and Helmut Kohl, events could have turned out very differently, and not for the better. Ambassador Edward Djerejian's chapter on Bush's recruitment of Hafez al-Assad, president of Syria, to get Syria to join the coalition to liberate Kuwait is a case study in this meticulous effort. In his chapter, Ambassador Dennis Ross details Bush's prudent policy in the Middle East, which was a direct result of his relationships with regional leaders, including King Fahd of Saudi Arabia, President Hosni Mubarak of Egypt, and King Hussein of Jordan. Bush was an attentive listener, always well briefed, and had an acute understanding of the character and personality of other foreign leaders. He put himself in other people's shoes to understand how far to push foreign leaders without forcing them to commit political suicide.

While hard-right populist conservatives have often held Bush ideologically suspect, his record reflects the political philosophy of Edmund Burke (the eighteenth-century British political philosopher and parliamentarian) more than any other president in post–World War II American politics. Burke founded the modern conservative movement.[9] Russell Kirk (Burke's greatest twentieth-century expositor) wrote: "A statesman's chief virtue, according to Plato and Burke, is prudence."[10] Bush himself used the word "prudence" to describe his manner of decision-making and of leadership. Burke also believed that healthy institutions were central to a stable and civilized nation. In his greatest work, *Reflections on the Revolution in France*, Burke defended the British political system with its emphasis on gradual incremental change to preserve, reform, and protect British institutions rather than the French model, which systemically destroyed institutions in the blood-drenched chaos of the French Revolution.

By worldview and disposition, George Bush was an institution builder and protector. Institutions are what distinguish weak, unstable, and dysfunctional countries (and international organizations) from strong, resilient, and enduring ones. Institutions count and they count a great deal. Douglass North, the father of institutional economics, has argued that institutions are what order the human landscape. The number, legitimacy, effectiveness, resilience, and dynamism of American institutions have been its greatest strengths over the past 225 years. Bush understood and internalized this better than most presidents. When he was the Republican National Committee chair (January 1973–September 1974), he gave a speech in Boston, Massachusetts, to party leaders and workers about the fundamental importance of American institutions to the stability, vitality, and strength of the country. He said in his talk that American institutions were under severe attack and this was hurting the country. The audience was surprised by the speech because it was not the kind of talk a party chair would give, but Bush obviously felt strongly about the subject.[11]

After he had given a talk at the Bush School, I asked Tony Mendez, a senior CIA operations officer (played by Ben Affleck in the 2012 movie *Argo*), who had rescued six American diplomats from Tehran during the hostage crisis, "Who was the greatest CIA director since its founding in 1947?" Without hesitation, he answered George H. W. Bush, which is why Mendez said the CIA Headquarters bears his name today. I responded that he answered that way because he was speaking at the Bush School; he replied without missing a beat, "That would be the answer most CIA officers would give, because it was Bush who saved the agency from being torn apart or, worse, abolished by Congress during the investigations of the 1970s."

According to Zelikow and Rice, during the critical negotiations on the reunification of Germany, the one central and unalterable position of President Bush was the inclusion of a unified Germany in NATO, the central institution protecting Europe from Soviet expansionism during the Cold War and avoiding another European war. The preservation of NATO was central to Bush's worldview because he knew from his own service during World War II the devastation that war caused across half the globe.

Brent Scowcroft's reforms of the National Security Council as an institution, described by Jane Holl Lute in her chapter, were carried out with the president's support and encouragement. The reforms had come out of the Tower Commission report, which was written by three people, including Scowcroft. The Commission was created to review the Iran-Contra controversy and propose reforms to better order the policy process. These reforms remain the model for the management of the interagency process: when they are ignored, bad policy has often been followed by flawed execution, leading to foreign policy mistakes or disasters.

The greatest challenge in public policy is not in the policy making itself so much as the execution of it. While Americans would say that the devil is in the details, an old Hungarian saying is that the "angel is in the details." If one were to carefully analyze the amount of time and effort presidents spend in policy making versus its implementation, I suspect the George H. W. Bush administration, more than any other in the post–World War II period, would be the most heavily weighted in the time and effort spent in the execution phase. This is why he had so many successes and so few failures.

Bush understood that the use of what is now called "soft power" was as important to American leadership in the world as hard power, which is why Bush valued the State Department and U.S. Agency for International Development's foreign aid programs. Chase Untermeyer reports that Bush named proportionally more career diplomats to ambassadorships than any recent president of either party. Bush carried out foreign policy through the State Department, not around it, even though he knew the weaknesses of the department. When he asked the department for a policy review to deal with a changing security situation in Europe, he received a set of recommendations that changed little, so he constructed his own set of options with Baker and Scowcroft.

On March 18, 1989, two months after taking office and one month after the last Soviet troops withdrew from Afghanistan, Bush signed an Executive Order (No. 5) ordering the U.S. Agency for International Development to draft legislation to authorize humanitarian and reconstruction assistance to the country: "AID should take the lead to develop, submit, and manage the legislation. The other departments and agencies should support AID as required."[12] This was the beginning of the post–Cold War era of whole-government approaches to development of assistance programs, but it was under the leadership of a single agency, AID. AID drafted the legislation, which passed the House with Congressman Dante Fascell's strong support but was held up by Senate Republicans, which Bush over time resolved.[13] Congress did eventually approve the program, with funding of between $60 and $100 million a year ($118 million and $177 million in 2019 dollars) from 1989 through 1993. It involved a cross-border program of humanitarian relief, food aid, education, health and agricultural services, and the repair of the road system.[14] The AID program used the seven-party alliance system of the Afghan Interim Government to involve local decision-makers, but the civil war with the Taliban destroyed much of the progress made by the program.

In November 1989, Bush signed the SEED law, the East European Democracy Act. In early 1990, this act began a foreign aid program to extend constitutional democracy, free markets and investments, and bring the rule of law and the protection of human rights into Poland and Hungary, both of which had begun the process of reform earlier than other Communist Bloc countries.

On October 24, 1992, Bush signed the Freedom Support Act to provide assistance to the states of the former Soviet Union, including Russia, having asked Senator Clayborn Pell (D-RI) to introduce the legislation on April 7, 1992. While Bush pushed the Freedom Support Act through Congress, he was reluctant to offer aid to the Soviet Union itself until Gorbachev presented a specific plan for economic reforms. Gorbachev, however, wanted the aid program before offering a serious plan for economic reform. Germany had provided generous aid packages to Gorbachev, which prevented bankruptcy, but none of this aid brought reform any closer. Bush's skepticism was, thus, well founded.[15]

Humanitarianism was also a focus of Bush's foreign policy. Bush's worldview, values, and family culture grew out of the notion of noblesse oblige, though he would not have used that term. He believed that to those whom "much is given, much will be required."[16] Since America had been given so much, much was required of it. The chapters on Bush's humanitarian leadership by Dayton Maxwell, Andrew Natsios, and James Kunder document, respectively, U.S. intervention among the Kurds in northern Iraq in 1991 and in Somalia's civil war and famine in 1992, which created new precedents for humanitarian response in protracted emergencies. Alex de Waal, one of the great famine scholars, studied famine deaths over a 150-year period in his recent book *Mass Starvation*. His research documents a significant decline in famine mortality since the mid-1980s, which he not only attributes to globalization, rising incomes, and the end of totalitarian regimes, but also to the evolution of the international humanitarian response system to which Bush lent his strong support and leadership, described by Nancy Bearg and Catherine Bertini in their essays.

As Zelikow and Rice have written, that the collapse of the Soviet Empire did not precipitate another international war between 1989 and 1992 was not a matter of random good fortune; it happened because the leaders of the two superpowers at the time—George Bush and Mikhail Gorbachev—made choices that allowed a peaceful transition. Robert Gates once wrote that George Bush greased the skids so that communism in Eastern Europe could slide peacefully into history, which is exactly what Bush also did for the Soviet Empire.[17] This serves as tribute to his prudent judgement, attention to diplomatic detail, and careful management of the foreign policy apparatus of U.S. government.

Virtually Bush's entire public career was devoted to slow and careful incremental reforms to open and stabilize free markets, to improve the National Security Council policy-making process, and to make the UN system more effective, as described in these pages by Ambassador Thomas Pickering, Catherine Bertini, and Nancy Bearg. These reforms to open markets and make the United States more competitive included the North American Free Trade Agreement (NAFTA) described by Carla Hills in her essay, the Maritime Reforms, the Brady Plan on Latin American debt relief mentioned earlier, and the Open Skies Agreement. Bush consistently and aggressively sought to preserve the NATO Alliance—which he had inherited from his eight predecessors—during the transformation of the European security system as the Soviet Union and the Warsaw Pact collapsed.

One aspect of NAFTA that is little understood today is that it profoundly changed the relationship between Mexico and the United States, not just economically but also geostrategically. This was no accident, as President Bush intended to change U.S.–Mexico relations into the distant future.[18] Mexico had been broadly hostile to U.S. political and strategic interests since the mid-nineteenth century. Now with the U.S. and Mexican economies tied so intimately with each other, Mexico has subtly adjusted its foreign policy over several decades to align more closely its national interests with those of the United States. Mexico in turn has benefited by having its national income increase by 40 percent, while the United States has benefited by having a much more cooperative relationship with its southern neighbor.

All this is not to suggest that Bush made no mistakes. But his mistakes or failures in foreign affairs were in choosing not to act when action might have been the better choice, which was a function of his prudential sense of presidential restraint. He should have intervened earlier in Panama when a coup attempt was underway to remove Manuel Noriega from office, but he corrected his mistake in late December 1989 when he successfully sent in U.S. troops to take out Noriega. Bush and Baker left the Europeans to resolve the breakup of Yugoslavia and subsequent Bosnian civil war, which they were unprepared, and perhaps incapable, of doing without the United States. These failures of omission were, perhaps, understandable given the rolling crisis spreading across the globe, which Bush did successfully resolve. As James Baker suggests in the first essay in this book, there are limits to what the United States can do.

Richard Haass argues persuasively in his essay that George H. W. Bush ranks with Harry Truman as the two greatest foreign policy presidents in the post–World War II period. Both presided over the collapse of the old order and the construction of a new international order, both made critically important decisions that turned out to be right, and both were guided by a sense of pragmatism and realism that saw the world as it was, not as they wished it to be. After his presidency, as described by Jean Becker, George Bush created the Bush School of Government and Public Service at Texas A&M University. President Bush often said that the Bush School would be his most lasting legacy. In the end, George Bush left all of the institutions he led or created greater than he found them.

This book of essays should be a reminder that the president who most embodied the old values and ideals in the modern era was the preeminent establishment Republican, George H. W. Bush, whose successes in managing a turbulent period in the international system are now being broadly acknowledged even by his former critics. It may be time to reflect on what we have lost and might cultivate again.

Scowcroft Institute of International Affairs
The Bush School of Government and Public Service
Texas A&M University

NOTES

1. Arnold Kanter, James Lilley, Richard Solomon, Larry Eagleburger, Admiral David Jeremiah, Princeton Lyman, Julia Taft, Peter Rodman, and General Norman Schwarzkopf have passed away, to name a few.

2. William Webster, the director of Central Intelligence, who retired from that post in 1991, was one of few senior foreign policy executives who left the Bush administration. He was succeeded by Robert Gates.

3. Eisenhower's list is part of the Bush Museum display at the Presidential Library.

4. Nelson Polsby published his extraordinary study *The Consequences of Party Reform* (Berkeley, CA: Institute of Government Studies Press, 1982), on the damaging effects these reforms had on the American political system.

5. Jeffrey A. Engel, *When the World Seemed New: George H. W. Bush and the End of the Cold War* (Boston: Mariner Books/Houghton Mifflin Harcourt, 2018), 451–54.

6. I was told as the director of the Office of Foreign Disaster Assistance in USAID by the Office of Soviet Affairs in the State Department that they were worried about a potential coup by the old order in Moscow against Gorbachev.

7. See Baker's remarks at the 1996 GOP Presidential Nominating Convention at: https://www.cnn.com/ALLPOLITICS/1996/conventions/san.diego/transcripts/0814/baker.fdch.shtml.

8. ABC News, *World News Tonight*, Sunday, January 22, 1989.

9. See Russell Kirk, *The Conservative Mind From Burke to Eliot*, 7th ed. (Washington, DC: Regnery Publishing, 1985).

10. Ibid., 9.

11. Interview with Andy Card on February 11, 2020. He attended the meeting where Bush gave the talk.

12. National Security Directive 5, March 18, 1989, https://fas.org/irp/offdocs/nsd/nsd5.pdf.

13. H.R.2655—International Cooperation Act of 1989, https://www.congress.gov/bill/101st-congress/house-bill/2655/all-actions?overview=closed#tabs.

14. See Asger Christensen, *Aiding Afghanistan: The Background and Prospects for Reconstruction of a Fragmented Society* (Copenhagen: Nordic Institute of Asian Studies, 1995), 129.

15. See USAID, *20 Years of USAID Economic Growth Assistance in Europe and Eurasia* (Washington, DC: USAID, 2013), https://www.usaid.gov/where-we-work/europe-and-eurasia/20-years-economic-growth-assistance.

16. Luke 12:48.

17. See Robert Gates, *From the Shadows: The Ultimate Insider's Story of Five Presidents and How They Won the Cold War* (New York: Simon & Schuster, 2007).

18. For a full description of the potential political and geostrategic consequences of NAFTA, see M. Delal Baer, "North American Free Trade," *Foreign Affairs* 70, no. 4 (Fall 1991): 132–49.

1

Ten Foreign Policy Maxims of a
Great President

James A. Baker III

When George H. W. Bush was sworn in as the forty-first president of the United States on January 20, 1989, he inherited a world that was poised for great opportunities and fraught with tremendous risk. Mankind was witnessing a seismic shift in the global landscape as people weary of authoritarian rule began a push for freedom. Between July and November of that year, human rights protests hopscotched from Tiananmen Square in China to the streets of Poland and other Warsaw Pact countries and finally to the Berlin Wall that divided East and West Germany. As the "Freedom Genie" escaped the lamp, civil disobedience was shaking the foundations of autocratic governments and leaders.

Perhaps no one was affected by this phenomenon more than Soviet president Mikhail Gorbachev. Already trying to dramatically alter the direction of his country against hardline domestic opposition to glasnost and perestroika, Gorbachev also had the complex task of keeping together a faltering economy. As his domestic problems mounted, the 1989 revolutions in Poland, Hungary, East Germany, Bulgaria, Czechoslovakia, and Romania heaped even more strain on the man in Moscow who had his finger on the nuclear button. George and Barbara Bush moved into the White House with the new president fully anticipating both the challenges and opportunities facing the United States and the world. During his first State of the Union address twenty days later, he talked about that moment as "a time of extraordinary hope," saying "Never before in this century have our values of freedom, democracy, and economic opportunity been such a powerful and intellectual force around the globe. Never before has our leadership been so crucial, because while America has its eyes on the future, the world has its eyes on America."

Indeed, all eyes were on America and its new president to see if he was ready for the job. And he was. No one came into the Oval Office better prepared for such complex foreign policy challenges than President Bush. A decorated World War

II navy pilot, he later served two terms as a congressman from Houston. He was the U.S. ambassador to the United Nations, America's de facto ambassador to the People's Republic of China, and director of the Central Intelligence Agency. Finally, his two terms as vice president had allowed him to participate in all National Security Council meetings. It was as if he had spent his entire life getting ready for the next four years.

President Bush had another advantage—a thorough understanding about how the nation's foreign policy apparatus could operate effectively. As others have noted, he assembled a strong-willed team of foreign policy advisors who were extremely loyal yet also empowered to speak honestly to their president and not spare him the truth. That team included Dick Cheney as secretary of defense, Brent Scowcroft as national security advisor, and me as secretary of state. We had all worked together in prior administrations and knew how to settle most of our differences without needing the Oval Office to referee.

Above all, President Bush understood the importance of America's leadership on the world stage. He recognized that a large component of American strength was being champion of a liberal world order that revolved around open markets, multilateral institutions, and liberal democracy. Allies mattered, and Pax Americana was his lodestar. American strength, however, was not limitless. At the time President Bush took office, America had the world's strongest economy, best military, and most effective alliances. Still, the Soviet Union remained a decided nuclear threat, as it had been for most his adult life.

Like his Cold War predecessors, however, the president recognized that Americans had something the Soviets didn't have—an ideology based on free market democracy. As the arc of history was tilting toward freedom, he believed the United States should be the role model for people suffering under totalitarian regimes in the Soviet Empire and elsewhere. As a result, President Bush had a clear-eyed view of America's role in world affairs. "We must continue to be freedom's best friend" he said at that first State of the Union address, adding that, under his guidance, the United States would serve "as solid a force for peace as the world has ever known." In the ensuing years, the Bush administration built strong diplomatic relations with the Soviet Union and negotiated the mother of all soft landings—the reunification of Germany inside NATO, freedom for the countries of the Soviet Bloc, and the peaceful breakup of the Soviet Union itself. Along the way, President Bush negotiated nuclear arms reduction treaties that greatly lessened the decades-longer specter of global annihilation.

As we reflect on the role President Bush played during his four years as president, it is instructive to remember ten maxims that guided his foreign policy. They not only permitted him to manage the peaceful end of the Cold War; they are also timeless reminders of how all presidents should practice international affairs.

First, President Bush understood the importance of bipartisan domestic support for his foreign policy. The policies of a president will eventually wither unless the White House has the backing of the American people. Absent such support, a president can quickly become a lame duck. With that in mind, President Bush wanted to move away from the politics of confrontation between the White House and Congress that had characterized much of the foreign policy debate of the previous eight years.

One of his first forays into foreign policy was to resolve the domestic dispute over the wars in Central America, an issue that sharply divided the left and the right in the United States. He negotiated a bipartisan accord on Central America, an agreement between Republicans and Democrats calling for an election that both sides in Nicaragua would pledge to respect. When the Sandinistas were voted out of power, they honored the elections results. Thus concluded a contentious domestic battle that had separated Americans for far too long.

Second, although Americans should encourage and support democracy and freedom in other countries, President Bush understood that we cannot force these values upon them. Yes, self-determination is a dynamic force that greatly benefits countries that practice it. History has demonstrated that democracies tend to have stronger economies than nondemocratic ones. And democracies engage in war with each other at lower rates than authoritarian governments. But President Bush believed that democracy best works if the people of a captive nation yearn for it and are willing to struggle and even fight for it, if necessary. Trying to impose democracy on a people resistant to that concept is a proposition fraught with pitfalls.

Third, President Bush appreciated the importance of allies and international support. After all, he had taken part in two of the three great global conflagrations of the twentieth century, first as a navy pilot in World War II and then as a U.S. official during much of the Cold War. Both of those conflicts, as well as World War I before them, were won by coalitions.

Knowing history, President Bush rejected domestic and international pressure to respond precipitously to the 1990 invasion of Kuwait by Iraq. Instead, he methodically sought and received a UN Security Council resolution authorizing the use of all necessary means to eject Iraqi troops from Kuwait. He then cobbled together a military coalition that included the United States, United Kingdom, France, even many Arab nations, and others. Not only did the coalition provide military and financial assistance, the fact that its actions were sanctioned by the UN Security Council gave those actions international legitimacy.

Fourth, an American president must be comfortable using the nation's power. During his life, President Bush had come to appreciate that in all global conflicts of the twentieth century, the United States played a historic role in defeating imperialism and totalitarianism. He also knew that if he did not exercise American power, then other countries would be eager to fill the power vacuum that would exist in our absence. Though he was prudent in exercising America's military force, the world understood his resolve when he responded to the August 1990 invasion of Iraqi troops into Kuwait by saying, "This will not stand, this aggression against Kuwait." Less than six months later, seven hundred thousand American troops joined two hundred fifty thousand troops from other countries to win the First Gulf War to liberate Kuwait.

Fifth, personal relationships matter. After the Berlin Wall fell, President Bush immediately went into full gear to take the next and much more monumental step of reuniting East and West Germany. He did so despite hesitancy and misgiving on the part of the other three occupying powers that had a say over Germany's future—the Soviet Union, the United Kingdom, and France. All were wary of reunification. In fact, all of Europe was wary of the prospect of a strong and united Germany—a country that had started two horrific world wars during the twentieth century.

President Bush ultimately overcame those international concerns. He understood the importance of trust between world leaders. He had developed strong relations with Soviet president Mikhail Gorbachev, British prime minister Margaret Thatcher, and French president François Mitterrand. Each of them trusted the president as a leader who kept his word. They also recognized that Bush would search for pragmatic solutions that would ease their concerns rather than ignore them.

Sixth, President Bush was a shrewd negotiator who understood the importance of timing. As the country-western song goes, he knew when to hold them and when to fold them. After the Gulf War, I sensed that the time was right to ramp up Arab-Israeli peace talks. As the Soviet Union was imploding, we were heading from a bipolar world that had been divided by old Cold War rivalries to a new unipolar world led by the United States. Further, American stature across the Middle East was at an all-time high after the Gulf War, and by dealing forcefully and effectively with Saddam Hussein, we had strong credibility with both Israel and many Arab nations. President Bush agreed that the timing was right for a peace initiative. He allowed me to begin negotiations that would lead to the Madrid Peace Conference, the first time Israel and all its Arab neighbors sat together to discuss peace.

Seventh, President Bush was prepared to alter his course if the circumstances demanded it. Consistency, of course, is an important element of foreign policy. It permits officials to move beyond crisis management and facilitates the development of long-term strategies. Consistency can also foster stability by reassuring allies and setting down clear markers for potential adversaries. But when events changed, President Bush was prepared to change with them. The rise of Mikhail Gorbachev in the Soviet Union, for instance, marked a dramatic shift in the worldview of the Soviet leadership. It was therefore only right that President Bush reach out to Moscow in ways unimaginable just years before.

Eighth, President Bush recognized and accepted that the United States sometimes had to deal with authoritarian regimes. In a perfect world, he could have worked only with other democracies. Unfortunately, this is not a perfect world. And so President Bush had to work with governments that fell short when it came to democratic practices and protection of human rights.

That tension was apparent as the Chinese government slew thousands of protesters in Tiananmen Square. President Bush joined with Congress to sanction the Chinese government for this assault on freedom. It was, after all, important that China and the world know where the United States stood with respect to the human rights abuses. At the same time, however, President Bush understood the importance of maintaining a relationship with China. He sent high-level emissaries to Beijing to reassure Chinese leaders that, despite the criticism from the United States, the White House still wanted to maintain a relationship with China.

Ninth, President Bush was prepared to talk with America's enemies. After all, he theorized, you don't make peace with your friends; you make peace with your adversaries. He knew that dialogue not only helped avoid misunderstandings and missteps, it also offered the prospects of reaching agreements. That was why we maintained an embassy in Moscow throughout the Cold War. And it was why Bush was prepared to negotiate with the Soviets. Talking to hostile states was not "appeasement," it was good foreign policy, and it remains so today.

And *tenth*, President Bush recognized that even U.S. power is limited. He understood that his country could not serve as the police force of the world. As strong as America was, it could not solve every problem around the globe. That was a reason he rightfully refused to permit U.S. troops to occupy all of Iraq and change the regime of Saddam Hussein at the end of the Gulf War. There were other reasons, as well. Doing so would have splintered the coalition that had just fought the war. In addition, it would have made a martyr out of Saddam Hussein.

There was another practical reason that President Bush did not want to occupy all of Iraq. That country's military had been virtually obliterated, leaving Hussein extremely weakened. Absent strong central authority, the president worried that Iraq might splinter into warring factions. If that were to happen, he believed that U.S. troops would have to remain in Iraq for a long time to resolve problems left behind. Still, for more than a decade after the war, President Bush heard criticism that he had made a mistake in not going to Baghdad. People stopped making that observation when President Bush's caution was vindicated by the grim experience of the Iraq War of 2003 and the subsequent civil war between Shia and Sunni, which opened the door for greater Iranian influence there.

Four years after he took office, the world President Bush left behind was markedly different from the one he had inherited. Instead of battling the forty-five-year Cold War, a "new world order" the president had foreseen was coming to fruition, one in which Pax Americana would prevail. He encapsulated his vision for that new order in the farewell speech he made at West Point on January 5, 1993: "Our objective," he said, "must be to exploit the unparalleled opportunity presented by the Cold War's end to work toward transforming this new world into a new world order, one of governments that are democratic, tolerant, and economically free at home and committed abroad to settling inevitable differences peacefully, without the threat or use of force."

Indeed, what followed was a dramatic shift in the global balance of power as the United States emerged as leader of a unipolar world. Absent the tension of the Cold War, there was a sense that collective efforts could address worldwide problems. International trade exploded. Europe became united after being separated since the end of World War II. The United States and Russia built diplomatic, business, and

cultural relationships that lasted well into the next century. The number of democracies almost doubled from fifty-one in 1989 to one hundred in 2009. For another
fifteen years or so, the possibilities seemed endless.

But, as always, history happens—and so it has. Almost three decades after President Bush left office, we have entered a new period of world history in which this
nation's stature on the global stage has become greatly diminished. American resolve
is being tested at home and abroad, particularly in the face of the emergence of
China as a global powerhouse. Bonds between traditional allies have become frayed
as nationalistic movements are sprouting up in the United States and elsewhere. We
are once again in a Cold War with Russia. And amid this changing world, political
discourse in America has become so polarized that it's almost impossible for our
elected leaders to get anything done.

Yes, it's a vastly different world from the one President Bush inherited in 1989.
The nation faces new challenges that demand new solutions. But the approach to
foreign policy practiced by President Bush is as vital to our national security today as
it was when he was in the White House. His pragmatic approach favored real-world
solutions to high-minded rhetoric and sought bipartisan deal making over politically
charged squabbling. Most importantly, it understood that America's active engagement in the world is critical to global stability. The adroit foreign policy practiced by
President Bush during that impressive time of global transformation is a reason he is
considered a great American leader and the very best one-term president of all time.
The foreign policy of President George H. W. Bush was—and remains—the gold
standard for all presidents seeking to maintain our nation's greatness.

2

The Compassionate Realist

An Overview

Richard Haass

The forty-first president, George H. W. Bush, was the last of the post–World War II presidents who was of World War II.[1] He was born a generation before it, fought and came of age in it, and, from a base in Texas, pursued a career in business and politics after it. He did not become president until nearly half a century more had passed, but he was very much a man of that war and the world it brought into being.

Bush was an unapologetic internationalist, someone who firmly held that American leadership was essential to building order, that the United Nations and multilateral institutions had an important role to play in promoting stability, and that America's network of alliances in Europe and Asia undergirded that stability. He also believed that free trade was the best way to promote prosperity for Americans, saw the necessity of maintaining a strong military along with a willingness to use it if need be, and appreciated the advantages of democracy and capitalism. He rejected the isolationism that had characterized American foreign policy in the run-up to World War II and likewise the protectionism and appeasement that characterized much of the interwar period. In all of this, he reflected, or better yet embodied, the essence of post–World War II American foreign policy.

Bush was as well an optimist, someone who embraced the notion that men and women of good faith could find common ground. He was temperamentally moderate and uncomfortable with ideology. He was much more a pragmatist than a visionary. While a proud Republican, he was not overly partisan; to the contrary, and even though he had served as chair of the Republican National Committee, he was comfortable working with Democrats.

Bush entered the Oval Office in 1989 more prepared to contend with foreign policy challenges than most of his post–World War II predecessors. A former U.S. envoy to China, permanent representative to the United Nations, director of Central Intelligence, and vice president, he brought far more knowledge of and experience with the world to the job than any of his successors would. It was no coincidence that he was the last American president elected during the Cold War, when foreign policy credentials conferred an advantage on anyone seeking the highest office in the land.

This background mostly served Bush well, as during his four years in the White House international developments frequently challenged his administration. What stands out most was his deft and to this day underappreciated handling of the Cold War's end, his stewardship of the bilateral relationship with China, and his measured but firm response to a blatant act of aggression in the Persian Gulf. Bush also resolved the domestic chasm that had bedeviled U.S. policy toward Central America for a decade, negotiated the North American Free Trade Agreement with Canada and Mexico that would later be signed and implemented under Bill Clinton, and convened the first ever face-to-face peace talks between Israel and its Arab neighbors. Bush also hammered out a budget agreement that, while not a foreign policy matter per se, had significant implications for national security, and while it cost Bush politically, it was a price he was willing to pay to place the government on a sustainable and responsible fiscal trajectory.

This is not to suggest that the forty-first president got everything right in the realm of foreign policy. For much of 1989, Bush struggled to come up with an effective policy for Panama, then led by Manuel Noriega, a drug-running strongman. Bush also came up against a number of other messy situations, including in Iraq after the liberation of Kuwait in 1991 and the former Yugoslavia in 1992. What these situations had in common was that they tended to involve increasingly dysfunctional and often violent conditions within countries rather than between them. The scenarios thus largely fell outside the purview of traditional diplomacy. Bush wanted to do good but was wary of devoting large American resources that were not justified by the U.S. interests at stake. He chose to act decisively in Panama, sending twenty thousand soldiers and midwifing a political succession, something that could be accomplished with relative ease given the lack of organized opposition and widespread local sympathy toward the United States. Similar conditions were not present in either Iraq or the former Yugoslavia, and he was criticized in both cases, mostly for what he did not do. Again, though, he got the biggest things right and as a result deserves high marks for his oversight of U.S. foreign policy at a critical juncture in modern history.

It should be added that Bush did well not just because of his own experience and judgment but also because of how he organized and staffed the machinery by which policy was formulated and carried out. The National Security Act of 1947 created a system on paper for making and implementing foreign and defense policy but had little to say about how it would work in practice. Different presidents, beginning with Harry Truman, chose different approaches with widely varying results.[2] Bush came to the job with considerable familiarity with the system and thus with strong views as to what he needed in the way of process and people alike. He aimed to thread the needle: more hands-on than Ronald Reagan, less of a micromanager than Jimmy Carter.

Two appointments proved central to Bush's foreign policy. The first was James A. Baker, the secretary of state.[3] Baker was first among equals. He had uncommon abilities as a negotiator and a rare ability to discern talent in others. Baker also had the necessary authority to do the job owing to his long-standing personal relationship with the president. People at home and abroad understood that when Baker spoke and acted, he did so with presidential backing.

Baker was the principal public voice of the administration's foreign policy, something agreed on from the outset. One result was that the tension or, worse yet, split between the State Department and the White House that at times emerged in other administrations rarely happened. It helped as well that others at the most senior level (including Dick Cheney at Defense, Colin Powell as chairman of the Joint Chiefs of Staff, William Webster at the CIA, and Nicholas Brady at Treasury), along with many who toiled below them, were experienced, capable, and in many instances familiar with one another from previous stints in government. Bush himself set the tone and example. He mostly depended on the formal process and avoided a culture of end-runs and leaks.

No less central was Brent Scowcroft,[4] who had previously held the job of national security advisor (under President Gerald Ford) and who proved to be better than anyone before or since at balancing the job's twin mandates of counselor to the president and honest broker, the guarantor of due process. It worked not because Scowcroft lacked strong views of his own, which he most decidedly did not, but because Scowcroft possessed the discipline and character not to allow his own preferences to get in the way of his job. Scowcroft ensured that the president heard from those who held other views, and that once the president made his decision his preferred policy was implemented, even if it was not the policy he, Scowcroft, preferred. It also worked because Bush and Scowcroft, who began the administration with a relatively modest personal connection, grew increasingly close over the following years.

Scowcroft headed a National Security Council (NSC) staff possessing several strengths. It was small in number (just a fraction of the size of the NSC staffs built by his successors), which meant it needed to work with the departments and agencies rather than try to substitute for them. Second, following on the guidance issued by the Tower Commission, established in the wake of the Iran-Contra scandal and on which Scowcroft had served, there was no appetite for an operational role. The NSC and those who served on it were there to coordinate and advise rather than implement policy. Third, many on the NSC staff, like Scowcroft, were scholar-practitioners, able to produce original thinking and oversee an interagency process. Scowcroft put into place a structured process, introducing the principals committee, where cabinet-level officials would meet without the president, something that encouraged more open debate and preserved the president's time. It helped too that in Bob Gates had a deputy who had the standing and the skill to oversee the deputies committee level and make sure the principals were well served and that implementation was disciplined.

I describe the forty-first president (and so name this chapter) as a compassionate realist. The description is not quite an oxymoron, but it does link two words and two foreign policy traditions rarely combined. *Realism* is used here not as a theory of international relations but rather as an approach to foreign policy that focuses on efforts to shape the foreign policies of other countries more than their internal nature. Such an approach to foreign policy stands in contrast to those, including such presidents as Woodrow Wilson, Ronald Reagan, Jimmy Carter, and George W. Bush, who tended to see the promotion of human rights and democracy as central or even paramount. It is as well different from an emphasis on alleviating humanitarian crises, which some presidents have chosen to focus on (Bill Clinton comes to mind), or promoting U.S. economic interests (Donald Trump). Realism is the foreign policy most associated with individuals such as Hans Morgenthau, George Kennan, and Henry Kissinger and presidents such as Harry Truman, Dwight Eisenhower, Richard Nixon, and Gerald Ford.[5]

Bush's realism, though, was not absolute. It was tempered by compassion, more than a little idealism, and a concern for human rights and human life itself. He was willing in specific circumstances to act on these concerns. This in part explains his determination not to allow Iraqi aggression against Kuwait to stand unopposed. As a realist, Bush was concerned that if Saddam Hussein's invasion of Kuwait stood, it would alter the balance of power in the Middle East, set a dangerous precedent for world order, and threaten the availability of oil. As a compassionate realist, he was also concerned by reports of torture and Kuwaiti children being left to die so that hospital equipment could be removed and sent to Iraq. This duality also partly explains the Panama invasion and the lengths the president went to in order to protect and feed Iraq's Kurds in the wake of the Gulf War and, in the closing months of his presidency, to make sure millions in Somalia did not starve.

THE YEAR AND A HALF OF EUROPE

After taking office, Bush and his administration first took up the issue of Afghanistan, as the last Soviet troops were due to depart that country by February 15, 1989, just shy of one month after his inauguration. This policy review was thus mandated by events more than choice. Not much in the way of a policy for post-Soviet Afghanistan emerged, as there was little appetite to get heavily involved in trying to determine the country's complexion or tip the balance between competing warlords, neither of which was seen as a vital U.S. interest. I thought then and think now that we might have tried harder to strengthen those who appeared to be more moderate, but there is no way of knowing whether doing so would have meaningfully affected Afghanistan's trajectory.

It was not long before Bush turned his focus to Eastern Europe and the Soviet Union. Again, it was a shift (one that dominated the first eighteen months of Bush's tenure) brought about more by events than by design. Bush became president some four years after Mikhail Gorbachev had become general secretary of the Communist Party of the Soviet Union, and by 1989 economic reform (perestroika) and even more political opening (glasnost) were well under way. Gorbachev's domestic initiatives were matched and then some by all he was proposing in the realm of foreign policy, where his many far-ranging proposals for restructuring security in a divided Europe created the widespread impression he was stealing a march on the United States and its Western allies, who, by comparison, seemed to many unimaginative and locked in Cold War thinking.

Bush, who as vice president had met Gorbachev, judged early on that Gorbachev represented a fundamentally different Soviet leader and therefore posed not just a challenge but an opportunity as well. Baker tended to agree. Scowcroft for his part admits he was "suspicious of Gorbachev's motives and skeptical of his prospects."[6] This caution (which Bush to some extent shared) was born of the impossibility of knowing how things would turn out; he and others did not want the United States and the West to let down their collective guard in case Gorbachev and his fellow reformers were overthrown by a group that sought to bring back the sort of Soviet Union that had existed for nearly seventy years. A related concern was that of being lulled into complacency if Gorbachev's reforms turned out to be less about bringing into existence a new and different (and more cooperative) Soviet Union than a means to an end with the objective being the reestablishment of Soviet power without any real change in either its methods or goals.

Bush's initial approach to the Soviet Union and Europe was one that sought to weaken the Soviet hold on Eastern Europe as a goal in itself (where there were already some signs local leaders were charting their own more liberal paths) and as a hedge in case political reform in Moscow went backward. At the same time, there was a desire to act with great care so as not to trigger the sorts of anti-Soviet rebellions that had led to massive repression in Hungary in 1956 and Czechoslovakia in 1968.

President Bush first articulated the new policy, in which aid would be extended to Eastern European countries as they liberalized politically and economically, in Hamtramck, Michigan, in April 1989.[7] Subsequent speeches that May in Texas, Boston, and at the Coast Guard Academy introduced and fleshed out a different approach to the Soviet Union, one that offered a future "beyond containment" in which the country could be integrated into the post–World War II international order.[8] The NATO summit that May saw the alliance come together around a U.S. initiative calling for reduced levels of military forces in Europe. Bush avoided a major rift within NATO by putting on hold a proposal to modernize short-range nuclear forces. Gradually, U.S. goals began to expand. A speech in Germany by the president in May put forward the idea of a post-Cold War Europe that could be "whole and free."[9] Presidential visits to Poland and Hungary in July 1989 further highlighted and advanced the new approach to an increasingly independent Eastern Europe.

Over the course of 1989, most of the Bush administration principals came to see Gorbachev as a bona fide reformer, someone who sought to change the Soviet

Union in fundamental ways. This view gained momentum at and after the December 1989 Malta Summit. That summit was critical for many things, none more so than what it did to pave the way for German unification within NATO, something Gorbachev finally signed onto in May 1990. The outcome is something that Bush and his closest advisors deserve special credit for. It was hardly preordained. There were any number of other options being debated, including keeping the two Germanies separate or combining them outside both the Warsaw Pact and NATO. Bush worked hard to overcome not just Soviet opposition but also British and to a lesser extent French reluctance. It also required painstaking, creative diplomacy, much of which took place in a special mechanism built just for this moment—the "2 plus 4"—consisting of representatives from both West and East Germany as well as the United States, the Soviet Union, United Kingdom, and France (the four occupying powers) to coordinate and implement policy.[10]

In his approach to German unification, Bush's realism was again at work. The president understood that how Germany's fate was decided could tilt the balance of power either toward the United States and its allies or away from it. While France and Britain feared a powerful united Germany, Bush saw that Germany had to be unified and integrated into the West and could not be left to stoke its resentment, as occurred following World War I. Overall, things could hardly have turned out better: a peaceful end to the Cold War, the breakup of the external Soviet Empire followed by the breakup of the Soviet Union itself, and the unification of Germany based on what had been West Germany followed by the admission of the new country into NATO.

It is difficult to exaggerate the intellectual challenge before the Bush administration. For forty years, American foreign policy had revolved around the question of how best to meet the threat posed by Soviet strength. By 1990, it was becoming increasingly clear that the challenge at hand was how to respond to Soviet weakness and possibly collapse. This was the backdrop to a speech Bush delivered in Kiev in August 1991. Bush, warning of the dangers of "suicidal nationalism," called on Soviet republics to work for autonomy from within the Soviet Union rather than push for independence.[11] This approach embodied Bush's realism, as he did not push for the Soviet republics to immediately democratize and break away, and instead sought to ensure that local leaders would avoid steps that could undermine Gorbachev. There was, as well, the desire to avoid the sort of violent instability that had come to the former Yugoslavia as component parts broke away. This caution was only jettisoned when, weeks later, it became clear the Soviet Union would not survive in the wake of a failed coup against Gorbachev, who emerged much weakened and essentially dependent on Boris Yeltsin, then the leader of the Russian Republic. Less than six months later the Soviet Union and Gorbachev were in fact gone, succeeded by Yeltsin's Russia and fourteen other countries that had been republics within the Soviet Union.

No single U.S president—including George H. W. Bush—deserves sole credit for this outcome, in that it reflected decades of concerted Western political, military, and economic effort to stand up to Soviet pressure, the defeat of the Soviet Union in Afghanistan, the deep-seated flaws within the top-heavy Soviet system, and the words and deeds of Mikhail Gorbachev. But Bush deserves tremendous praise for his handling of the final months and years of the Cold War.[12] Much of history centers on the rise and fall of great powers. Central to the backdrop of World War I, for example, was the rise of Imperial Germany along with the demise of the Ottoman and Austro-Hungarian Empires and the collapse of authority in czarist Russia. The collapse of the external Soviet Empire that gave Moscow control over Eastern Europe and the internal empire that gave Russia control of the other republics could have triggered outcomes that would have threatened the peace. That they did not was anything but inevitable.

Interestingly, Bush was more criticized than lauded at the time for his low-key response to what proved to be truly historic events. He avoided dramatic public statements or talk of victory lest he humiliate Gorbachev and risk bringing about a situation in which he and others associated with his reforms were forced to stand up to the United States to demonstrate their nationalist credentials or, worse yet, were overthrown by those who claimed they had sold out their country. Here Bush and his record have stood the test of time far better than most of his critics.

THE CHINA MOMENT

Events in China in May and June 1989 temporarily interrupted the Bush administration's European focus. The proximate cause was events in China itself, namely, the student-led protests in Tiananmen Square calling for increased political reform in the wake of Hu Yaobang's death in mid-April 1989. (Hu, a former general secretary of the Communist Party, was widely seen to have favored reform.) The stakes mounted as the protests spread throughout China, and the Chinese Communist Party increasingly came to view them as an existential challenge to its rule and role. A month later, martial law was imposed. Finally, some six weeks after the protests first began, in early June, Deng Xiaoping and the senior cadre of party leaders determined they could no longer countenance the standoff and moved against the protesters, killing several hundred and by some accounts many more.

These events came at a critical time of transition. The United States and China were coming out of what can best be understood as the second era of their relationship. The first era was one defined by open hostility and clashes: the two were on opposite sides of the Chinese civil war and fought one another in Korea once President Truman made the fateful and ill-advised decision to allow General Douglas MacArthur to attempt to reunify the entire peninsula by force. The second era was one born of common American and Chinese animosity toward the Soviet Union and saw the two countries partner to counter the Soviet Union. The opportunity for rapprochement presented itself with the emergence of the so-called Sino-Soviet split in the late 1960s and was harvested by the diplomacy of Richard Nixon and Henry Kissinger.

But under Bush's watch the rationale for the U.S.–China relationship was fading along with the Cold War. The question then was whether—and if so, how—the two countries would find a way to continue to work together in some areas while at the same time make sure their continuing differences did not cause a rupture. Given the complementarity of the American and Chinese economies, increased economic ties were the most likely path ahead, but the Chinese response to Tiananmen Square threatened this and much more. Indeed, many in Washington in both parties called for applying draconian sanctions, recalling the American ambassador, and more.

Bush, who knew China well from his time there, understood China had to pay a price for its brutal crackdown, but rejected taking steps that could do lasting harm to the relationship. Here again his realism was at work, as Bush believed that however tragic Tiananmen might have been, it could not be allowed to consume the entire Sino–U.S. relationship. To the contrary, Bush believed the United States had to maintain a working relationship with China given that it was in the process of becoming a powerful country with enormous influence. The administration criticized the Chinese authorities, imposed sanctions, and allowed Chinese students studying in the United States to remain in the country, but both the criticism and the sanctions were modulated.[13] Bush explained all this in an extraordinarily personal letter to Deng Xiaoping, the effective ruler of China, and then secretly dispatched Scowcroft to Beijing as his personal emissary.[14] Meeting with Deng in early July, Scowcroft made clear that how the Chinese government dealt with the students was their internal matter, but how the United States reacted was an internal matter for Americans.[15] A good many Americans criticized Bush's decision to reach out to China's leadership, and during Bush's reelection campaign his challenger Bill Clinton accused him of coddling the "butchers of Beijing." But Bush's measured response (one President Clinton came around to) was wise, as he created a context in which the U.S. relationship with the world's most populous country and a rising power could continue to develop in a positive way absent what had brought them together.

THE GULF WAR

The other great crisis of George H. W. Bush's tenure began a year and a half into his presidency, in July 1990, when intelligence showed Saddam Hussein was massing military forces along Iraq's border with Kuwait.[16] The prevailing view was that Saddam was saber-rattling in an effort to persuade Kuwait and other Arab governments to reduce their oil output so that prices would rise, something Saddam desperately needed, given his ambitions and the costs of Iraq's decade-long war with Iran. In the first days of August, however, this conventional wisdom was proven wrong as Iraq invaded and quickly overwhelmed Kuwait and then incorporated it into Iraq as its nineteenth province.

The administration had to forge a response to a situation for which there had been little anticipation. Indeed, for the better part of the previous year, the administration had engaged in a degree of outreach toward Iraq in an effort to bring Saddam Hussein into the circle of so-called moderate Arab countries that would resist the ambitions of an imperial Iran. This effort showed unmistakable signs of failing as Saddam's language and behavior grew increasingly bellicose, and by the spring of 1990 the Bush administration had turned to a more confrontational approach toward Iraq.

The initial meeting of the National Security Council in the wake of the Iraqi invasion reflected this lack of readiness and the absence of any consensus. For Bush, though, it was all relatively clear-cut. What happened was wrong and could not be allowed to stand for strategic and moral reasons alike. He felt so strongly about this that he was prepared to go to war without the backing of Congress and in the face of predictions by a good many pundits that thousands of American soldiers would be killed on the battlefield.

Here the president was ahead of many in his administration. His statement to the world on the South Lawn of the White House on August 5 upon his return from Camp David—"This will not stand, this aggression against Kuwait"—had not been scripted or formally adopted.[17] What set him off were reports that Saddam was not standing down and that many Arab leaders wanted Bush to give them and "Arab diplomacy" more time to work out a resolution. He was having none of it. The notion that has become something of an urban legend, that it was Prime Minister Margaret Thatcher who stiffened his spine, is simply untrue. Yes, she did tell Bush "this is no time to go wobbly," but she said it when the issue at hand was only whether to enforce sanctions absent a UN resolution specifically authorizing military action.[18] Bush, Baker, and Scowcroft all judged that it made more sense to try to maintain a united international front against Saddam before acting independently, which they were all prepared to do. Their patience was rewarded, as the Security Council quickly voted in favor of sanctions enforcement.

The U.S. response was a model of American leadership and of multilateralism. The administration went to the United Nations repeatedly and successfully in an effort to gather international support for rejecting what Saddam had done, for the imposition and enforcement of crippling sanctions, and ultimately for the use of "all necessary means"—a euphemism for military force—to evict Iraq from Kuwait and reestablish the latter's sovereign independence. Dozens of countries, among them not only the Soviet Union and China but also numerous members of the Arab world, lent the United States diplomatic, economic, and military support. Years of investing in relationships through meetings, letters, and phone calls with his foreign counterparts paid off handsomely for Bush. He sent half a million American soldiers to the region in Operation Desert Shield, where they were joined by some two hundred thousand troops from other coalition members to deter further Iraqi aggression and prepare to roll back the occupation of Kuwait. Once it became clear that sanctions and diplomacy were not enough, Operation Desert Shield gave way to Desert Storm, a full military campaign to eject Iraq from Kuwait.

Bush also deserves special praise for what he did not do. Desert Storm far exceeded expectations in both the scale of what it accomplished and the modesty of its costs.

The question was whether the United States would limit itself to what it set out to do (liberate Kuwait) or whether it would use this opportunity to go on to Baghdad and oust Saddam in an effort to bring about a democratic Iraq.

Bush stuck to his realist guns. The precedent here was Korea and President Truman's decision to go north of the 38th parallel once South Korea was liberated. The attempt to reunify the entire peninsula by force in the fall of 1950 met with fierce Chinese resistance, as hundreds of thousands of Chinese soldiers helped to push back the advancing UN force dominated by the United States. An additional twenty thousand Americans lost their lives in the process.

Almost half century later, Bush opposed marching north, in this case to Baghdad. He was persuaded that the effort would be difficult and expensive by every measure. The American experience in Iraq beginning in 2003 suggests the forty-first president was far more right than wrong here. He also felt he had given his word to the American people, to the world, and to Arab leaders in particular—that U.S. goals were limited—and that it was essential he not go back on his word.

Bush also thought there was a good chance military victory could create a context in which Arab-Israeli diplomacy would prosper. He turned out to be right in his view, as in October of 1990 representatives of Israel, Arab governments, and the Palestinians (formally participating as part of the Jordanian delegation) came together in Madrid as part of the first ever face-to-face peace talks. The talks themselves did not thrive, but an important precedent had been set.

Like most others in the administration, though, Bush was wrong in believing that the defeated Saddam would be replaced by his fellow Iraqis. (For the record, those of us who thought he would likely be removed thought his regime would be succeeded not by a democracy but by a general who would govern in the authoritarian mode common to much of the Arab world.) What happened instead is that Saddam hung on to power. The terms of the Iraqi surrender negotiated between American and Iraqi generals were not sufficiently thought through, and the ability of the defeated Iraqis to fly helicopters helped them brutally put down a Kurdish rebellion in the north of the country and a Shia rebellion in the south. Bush and his senior advisors were wary of getting involved and judged subsequently that even if helicopters were grounded Saddam would be able to crush domestic opposition so long as the army and intelligence personnel remained loyal. As a result, the United States did not intervene to oust Saddam but limited itself to saving lives in the north as millions moved toward the border with Turkey. The ending took some of the glow off all that had been accomplished, but it remains fair to say that what was done and how it was done was for the most part a textbook example of effective international leadership.

THE FINAL THIRD

If Europe and the end of the Cold War dominated the first eighteen months of the Bush presidency, and the Gulf crisis and its aftermath the next year to eighteen months, the last twelve to fifteen months, which began in late 1991 and ran through the end of his presidency in January 1993, took place in the context of the reelection campaign and its aftermath. The focus was less on foreign policy, as the country was experiencing a mild recession and as politics argued for the president to place greater emphasis on domestic issues.

This mindset that less was more when it came to foreign policy played itself out in the former Yugoslavia, then experiencing a series of conflicts in the wake of the breakup of the Soviet Union and the associated disappearance of a strong central government and leadership in Belgrade. Following the departures of both Slovenia and Croatia, Bosnia announced its independence in March of 1992. Serbia resisted this step and civil war began in earnest. Under Bush, the United States was reluctant to get involved, a bias reinforced by skepticism that military intervention would achieve results commensurate with the costs and risks. The preference was to leave Europe to sort things out, something it was clearly not up to. Years later, the Clinton administration ultimately embraced a far more active policy (both diplomatically and militarily) toward the former Yugoslavia and achieved a significant result. The question is whether the Bush administration underestimated the human and strategic costs of remaining aloof as well as what could be accomplished by the United States if it were prepared to commit itself. Subsequent events suggest that it was wrong to hold back as much as the administration did.

Somalia was different. After his defeat in the 1992 presidential election, and amid reports of widespread starvation, Bush ordered U.S. forces to participate in Operation Restore Hope. The goal was to alleviate the humanitarian crisis that had developed amid civil war. The mission was kept narrow and mostly worked. The Clinton administration, though, expanded the mission and attempted to sort out the struggle for political power in Somalia, with tragic consequences.[19] Again, Bush's caution when it came to trying to engineer the internal workings of foreign societies proved wise.

I began this chapter by favorably comparing the forty-first president with almost all of his post–World War II predecessors and successors when it came to being prepared for the international challenges of the office. I want to end this chapter with another assessment, namely, one that compares George H. W. Bush with the twelve other presidents of the post–World War II era in terms of their foreign policy accomplishments.

Here I would again rate him near the top of the list, with only Harry Truman higher. There was no Bush Doctrine—again, the forty-first president was more a builder than an architect—but Bush notched two major accomplishments (the end of the Cold War on extraordinarily favorable terms and the liberation of Kuwait) and a number of additional important ones. His mistakes were modest in comparison. Most of the other post–World War II presidents either did not accomplish major things (because of their own shortcomings or a lack of opportunity) or had significant foreign policy failures.

Few of the thus far forty-five American presidents are judged to be great and then tend to be in contention if one and possibly two conditions are met. First, sufficient time needs to have passed to allow for perspective—to allow passions to cool and fondness (or in some cases distaste) for the individual to fade. Time also allows for the effects of decisions to become clearer. And second, greatness is normally associated with their having served two terms (or close to two terms) in office, an amount of time judged to be sufficient to allow someone to make a meaningful impact on enough history to warrant the adjective. There are exceptions—Lincoln the most obvious—but most of those I would judge as being great or near great (including George Washington, Franklin Delano Roosevelt, Harry Truman, and possibly Theodore Roosevelt and Ronald Reagan) occupied the Oval Office for more than four years.

When evaluating the presidency of George H. W. Bush, enough time has passed. It is now more than a quarter century since he left office. As for not having served two terms, Bush is arguably an exception to the rule that one-term presidents do not deserve a high ranking. To the contrary, and as was explained here, he merits being judged as great or near great in the foreign policy realm given all he managed to do on the world stage in just four years.

A final point. Bush's compassionate realism turns out to be a good match for the United States and the American people. It constitutes an active and principled foreign policy that emphasizes what foreign policy can best accomplish and avoids difficult and costly undertakings that might be desirable but are not essential. It offers an alternative to isolationism, unilateralism, and attempting to transform the world. It served Bush well and offers a model that future presidents would be wise to consider making their own.

NOTES

1. For a general portrait of George H. W. Bush, the best book is Jon Meacham, *Destiny and Power: The American Odyssey of George Herbert Walker Bush* (New York: Random House, 2015). For a firsthand account of President Bush's foreign policy, see his coauthored memoir, George H. W. Bush and Brent Scowcroft, *A World Transformed* (New York: Alfred A. Knopf, 1998).

2. For those interested in a broader treatment of the National Security Council, see David Rothkopf, *Running the World: The Inside Story of the National Security Council and the Architects of American Power* (New York: PublicAffairs, 2005).

3. For more on Secretary of State James Baker's role, I would recommend his memoir, *The Politics of Diplomacy: Revolution, War and Peace 1989–1992* (New York: G. P. Putnam's Sons, 1995).

4. For more on Brent Scowcroft, see Ivo H. Daalder and I. M. Destler, *In the Shadow of the Oval Office: Profiles of the National Security Advisers and the Presidents They Served—From JFK to George W. Bush* (New York: Simon & Schuster, 2009), 168–204.

5. For more on realism as a theory of international relations, the canonical text is Hans J. Morgenthau, *Politics among Nations: The Struggle for Power and Peace* (New York: Alfred A. Knopf, 1948). For profiles of Hans Morgenthau, George Kennan, and Henry Kissinger

that focus on their realism, see Michael Joseph Smith, *Realist Thought from Weber to Kissinger* (Baton Rouge: Louisiana State University Press, 1986).

6. Bush and Scowcroft, *A World Transformed*, 13.

7. In his speech, Bush focused on Poland, pledging to support the country's reforms by providing it with selective tariff relief. Bush also proposed coordinating with other members of the Paris Club to restructure Poland's debt and authorizing the Overseas Private Investment Corporation to operate in Poland, among other initiatives. Bush then opened the door to similar initiatives throughout Eastern Europe, stating, "If Poland's experiment succeeds, other countries may follow. . . . Poland offers two lessons for all. First, there can be no progress without significant political and economic liberalization. And second, help from the West will come in concert with liberalization." President George H. W. Bush, "Remarks to Citizens in Hamtramck, Michigan," April 17, 1989, Public Papers, George H. W. Bush Presidential Library and Museum, https://bush41library.tamu.edu/archives/public-papers/326.

8. In his commencement address to the graduates of Texas A&M University, President Bush stated, "Forty years of perseverance have brought us a precious opportunity, and now it is time to move beyond containment to a new policy for the 1990s—one that recognizes the full scope of change taking place around the world and in the Soviet Union itself. In sum, the United States now has as its goal much more than simply containing Soviet expansionism. We seek the integration of the Soviet Union into the community of nations. And as the Soviet Union itself moves toward greater openness and democratization, as they meet the challenge of responsible international behavior, we will match their steps with steps of our own. Ultimately, our objective is to welcome the Soviet Union back into the world order." President George H. W. Bush, "Remarks at the Texas A&M University Commencement Ceremony in College Station," May 12, 1989, Public Papers, George H. W. Bush Presidential Library and Museum, https://bush41library.tamu.edu/archives/public-papers/413.

9. President Bush remarked, "The world has waited long enough. The time is right. Let Europe be whole and free." President George H. W. Bush, "Remarks to the Citizens in Mainz, Federal Republic of Germany," May 31, 1989, Public Papers, George H. W. Bush Presidential Library and Museum, https://bush41library.tamu.edu/archives/public-papers/476.

10. For more on this diplomacy, see Philip Zelikow and Condoleezza Rice, *To Build a Better World: Choices to End the Cold War and Create a Global Commonwealth* (New York: Twelve, 2019).

11. In his speech, Bush warned, "freedom is not the same as independence. Americans will not support those who seek independence in order to replace a far-off tyranny with a local despotism. They will not aid those who promote a suicidal nationalism based upon ethnic hatred." President George H. W. Bush, "Remarks to the Supreme Soviet of the Republic of the Ukraine in Kiev, Soviet Union," August 1, 1991, Public Papers, George H. W. Bush Presidential Library and Museum, https://bush41library.tamu.edu/archives/public-papers/3267.

12. The best study of President Bush's handling of the Cold War's end is Jeffrey A. Engel, *When the World Seemed New: George H. W. Bush and the End of the Cold War* (New York: Houghton Mifflin Harcourt, 2017).

13. For an in-depth look at the Bush administration's response to the Tiananmen Square massacre, see Robert L. Suettinger, *Beyond Tiananmen: The Politics of U.S.-China Relations 1989–2000* (Washington, DC: Brookings Institution Press, 2003).

14. The text of President Bush's letter to Deng Xiaoping can be found in Bush and Scowcroft, *A World Transformed*, 100–102. Scowcroft describes his trip to Beijing at 105–11.

15. Ibid., 108.

16. For those interested in the Gulf War, see my book, *War of Necessity, War of Choice* (New York: Simon & Schuster, 2009), especially 17–153.

17. President George H. W. Bush, "Remarks and an Exchange with Reporters on the Iraqi Invasion of Kuwait," August 5, 1990, Public Papers, George H. W. Bush Presidential Library and Museum, https://bush41library.tamu.edu/archives/public-papers/2138.

18. President Bush recalled their conversation and confirmed Thatcher said this in Bush and Scowcroft, *A World Transformed*, 325. Margaret Thatcher also recounted this conversation in her memoir, *The Downing Street Years* (New York: HarperCollins, 1993), 823–24. Excerpt available at https://www.margaretthatcher.org/document/110711.

19. These tragic consequences were famously told in Mark Bowden's *Black Hawk Down: A Story of Modern War* (New York: Grove Press, 1999).

3

The Accidental Diplomat

Staffing Foreign Policy

Chase Untermeyer

George Herbert Walker Bush was the first president in 128 years to have been a diplomat earlier in his career. Diplomatic service was practically a requirement for presidents from the first Adams through the second one, yet this admirable preparation had been absent from the White House since 1861 when the unloved James Buchanan (former secretary of state and minister to both Russia and Great Britain) departed the premises.

Bush's experience in foreign affairs prior to assuming the presidency in 1989—two years as ambassador to the United Nations, one as envoy to China, one as director of Central Intelligence, and eight as vice president—resulted from the accidents of politics, not from career choice. Yet these experiences profoundly shaped his approach to foreign policy and the people he chose to run it. He acquired not only a worldview but also an acquaintance with world leaders. He learned to parlay with Russians, Chinese, and America's long-standing allies. He also came to value the dedication and knowledge of career military, Foreign Service, and intelligence officers, routinely and unfairly dismissed as "bureaucrats" or "the deep state" by many other Republican politicians.

Foreign affairs was not George Bush's area of expertise until he went to the United Nations in 1971. He never crossed an ocean until the U.S. Navy sent him. The Bushes of Greenwich spent their summers on the Maine coast rather than on grand tours of "the Continent." Prior to his election to Congress in 1966, George Bush had no greater knowledge of the world than other Americans of his background and education did. His interest since college days had been economics, not foreign relations, and his business career was purely domestic. The Gulf where he planted his oil rigs was of Mexico, not of Persia. When he got to Congress, he wanted to be on—and was a rare freshman appointee to—the House Committee on Ways and Means, not Foreign Affairs. (As a rule, Texans in Congress want to be on "money" committees like Ways and Means and Appropriations; New Yorkers want to be on Foreign Affairs.)

Bush was blissfully happy on Ways and Means, learning federal tax policy from its House master, Chairman Wilbur Mills (D-Arkansas). When, in 1970, Texas voters dealt him a second defeat for the Senate, not a little due to the state's former Democratic governor, John B. Connally, Bush hoped for a presidential appointment to the Treasury, as deputy secretary if not as secretary. It was a searing blow when Richard Nixon chose Connally (with whom Nixon was much smitten) to be his finance minister. Bush was given the consolation prize of the UN, thought by friends and supporters as the end of the political road for him. When Bush's nomination was announced, the *New York Times* sniffed, "There seems to be nothing in his record which qualifies him for this highly-sensitive post."

The new ambassador went about his job with typical Bushian energy and enthusiasm. Everyone knew that foreign policy was decided by President Nixon and his national security advisor, Henry Kissinger. The UN ambassador had a seat at the cabinet table, but he was a mere agent of decisions made in Washington, not a participant in them.[1] The nadir came when Bush fought to retain Taiwan's seat in the world body at the very moment Kissinger was meeting with those who wanted that seat, the communist Chinese. It had not occurred to Kissinger even to notify, much less consult, the man on the scene in New York.

Bush used his less-than-good situation as UN ambassador to do what he always did best—to make friends. He saw his counterparts the same as he had his classmates at Andover and Yale or his colleagues in the U.S. House: as people to get to know on a personal basis. Tennis, cocktail parties, informal dinners, and simple conversations over coffee in the lounge were his tools, and they were enormously successful. Winning the friendship of his fellow ambassadors may not have swung many votes to the U.S. position in those chilly days when "neutrals" regularly bashed America, but they were friendships banked for a better day, when he and they held much higher offices in their countries.

After Nixon's reelection in 1972, Bush was called back to Washington to chair the Republican National Committee, another "loser" job he resolutely occupied as the tides of Watergate mounted, crested, and finally broke. When Nixon resigned two years later, Gerald Ford wanted to reward Bush for his tireless, thankless service to the party by offering him the ambassadorship to either London or Paris. The new president was surprised when Bush asked to go to Beijing instead. Because the United States and the People's Republic of China had not yet "normalized" their new relationship, the job Bush requested was not that of ambassador but of "chief of the U.S. liaison office" in the Chinese capital.[2] Ford agreed to the request, and Barbara Bush packed for another household move.

As at the UN, Bush in Beijing was disregarded by Henry Kissinger, who dominated China policy to the point of making even Richard Nixon jealous. When the newly named envoy asked to see the top secret cables Kissinger had sent after his epochal meetings with Mao Zedong and Chou Enlai, he was permitted to do so only if he read them in the presence of Kissinger's assistant, Richard Solomon.

Once in Beijing, Bush proceeded to do as he had done at the United Nations, making friends with his fellow foreign diplomats and, to the extent possible, his Chinese interlocutors. The terrain for such contact in those days was limited chiefly to formal receptions and to informal games of tennis at the International Club. George and Barbara Bush practiced "public diplomacy" on their celebrated rides around Beijing on Flying Pigeon bicycles. Otherwise, their lives were extremely circumscribed.

They also lived in isolation. In those pre-Internet, pre–cable TV days, the U.S. mission in Beijing had little idea of what was happening at home or elsewhere in the world. It was very much like being on the dark side of the moon. One effect of this isolation was to knit the members of the mission and their families much more tightly together. Bush came to know well and to admire the Foreign Service officers with whom he lived and worked in their hardship post. This group of Asia hands—most notably John Holdridge, Harry Thayer, and Lynn Pascoe—would later occupy senior posts during the Reagan and first Bush administrations. The CIA station chief during Bush's tenure in Beijing, James Lilley, would become his good friend and his ambassador to China at the time of the Tiananmen crisis of June 1989.

During a bicycle ride on Sunday, November 1, 1975, Bush was hailed by a messenger and asked to return to the liaison office. Waiting there was a short cable from Secretary of State Kissinger, the heart of which said, "The President asks that you consent to his nominating you as the new director of the Central Intelligence Agency." There was no explanation as to what lay behind the summons—and no CNN to turn on for leaks out of the White House. Feeling "there was only one answer I could give," Bush accepted Ford's call to new service.

At the time, it seemed odd that Bush, the former businessman and congressman, was picked to head the scandal-plagued CIA and that Elliot Richardson, Mr. Probity during Watergate, was chosen to be secretary of commerce—not the other way around. In his authoritative biography of Bush, *Destiny and Power* (2015), Jon Meacham cited Richard Cheney's explanation that it had indeed been Ford's plan to put Richardson at the Agency and Bush at Commerce but that Kissinger felt he could not work with Richardson. So the switch was made.

Once again, the odd workings of politics had given Bush a job that appeared to doom his political future but that proved of immense value. Although Kissinger's cable had called it director of the CIA, the job was much more than that. More properly called director of Central Intelligence (or DCI), it put Bush in charge of all intelligence-gathering and -weighing functions of the U.S. government, with the task of making sense of the mass of information and giving the president the best possible analysis. Bush threw himself into this immense responsibility with his trademark energy, gaining new knowledge and a deeper appreciation for the work of the dedicated professionals with whom he worked. They in turn came truly to love their boss, under whose leadership their morale rebounded.

Alas for Bush, his fascinating education in intelligence proved short. Scarcely a year into the job, he was heaved out of it upon Ford's defeat by Jimmy Carter. It was Bush's dearest wish that Carter, in a spirit of bipartisanship and perhaps in appreciation for all the positive changes at Langley, would retain him as DCI. But the new president replaced him with Admiral Stansfield Turner, who snidely called the agency "the Bush league."

Wounded though Bush was by Carter's decision, he had actually been given a great political blessing—or, more correctly, spared a true political deathblow. Had Carter asked him to remain at CIA, Bush would have done so, gratefully. But by taking the peanut king's coin, he would have been condemned and ostracized by Republican activists. This in fact happened to Elliot Richardson, a nonpartisan public servant par excellence, after he accepted Carter's offer to become ambassador-at-large for the Law of the Sea.

Just as the British say someone "had a good war," George Bush had a good Nixon-Ford era, a time when many former colleagues were disgraced and even incarcerated. In January 1977, George Bush could look back on eight years of professional growth and the acquisition of solid expertise in intelligence and diplomacy, especially the crucial Sino-American relationship. He also ended the Ford administration with a closer friendship with three men who would be his primary comrades-in-arms in the liberation of Kuwait fourteen years later: Brent Scowcroft, successor to Kissinger as Ford's national security advisor; Dick Cheney, Ford's chief of staff; and especially James A. Baker III, his former tennis partner in Houston, who had been undersecretary of commerce.

It was as "a president we won't have to train" that Bush waged a titanic, see-saw battle against Ronald Reagan in the Republican caucuses and primaries of early 1980 for the party's presidential nomination. As de facto leader of the GOP's "moderate" wing, Bush was pilloried by the GOP's farther-right wing for his membership in the "Eastern elitist" Council on Foreign Relations and especially the ominous-sounding Trilateral Commission.[3] It was with reluctance that Reagan made Bush his running mate, which he did to balance the GOP ticket and beat Carter in the fall. But first he wanted (and received) assurance that Bush could and would support his conservative agenda. More positively, Reagan recognized and needed Bush's savvy in foreign affairs and the workings of Washington, something that as a former governor he conspicuously lacked. In short order, the two men, with their immense founts of friendship and goodwill, came to be fond working partners, overcoming the rivalry and doubts of the recent intraparty campaign.

Bush had a disastrous debut as Reagan's running mate when he was given the diplomatic equivalent of a suicide mission: to persuade Chinese maximum leader Deng Xiaoping that Reagan's desire for a higher-level relationship with Taiwan (downgraded upon the "normalization" of relations with the mainland) would not be at Beijing's expense. Deng bought none of it: to the Chinese, Taiwan was a renegade province that deserved no international recognition beyond the barest commercial and cultural connections; anything above this was viewed as a direct affront to the

People's Republic. Bush got a very public shellacking in Beijing that singed the nascent Reagan-Bush campaign but at least served to show staunch Reaganites that Bush was willing to embrace (and take brickbats for) the Gipper's agenda.

After the big Republican victory in November, Bush got two major boosts, one immediately obvious and one that took a little more time. The first was when Reagan chose, to the shock of his California crowd, Bush's close friend and former campaign manager, James Baker, to be White House chief of staff. The selection of Baker was a clear statement by the new president that he wanted an administration of quality and ability, not simply one of long-standing loyalty. Bush and Baker never conspired to subvert Reaganism, as many conservative activists claimed in an eight-year state of hyperventilation, but it was without question helpful for the vice president to have a true friend next door keeping him fully informed on administration developments and political crosscurrents.

The other boost for Bush—and another fortuitous accident—was Reagan's less-than-well-considered selection of Alexander Haig to be secretary of state. The general believed, and actively promoted, the notion that he had been the nation's savior as White House chief of staff at the end of the Nixon presidency. Having subsequently become NATO commander, with four stars on his shoulder, Haig saw himself—worse, proclaimed himself—the "vicar of foreign policy" for the aged and inexperienced actor in the Oval Office.

In mid-March 1981, Reagan made the logical and constitutionally sensible decision that Vice President Bush would preside over meetings of the National Security Council in his absence. Not being chosen "crisis manager" prompted Haig to explode in public. This occurred at the very moment he was on the cover of *Time*, hands on hips, in an evocation of his idol Douglas MacArthur, a man not much known for respecting presidents.

The climax came ten days later, with the attempted assassination of President Reagan. In the press briefing room shortly after the shooting, Haig said he was "in control here in the White House" pending Bush's return from a trip to Texas. These ill-chosen words seemed to validate Haig's image as a power-grabber. To the surprise of no one who knew him, Bush acted by contrast with the utmost decorum, circumspection, and genuine concern for his new friend Ronald Reagan. If there were any lingering doubts about Bush among Reagan's staff, they were dashed during these days. He was seen as a "team player," and Haig was most definitely not. The wonder is that fully fifteen months would pass before Haig finally departed the administration. Until this happened, Bush was careful not to step on Haig's spit-shined shoes—for example, never visiting a foreign country unless the secretary of state had been there first.

It was Bush's style and wise practice to give his advice to Reagan discreetly. He was quick to quash any talk by his staff about how influential the boss was. Though this led to news stories wondering "whatever happened to George Bush," the VP himself was unconcerned. He was content to serve the modern vice presidential role as the most senior, most respected, and final voice heard in the Oval Office.

He also undertook many important tasks in the realm of national security for the administration. One was successfully lobbying the Senate in 1981 to permit the sale of Airborne Warning and Control System (AWACS) surveillance aircraft to Saudi Arabia. Another was his mission to Europe in January–February 1983 to stiffen the resolve of NATO allies to deploy the Pershing intermediate-range missile system. Yet another was his trip to El Salvador in 1985 to tell that country's military dictators to quit their private war against leftist opponents.

There were his three trips to Moscow (in 1982, 1984, and 1985) for the funerals of Soviet leaders, followed immediately by conversations with their heirs. And there were numerous trips abroad for the funerals of other notables, leading to Bush's joke, "You die, I fly." But funerals, inaugurations, conferences, and goodwill tours were opportunities to meet and take the measure of foreign leaders. A CIA officer once noted, not really exaggerating, that "George Bush put together the coalition that won the Gulf War at all the funerals he attended as vice president."

On occasion, the Reagan personnel office sought the names of potential appointees from the vice president, with his excellent connections in the worlds of business and national security. For example, in 1982, as part of its Caribbean Basin Initiative to shore up nonsocialist governments in the region, the White House wanted a major business leader as ambassador to Jamaica. Bush recommended—and Reagan eventually appointed—William A. Hewitt, chairman of Deere & Company. For the most part, though, Bush kept out of personnel matters, not least to avoid strengthening the claim of detractors that he was manipulating the president.[4]

Bush's weight on national security matters was such that "the chattering classes" of Washington found it hard to believe his statement that he was "out of the loop" when decisions were made to arm the Contras in Central America using the proceeds of arms sales to Iran. Yet the special counsel, Judge Lawrence Walsh, was never able to tie Bush directly to the Iran-Contra imbroglio of the later 1980s, much as he may have dearly wanted to do so.

Throughout the Reagan years, foreign leaders and journalists simply assumed that George Bush would be the next president of the United States, and in all his international dealings during this time he was treated as such. Actually becoming president would require a hard slog through the Republican primaries and the general election campaign of 1988, and through much of that year he lagged seriously behind in the polls. The tactics used by Bush's campaign and his outside supporters may not have been pretty, but they were the price that bare-knuckled American politics required to put "the president we won't have to train" in the Oval Office at long last.

After winning 54 percent of the popular vote and 79 percent of the electoral vote, Bush left personal politics behind and focused on the task ahead. His first act, announced the very morning after the election, was the selection of James Baker to be secretary of state. He also named his vice presidential counsel (lawyer) C. Boyden Gray as White House counsel and the author of this chapter, Chase Untermeyer, as director of presidential personnel. Bush saw these two jobs as critical to staffing his administration, with the need to get started right away and to work together. (The

Presidential Personnel Office recommends individuals to the president for nomination to the Senate after the White House counsel checks their backgrounds and finances and "clears" them.)

Because of Baker's close relationship to the new president, he was given carte blanche in filling the subordinate ranks of the State Department. The positions about which Baker cared most intensely were those he proceeded to fill with an able coterie of trusted aides: Robert (Bob) Zoellick as counselor of the department; Robert (Bob) Kimmitt as undersecretary for policy; Dennis Ross as director of policy planning; John F. W. Rogers as undersecretary for management; Janet Mullins as congressional liaison; and Margaret Tutwiler as assistant secretary for public affairs, departmental spokesperson, and all-round political advisor. With an eye toward achieving a bipartisan consensus on ending the conflict in Nicaragua, Baker recruited a Democrat, Bernard Aronson, as assistant secretary for Western Hemisphere affairs, and recommended the retention of another Democrat (initially appointed by Reagan), Richard Schifter, as assistant secretary for democracy, human rights, and labor.

Even though Baker chose the eminent Foreign Service officer Lawrence (Larry) Eagleburger to be deputy secretary and Foreign Service officers (FSOs) to fill other senior posts,[5] the immediate reaction in Foggy Bottom was fury at Baker's putting "outsiders" in offices on the sacred seventh floor instead of career diplomats like themselves. Later, these same people would hail the leadership of Baker and his team, who made the whole department look good. Baker respected the Foreign Service, and his boss at 1600 Pennsylvania Avenue certainly did. But the Constitution gives the president unrestricted authority to pick whomever he wishes for every post, subject to the confirmation of the Senate. There is no clause with reference to "ambassadors, other public ministers, and consuls" that requires him to choose career diplomats.

It was in the category of ambassadorships that President Bush most dramatically demonstrated his regard for the Foreign Service. Having worked with FSOs at the UN and in China, as well as collaterally at CIA, he deeply valued their expertise in policy, languages, and the craft of diplomacy. This was in contrast to many in the Reagan high command, who viewed FSOs and all other "bureaucrats" with suspicion. It was a Reagan administration goal to decrease the number of FSOs serving as ambassadors and to increase that of non-career (or "political") appointees. By the end of Reagan's second term, the number of non-career ambassadors stood at 40 percent.

Bush as president boosted the ambassadorial ratio to two-thirds career, one-third noncareer. He moved early to accomplish this by placing FSOs in embassies that either always or almost always took noncareer appointees. For example, he sent John Negroponte to Mexico, Terence Todman to Argentina, Michael Armacost to Japan, William Clark to India, Thomas Pickering to the United Nations, and, most significant of all, Raymond Seitz to the United Kingdom, the cynosure political post. To China he sent his friend James Lilley, who had been at CIA instead of State but possessed a native knowledge of Chinese and had previous service as envoy to Taiwan and South Korea. Two other CIA veterans whom Bush knew well were also given ambassadorships: Donald Gregg, his vice presidential national security advisor, went to South Korea, and Frederick Vreeland, who had been station chief at the United Nations during Bush's time there, went to Morocco.

Having been a noncareer ambassador himself, Bush had no problem giving foreign posts to able people outside the State Department. In three interesting instances, Bush put noncareer appointees in posts normally held by FSOs. He named Shirley Temple Black as ambassador to Czechoslovakia; Alan (Punch) Green as ambassador to Romania; and Smith Hempstone as ambassador to Kenya. Each proved a great success under trying circumstances. Black, who had been ambassador to Ghana and chief of protocol during the Ford administration, asked to go to Prague, where she had happened to be in 1968 as Soviet tanks occupied the city. When the "Velvet Revolution" broke out in 1989, she was a valiant voice in its support. Likewise, when Romania at the same time rose against the Ceaușescu dictatorship, Green was a strong advocate for societal reform. And in East Africa, Hempstone, a journalist, was outspoken on behalf of democracy, earning great credit for America on the street if not in the government to which he was accredited.

Because he had headed Bush's campaign, Jim Baker not only accepted but fully endorsed putting noncareer appointees in a third of ambassadorial posts, and he was personally acquainted with many of the people Bush wanted in them. He and Untermeyer, with Margaret Tutwiler sitting in, would meet in a small room off the main secretarial chambers on the seventh floor of State to go over Untermeyer's list of prospects. Once they had agreed on a name, it would go forward to the president. The national security advisor, Brent Scowcroft, had no desire to get involved in ambassadorial selection. With an entire globe to watch, he had more important things to do with his time and energy. Theirs was therefore a very harmonious arrangement, in contrast to the endless warfare between the White House staff and Secretary of State George Shultz during the Reagan administration.

Personnel was handled quite differently at the Department of Defense (DOD). Bush's original choice to head the Pentagon was his fellow Texan, John Tower, who had specialized in national security affairs during a career of nearly a quarter century in the Senate. Tower agreed to serve with the proviso that he staff the department with people of his own choosing; Bush concurred. Among Tower's choices were Paul Wolfowitz as undersecretary for policy and Stephen Hadley as assistant secretary for global strategic affairs. When Tower was denied confirmation by his former colleagues—the first time the Senate voted down a new president's nominee for a cabinet post—Bush promptly chose Congressman Dick Cheney of Wyoming as "SecDef." Thus were four friends and productive working partners from the Ford administration—Bush, Baker, Scowcroft, and Cheney—reunited after more than twenty years and charged with the formation and execution of American foreign policy.

A former White House chief of staff, Cheney was wise in the business of political appointments and secured from Bush the same promise he had given Tower, that of staffing DOD as he chose. He retained Tower's selections of Wolfowitz and Had-ley—creating a partnership that would prove consequential—but discarded those of former Tower Senate staffers as secretaries of the three military departments.

Whereas Baker wanted to control only a top few critical positions at State and was quite willing to work with the White House on all others, Cheney wanted to control *all* civilian appointments at Defense. This led to confrontations with Bush's director of the Presidential Personnel Office, backed by White House chief of staff John Sununu. Undaunted, Cheney took fights even for third-level positions into the Oval Office, where he prevailed. (Presidents, Bush included, hate personnel wrangles and usually accede to a cabinet secretary's wishes.)

In 1992, when Cheney's first secretary of the Navy resigned during the Tailhook scandal, Cheney circumvented the Presidential Personnel Office altogether. He went straight to Scowcroft, accompanying the president on a foreign trip, with the name of man he wanted. This technique Cheney called "short-circuiting the system."[6]

A prominent exception occurred the previous year, when the position of assistant secretary of defense for international security affairs fell open. Before Cheney could propose advancing the deputy assistant secretary into the job, Presidential Personnel did some short-circuiting of its own, going straight to President Bush with the name of his friend, James Lilley. Bush of course agreed and sent Lilley's name to the Senate. Though rebuffed, Cheney came to value Lilley as the extraordinary public servant and patriot he was—and as Cheney himself was.

Such struggles over personnel occur in every administration, and those of the first Bush administration probably were fewer and milder than most, owing to the high standards of collegiality and professionalism set by the president himself. Professor Richard Neustadt of Harvard, the eminent scholar of the presidency, noted the excellent working relationship of Baker, Cheney, and Scowcroft, saying, "The only time there was such cooperation among the secretary of state, the secretary of defense, and the national security advisor was when Henry Kissinger held two of the three positions." The three of them also had excellent working relationships with the rest of the National Security Team—Dan Quayle, Colin Powell, John Sununu, Robert Gates, and Andy Card.

The first Bush presidency gave special lift to the careers of two members of his National Security Council staff: Robert Gates, who became his director of the CIA and would become secretary of defense for both Presidents George W. Bush and Barack Obama; and Condoleezza Rice, who would become George W. Bush's national security advisor and secretary of state.

George H. W. Bush had reason to be proud of those who staffed the foreign policy and broader national security apparatus during his single term as president. That he did so without regard to background or party was a reflection of his own long career in public service, the deep knowledge of foreign affairs he had gained, and his earnest desire to put the best-possible people to work for the good of the nation.

NOTES

1. This curiosity originated when President Eisenhower gave the UN ambassadorship to Henry Cabot Lodge Jr., who in 1952 had helped elect Ike at the cost of his own reelection as senator from Massachusetts. To embellish the portfolio, Eisenhower made Lodge a member of the cabinet, even though as an ambassador he was down the ranks from the man up the table, Secretary of State John Foster Dulles.

2. It is commonly misstated that Bush was the first chief of the liaison office, but this distinction belongs to the veteran diplomat David L. K. Bruce, whom Bush directly succeeded. In Beijing, he would be called Ambassador Bush, but only out of courtesy for his prior service at the UN.

3. He resigned from both.

4. During the 1980–1981 transition, Bush did intervene in behalf of Dr. John F. Lehman to be secretary of the Navy. Rebuilding the nation's defenses was a cornerstone of Reagan administration policy, with the Navy most in need of renewal. Bush the former naval aviator felt strongly that the nation needed Lehman's expert knowledge of the fleet, in contrast to the skillset of the Reaganites' sentimental favorite, Robert Nesen, a Southern California auto dealer. Lehman went to the Pentagon as "SecNav," and Nesen went to Australia as ambassador.

5. A noteworthy instance was Baker's proposal of Richard Solomon—the instrument of Henry Kissinger's pettiness involving the Mao/Chou cables—as assistant secretary of state for East Asian and Pacific affairs. If Bush remembered the slight at all, he endorsed the recommendation, not simply because Baker made it but also because he knew and valued Solomon's long experience and expertise.

6. James Rosen, *Cheney One on One* (Washington: Regnery Publishing, 2015), 121 and 234. On page 290, Rosen quotes Cheney as saying, "If you want to be loved, go be a movie actor. But you don't belong in the business I've been involved in most of my life."

4

The Remaking of National Security Council Staff

Bush, Scowcroft, and Institutional Reform

Jane Holl Lute

On November 5, 1992, Brent Scowcroft, retired U.S. Air Force lieutenant general and national security advisor to President George H. W. Bush, summoned all of the directors and senior directors of the National Security Council (NSC) staff to the Cordell Hull conference room on the second floor of the Old Executive Office Building. As the group of roughly forty-five settled into their seats, Scowcroft took in the whole of the room and minced no words: "We've all been fired," he said. He then went on in his customary, understated way and told the staff that despite the unwanted outcome of the presidential election, there was some good news: as far as anyone could tell, foreign policy had played no role in the results. "I suppose we can take some satisfaction in that," he said dryly.

Don't start clearing out your desks just yet, Scowcroft told them; there was still plenty of work to do. President Bush intended to remain fully engaged up to the very end of his administration. The most pressing issues for the remaining ten weeks of the president's term included ongoing efforts to navigate the fallout from the collapse of the Soviet Union, shore up the NATO alliance, manage continuing tensions with China, address the humanitarian catastrophe in Somalia, and help control the intensifying war in Yugoslavia. Andrew Card, the secretary of transportation and former deputy White House chief of staff, would lead the transition for the president to the new administration. He and Scowcroft agreed that the president's foreign policy program would stay busy and full for the waning period of his term.

Scowcroft instructed that the handover to the incoming Clinton administration be as smooth as possible—a phrase that decidedly did not apply when he and his colleagues took over from the Reagan White House four years earlier. In contrast to what he experienced in that change of administrations, Scowcroft insisted that when dealing with the incoming team, his staff exercise the full measure of expert ability, care, and discretion that had characterized their efforts throughout President Bush's tenure.

Leading the transition for the president-elect would be Tony Lake, who himself had served on the NSC staff under Henry Kissinger during the Nixon administration and whom Scowcroft knew passingly from his time as Nixon's military aide. Scowcroft wanted the incoming crowd to have the information and insights they needed to ensure that the new president would have every advantage as he assumed responsibility for stewardship of U.S. national interests in the dramatically changed world he had just inherited.

Today, nearly thirty years later, foreign affairs experts, policy makers, and academics alike elevate this NSC staff handover from Bush to Clinton above all others as the model of a presidential transition at its finest, marked by professionalism and a generous spirit. Even more than this specific transition, however, the Bush and Scowcroft vision and version of the role, organization, and processes for the NSC staff, and, indeed, for U.S. national security decision-making overall, still serve as the gold standard against which other efforts are judged.[1] The Scowcroft NSC (as it came to be known) has, as the saying goes, been often imitated, but never duplicated. What made it so special? How did it come about? Why has it been so hard for succeeding generations of policy makers to equal its performance? To answer these questions, one must examine the NSC staff and process not at its best, but at its worst. This story begins in crisis.

THE IRAN-CONTRA SCANDAL

Serious students of national security may find it difficult to believe that a handful of indistinct U.S. military officers could join up with mid-level civilian bureaucrats who should have known better to undertake a self-appointed scheme of international intrigue, undetected for months, in the name of the president of the United States.[2] Their plan sought to secure the release of seven American hostages held by Hezbollah in Lebanon while funneling support to Nicaraguan rebels locked in a protracted civil war against their government.

For months between 1985 and 1986, an unlikely cast of characters led by Marine Lieutenant Colonel Oliver North, who largely managed the secretive, highly centralized operation, misdirected tens of millions of U.S. dollars and organized the covert delivery of hundreds of U.S. missiles and other weaponry to Iran. Discovery of the operation triggered multiple investigations and generated considerable political controversy for the president.[3]

THE TOWER COMMISSION

Toward the end of 1986, Scowcroft joined former U.S. senator John Tower and former senator and U.S. secretary of state Edmund S. Muskie to form the commission established by President Reagan to get to the bottom of the Iran-Contra

Affair.[4] The commission also had the mandate to understand how the national security decision-making apparatus, including the NSC staff at the heart of foreign policy in the executive office of the president, had gone so far off the rails. This aspect of the commission's charter, in fact, represented a rather more important issue for the overarching national security of the country.[5] Completing their work in roughly sixty days, Tower, Muskie, and Scowcroft, along with minimal staff, pored over thousands of documents and conducted dozens of firsthand interviews.[6] The commission had no subpoena power, however, and could not compel witnesses to testify or documents to be produced. Key advisers to the president refused to appear before the commission, and important documents remained unavailable for inspection or analysis.[7]

Scowcroft himself wrote the recommendations of the commission's report related to the national security system. He joined with his colleagues in an unsparing assessment of what had gone wrong, feeling more than a little reflected pain and embarrassment at the shoddy performance of an organization that he himself had led previously.[8] But Scowcroft was determined to prevent the dismantling of an organization and system that he knew could function well and honorably. He was equally determined to protect the position of the national security advisor from congressional micromanagement, and he sought to preserve the president's latitude to select and rely on the private advice he would need from his top foreign policy aide. Having served as deputy national security advisor during the Nixon years and as national security advisor himself to Gerald Ford, Scowcroft held well-developed ideas regarding how to organize not only the office of the national security advisor, but also the entire national security decision-making system to safeguard and advance the national interest while serving the president's interests.

The commission's report outlined two key elements deemed necessary for the national security system to work best: first, the need to organize thoughtfully and specifically for presidential strategic decision-making in national security, and, second, the imperative that the national security advisor discharge the responsibilities of that position with competence, diligence, and accountability to the president.[9] The report took pains to highlight unambiguously the importance of the president's own role to ensure a well-functioning and accountable process.[10]

Citing the National Security Act of 1947 that created the National Security Council and the position of the national security advisor, the commission underscored the absolute necessity of an established, inclusive, and deliberate process to allow principals—in modern times, customarily including the secretaries of state and defense, the director of central intelligence, the national security advisor, and the chairman of the Joint Chiefs (with other cabinet secretaries and senior foreign and defense officials, joining ad hoc as necessary)—to provide the president with their frank advice.[11] The commission also underscored the particular importance of the role of the national security advisor, not only to oversee this process, but also to establish sound operating systems and secure the best possible expertise to support the president in foreign policy making. The commission believed that collectively these tools constituted an essential arsenal for the president in discharging his constitutional powers in the area of foreign policy and national defense.[12]

When Frank Carlucci assumed responsibilities as Reagan's fifth national security advisor at the end of 1986, he slashed the NSC staff nearly in half and imposed other changes consistent with the commission's recommendations.[13] But the damage done was deep and deadly to President Reagan's foreign policy agenda for the remainder of his term. A year after he was appointed, Carlucci became secretary of defense and was replaced by General Colin Powell, who proved an able steward of a system still reeling from scandal.[14]

TURNING THINGS AROUND

As the commission's report made plain, no president could succeed without sound process and highly competent people of integrity imbedded in that process. Following his election in 1988, Bush applied his own considerable experience, policy expertise, and political instincts to put good people and practice into place.[15]

For Scowcroft, the lessons of Iran-Contra reinforced years of his own experience working strategy and policy execution (along with recollections of his tenure as national security advisor under Ford) to convince him of what did not work for U.S. foreign policy making—a disengaged and poorly staffed president; slipshod, irregular process; inattentive advisors; self-promoting, suspicious, and self-protective senior policy makers; and poor choices for staff. He would not repeat these mistakes. Thus, when he agreed to serve again as national security advisor under President-elect Bush, he knew what it would take to restore fully the integrity and performance of the NSC staff: a committed president, a rock-solid process, and excellent people.

THE PRESIDENT

How does any person about to become president of the United States ready him or herself to lead the nation's foreign policy? By many experts' accounts, no president before or since has been as well prepared to assume the foreign policy responsibilities of the presidency as was President George H. W. Bush.[16] In addition to an impeccable classical education, he saw combat duty as a naval aviator during World War II, and was elected to Congress. He served as United States ambassador to the United Nations and as U.S. envoy to China. He led the Central Intelligence Agency and served the full eight years of the Reagan presidency as vice president. With this background, not only did Bush have a firm grasp on the policies and politics that drove U.S. engagement in the world, but he actually knew how the machinery worked (or didn't) in the federal government, in Congress, in the United Nations, and in NATO. He was an instinctive politician and knew many world leaders personally, as well as their foreign and defense ministers and ambassadors.

Bush made two calls immediately following his election as president in 1988—the first to James A. Baker III, his longtime friend, to ask that he serve as secretary of state. The president-elect next called Scowcroft. Bush had worked with Scowcroft over the years, and he knew and admired the Air Force general for his competence, strategic thinking, bureaucratic abilities, and discretion.[17] Scowcroft reciprocated the admiration and easily agreed to take the position. No East Coast Brahmin, Scowcroft hailed from Ogden, Utah. After attending public schools, he graduated from West Point and then joined the Air Force where he spent a career in planning and strategy.

As superficially dissimilar as they may have seemed, they were actually a lot alike. Scowcroft shared the president's values, devotion to country, and self-deprecating sense of humor.[18] While a cadet at West Point, Scowcroft studied Russian and foreign affairs. From his early days on active duty in the military, he became known among his peers and superiors for his razor-sharp intellect, dry sense of humor, and mastery of strategic thinking as well as attention to detail. Scowcroft excelled at powering through complex intellectual challenges and quickly rose through the ranks. Like the president, Scowcroft was also a pilot, but a near-fatal plane crash grounded him for nearly two years. He taught in the Social Sciences Department at West Point, served in Belgrade as attaché, and had tours in the Pentagon. In 1971, President Nixon selected him to be his military aide where Kissinger took notice and asked that Scowcroft join the NSC staff as his deputy in 1973. During these years, Bush and Scowcroft got to know and respect each other.

From his decades of experience at the center of U.S. foreign policy making, Scowcroft believed deeply in the importance of clear, principled strategic thinking to advance the interests of the United States in a complex world. A patriot to his core, he believed loyalty to those interests could travel comfortably with loyalty to the president's agenda. And he placed great importance on coherent, deliberate process and on the value of close personal relationships with people of character and competence.[19]

Most people with close-hand knowledge of the relationship between George H. W. Bush and Brent Scowcroft cannot help but comment on how well they meshed. Comprehensively compatible, no one recalls that they ever really clashed—and not just because Scowcroft knew his place.[20] They were cut from the same cloth, born to the "greatest generation" just ten months apart, and shared the same worldview. They both believed in assertive but prudential U.S. global leadership and, at the same time, on the need for the United States to be able to call and rely on strong friends and allies.

They observed the same work habits and functioned especially well with those for whom they held deep personal connections. Their networks and close ties to counterparts reached far and wide—across the government and around the world. Remarkably, in a town where grace has ever been in short supply and at a time when the international stakes were as high as tempers were short, both men related to others with a deep sense of humanity and kindness, despite wrestling with some of the most consequential issues that plagued the late twentieth century.

Unrelenting pressure and unsparing scrutiny landed on their desks daily. Yet, they both remained unfailingly polite, generous, and, perhaps above all, modest, possessing a genuine and deep personal humility. Beneath the exterior, however, both men were clear-eyed realists, who met the world where it was. They believed firmly in American exceptionalism and in the strength of the United States to lead. At the same time, they valued strong friends and allies and in coalition building. They strove continually to counter obstructions to U.S. interests and to position the United States to best advantage—without provoking crisis or open conflict that invariably lead to unforeseeable consequences.

But Scowcroft knew that the decisions the president made would be only as good as the process that delivered up the options to him. Moreover, he was prepared, as was his deputy Robert Gates, to discipline the federal bureaucracy to ensure that the president was well served.

THE PROCESS

When Scowcroft resumed responsibilities as national security advisor to the president, he brought with him a principled sense of not only how to prioritize issues affecting the national interest, but also how to organize and run the processes necessary to advance those issues. Scowcroft had seen a well-functioning NSC system up close—when he served as deputy to Kissinger from 1973 to 1974. He admired that model, in which Nixon and Kissinger incorporated some of the best practices from previous administrations: bringing advice closer to the president from a small circle of advisors and regularizing the committee structure and staff process across the various departments and agencies of the executive branch under the firm direction of the White House.[21]

Scowcroft and Gates moved rapidly to imprint the systems and processes with the clear expectation that the president would be best served from advice given directly by his closest advisors who formed the Principals Committee. To prepare issues for consideration by the principals, department deputies met regularly in Deputies Committee meetings that shouldered the load of issues across the foreign policy spectrum. As deputy national security advisor, Gates ran these meetings, which often convened multiple times daily. To prepare the deputies meetings, interagency groups were formed at the working level, drawing in all relevant agencies and offices to ensure that issues were thoroughly examined and refined for presidential decision. For especially sensitive matters, "small groups" were created to provide the president directly with advice from his most senior advisors. But Scowcroft wanted a system that fully engaged the bureaucracy—despite his scaled-down expectations of what it could ultimately deliver, following an experience with a series of unimpressive studies he had requested to examine the major issues facing the new president.[22]

Scowcroft, aided mightily by Gates, who actually plowed through most of the paper generated every day, served as a watchful steward of it all. He saw his own role as twofold: foremost, to "run the system, to make the process work, and work efficiently" in order to provide the president with the timely information and analysis he needed to make decisions. Second, Scowcroft believed his job was to serve the president with his best advice and counsel, untethered to any one department's agenda. Whenever presenting the president options, Scowcroft would always represent the other principals' views first. Then, free of any bureaucratic or institutional bias, Scowcroft would also share his own views.[23]

Serving the nation and the president well required judicious management not only of the larger bureaucracies, but also of the large personalities that headed State, Defense, and intelligence. Both Bush and Scowcroft were determined not to recreate the acrimony that had characterized these key relationships in previous administrations. Fortunately, Scowcroft had excellent relations with both Jim Baker and Dick Cheney, whom he had known for years, and, consequently, personal politics created little to no turmoil among them. Scowcroft never impeded their access to the president, often carried their water, and never sought the limelight.

Scowcroft was also quite close to Baker's deputy secretary of defense, Lawrence Eagleburger, with whom he had shared the experience of living in Belgrade. To keep the wheels of government turning, Scowcroft and Eagleburger would speak daily, often multiple times. Gates, too, engaged continuously with the members of the Deputies Committee.[24] These close personal associations allowed small things to stay small and helped clear the path when the president's time and focus were urgently needed.

Not surprisingly, Scowcroft also had excellent relations with the wider bureaucracy, chatting regularly with the heads of Justice, the FBI, Treasury, and other cabinet officers who needed his guidance, advice, or help with access to the president. He felt strongly that, despite the likelihood the bureaucracy would not of itself reach the level of performance the times demanded, excluding important agencies from having a say in decisions and process that affected their interests would provoke a worse outcome. He skillfully managed the powerful egos surrounding the president, in part because he had a long history with many, a reputation for absolute integrity and discretion, and was known to all as an honest broker.[25] He also had the president's unwavering support throughout.

Scowcroft took very seriously the responsibility to staff the president properly and professionally. He met with Bush daily and had breakfast with the secretaries of the State and Defense Departments regularly. He held weekly meetings with the NSC staff. Whenever a member of the NSC staff was summoned to the Oval Office to take notes for a presidential phone call or meeting, Scowcroft—who did not always accompany the staffer—expected that individual to drop into his office for a pre-brief check-in and post-meeting debrief.[26] He insisted on brevity, clarity, and purpose in every piece of correspondence that went to the president. "Remember," he would regularly tell the staff, "when you type in 'Memorandum for the President' . . . that's where it goes. So be right."

Scowcroft also guarded the prerogatives of his office with care, believing the responsibility to prepare and equip the president to discharge the foreign policy of the United States required discipline and focus. He became impatient, for example, if senior officials from other parts of the White House tried to poke their noses in matters of national security. He accepted with reluctance the deputy White House chief of staff's attendance in Deputy Committee meetings because he knew it was a direct legacy of the Iran-Contra affair. But Scowcroft took a back seat to none when it came to knowing what the president needed and when he needed it regarding foreign policy, and had no patience for those who sought to dabble.[27]

Life on the National Security Council staff was not for the distracted or faint-hearted. Staffers typically worked six and seven days a week and were constantly on call. Massive geostrategic upheaval took place during the years of the Bush administration, as the Soviet Union collapsed, Germany unified, the Chinese cracked down on pro-democracy rallies in Tiananmen Square, Saddam Hussein invaded Kuwait, war erupted in Yugoslavia, and a devastating humanitarian crisis unfolded in Somalia.

These years also saw innumerable other major events and crises that pressed demands constantly on the president as well as the NSC apparatus: the U.S. invasion of Panama, an attempted coup in Russia, the overthrow of communism in Poland and Romania, the death of Japanese emperor Hirohito, Rajiv Gandhi's murder in India, Nelson Mandela's emergence from prison, the end of the fifteen-year war in Angola, the sudden influx of Haitian refugees, the murder of American hostages William Buckley and Colonel William J. Higgins in Lebanon, and the end of military rule in Chile, to name but a few. Every week held a new challenge, both internationally and domestically. A major earthquake in San Francisco, the environmental catastrophe resulting from the grounding of the Exxon tanker *Valdez* in Alaska, and a fitful economy all served to remind that foreign policy was not the president's only priority.

Typically, Scowcroft accompanied the president on travel and often on weekends when the president would retreat to Camp David. The president began each day with an intelligence briefing and a review of major foreign policy matters. When Scowcroft could not be with the president, an NSC staffer was always available, approved and empowered by Scowcroft. If a staffer were new, Scowcroft would leave nothing to chance: "Take good notes. You're not being invited in for a chat. But if the president asks you what you think about something, don't say, well, Mr. President, that's your decision—*he knows that*. Be ready with the information you know he is going to need. And if you don't know something, for God's sake, say you don't know, but that you will get the information right away."

The high stakes and low tolerance for error placed a premium on populating the National Security Council staff with individuals with a demonstrated track record of performance. No blind hires, no on-the-job-trainees. Scowcroft hired those whom he knew personally or those who were recommended by people he trusted implicitly. The result was a remarkable collection of professionals who helped bury the bones of Iran-Contra and establish the National Security Council staff at the apex of the U.S. foreign policy process.

THE PEOPLE

Scowcroft expected excellence from his staff. They had to be knowledgeable, not just intellectual. They had to be willing to work very hard and put in really long days. They had to be able to think strategically and substantively, not just procedurally. Nevertheless, there were lots of procedures and mounds of paper.[28] Countless briefing notes and decision memoranda made their way through the NSC staff system to the president every week. Scowcroft's standards were high: "Don't send the president a memo with the subject 'Your Meeting with So-and-So,' he knows he's got the meeting. Tell him what the meeting is about: 'Advancing the U.S.-Turkish relationship' or 'Next Steps in Yugoslavia.' Take seriously your responsibility to prepare the president to act in the best interest of this Country."

When the Berlin Wall fell in 1989 and the Soviet Union began its massive disintegration, the world had no right to expect that this transformation of the global order that had stood for half a century would have been as relatively peaceful as it was. And yet it was, in no small part due to the prudence, judgment, and involved management exercised by the president and his national security team. This remarkable achievement saw the orderly reunification of Germany, the emergence of Russia and other successor states, and recognition of and admission to the United Nations for the largest number of new states since the end of colonialism. This peaceful management of the end of the Cold War ranks among the best-known legacies of the Bush era. A much less well-known legacy of these years is the extraordinary record of continued service to the nation over decades by the cadre of individuals who served President Bush under Scowcroft on the NSC staff.

Scowcroft has remarked that the process of choosing people is "one of the most crucial, and one of the most error-ridden" imaginable. He also believed that getting people right is deeply important to the effective running of the U.S. government.[29] Even as brilliant a strategist as Kissinger, for example, struggled with his first round of picks for the NSC staff.[30] Still, Scowcroft found much to admire in the way Kissinger ran process and sought out the views of his staff to engage them vigorously in debate. Scowcroft, too, admired General Andrew Goodpaster, who served as an advisor to Eisenhower, but he took after no single role model. Rather, he conformed himself to what President Bush needed and to the task of making the bureaucracy work.

Scowcroft did not believe that "people picking" was a science; rather, he trusted his own instincts and judgment when it came to choosing those with whom he would work. He, like President Bush, placed a good deal of importance on personal relationships to get things done. He chose Bob Gates immediately as his deputy, and made one of his first calls to Condoleezza Rice, a young Stanford professor with whom Scowcroft had become impressed during an academic conference on the Soviet Union and nuclear weapons.[31]

Scrowcroft also knew instinctively that high-speed people are high-maintenance. Somehow, he managed to cultivate in everyone he oversaw a sense of the greater im-

portance of mission over self. He could genuinely empathize—because he had served
in the same trenches himself—with the staff toiling endless hours under the continual
strain of rapidly unfolding world events of great consequence.

Scowcroft drew on his roots at West Point and the Air Force as well as his long
experience in government to populate the ranks of the NSC staff, personally ap-
proving every professional who joined the staff. Nearly half a dozen alumni from
West Point's Social Sciences Department alone served under Scowcroft during these
years.[32] He held fast to those whom he valued most, taking several senior members
of the staff with him when he returned to the private sector and reestablished his
successful international consultancy.[33]

During the period 1989–1993, the NSC staff stayed steady at roughly forty-five
to fifty professionals—including Scowcroft and Gates. Over the course of the entire four-year term of the Bush presidency, slightly more than one hundred officers
served on the NSC staff. Despite the grueling work and tremendous pressure, there
was strikingly little turnover.[34] The Executive Office of the President had only a
relatively modest budget for the NSC staff, and most of the directors and senior
directors came from across the federal government. State Department Foreign Service officers, CIA professionals, military officers from every branch of service, and
officials from other agencies all served.

And while the Bush NSC staff remains a standout example of a professionally
run organization at the highest levels of government, at least equally extraordinary
has been the record of continued service by the members of this same staff. Three
individuals attained cabinet rank (Gates, Rice, Hayden), and, remarkably, Gates and
Rice each held two cabinet-level posts, while Hayden is the only individual to have
served both as the director of the National Security Agency and as director of the
Central Intelligence Agency. Five individuals became department or agency deputy
secretaries—serving as the number two and chief operating officer in the Department
of State, the Central Intelligence Agency, the Department of Energy, Directorate for
National Intelligence, and the Department of Homeland Security. In fact, at the outset of the Obama administration, three of the six individuals who made up the core
of the national security Deputies Committee had served on Scowcroft's NSC staff.[35]

Many others went on to reach ambassadorial, four-star, or equivalent ranks.[36] Some
colleagues advanced to more senior positions in the George W. Bush and Obama
administrations, while others returned to the private sector to become partners in
major law firms, prominent lobbying firms (Kissinger's and Scowcroft's own among
them), or senior academics at leading universities. Collectively, they have contributed
over two thousand years of public service to the nation and the public good—a quiet,
powerful legacy in which any president might justifiably take great pride.

CONCLUDING OBSERVATIONS

What accounts for the unique performance and reputation of the NSC staff under
Scowcroft during President Bush's tenure? The short answer can be found in the

extraordinary foreign policy capability of the president, combined with the effective processes and people put in place by Scowcroft. A longer answer no doubt rests on the importance that Bush and Scowcroft placed on the steady, principled advancement of U.S. national interests in a world undergoing enormous strategic change and on the care and value they put into their relationships with colleagues—at home and abroad—to get things done. Equal weight must be given, however, to the personalities of these two men that drove them both to a lifetime of public service and equipped them with the skills to craft a thoroughgoing process and the personal qualities to attract the best people and extract the best from them.

President Bush and General Scowcroft each brought considerable knowledge, experience, and bureaucratic savvy to the challenge of remaking the national security decision-making process following the Iran-Contra controversy. Indeed, much of the power of the so-called Scowcroft model rests in this remarkable, perhaps unique, combination of president and advisor. They applied considerable thought and effort to the challenge of stewarding U.S. foreign policy in a world truly transformed: how to accept the baton, how to carry the baton, and how to pass the baton. As the Bush administration was ending in that winter of 1992, its most important legacies had already begun.

BIBLIOGRAPHIC NOTE

This brief reflection on the period, people, and issues surrounding the Iran-Contra affair and subsequent process of restoring integrity to U.S. foreign policy making under the Bush presidency cannot do justice to the vast literatures that exist on all of these matters by firsthand participants and expert scholars. The following sources offer some suggested reading for the curious reader interested in learning more.

The Iran Contra Affair

Draper, Theodore. *A Very Thin Line: The Iran-Contra Affairs.* New York: Hill and Wang 1991.
Tower, John, Edmund Muskie, and Brent Scowcroft. *The Tower Commission Report.* New York: Random House, February 1987.
Walsh, Lawrence E. *Firewall: The Iran-Contra Conspiracy and Cover-Up.* New York: W.W. Norton 1997.

George H. W. Bush and His Presidency

Bush, George W. *41: A Portrait of My Father.* New York: Random House 2014.
Bush, George H. W., and Brent Scowcroft. *A World Transformed.* New York: Random House 1998.
Meacham, Jon. *Destiny and Power: The American Odyssey of George Herbert Walker Bush.* New York: Random House 2015.
Nelson, Michael, and Barbara A. Perry, eds., *41: Inside the Bush Presidency.* Ithaca, NY: Cornell University Press 2014.

The National Security Council Staff and Process

Best, Richard Jr. *The National Security Council: An Organizational Assessment.* Washington, DC: Congressional Research Service, December 2011.

Daalder, Ivo H., and I. M. Destler. *In the Shadow of the Oval Office: Profiles of the National Security Advisers and the Presidents They Served—from JFK to George W. Bush.* New York: Simon and Schuster 2009.

Gans, John. *White House Warriors: How the National Security Council Transformed the American Way of War.* New York: W.W. Norton & Company 2019.

Hooker, Richard. *The NSC Staff: New Choices for a New Administration.* Washington, DC: National Defense University Press, November 2016.

Whittaker, Alan G., Shannon A. Brown, Frederick C. Smith, and Elizabeth McKune. *The National Security Policy Process: The National Security Council and Interagency System.* Washington, DC: National Defense University Press, August 2011.

Wilcox, Mark. "The National Security Council Deputies Committee: Engine of the Policy Process." *Interagency Journal*, 5, no. 1 (Winter 2014): 22–32.

Zegart, Amy. *Flawed by Design: The Evolution of the CIA, JCS, and NSC.* Stanford, CA: Stanford University Press, 1999.

Brent Scowcroft

Lauter, David. "The Man behind the President: Brent Scowcroft Serves as Bush's Counselor and Sounding Board." *Los Angeles Times*, 14 October, 1990. https://www.latimes.com/archives/la-xpm-1990-10-14-mn-3592-story.html.

Scowcroft, Brent. "Brent Scowcroft Oral History. Interview with Philip Zelikow, *Presidential Oral Histories Project*, The Miller Center, University of Virginia 1999, https://millercenter.org/the-presidency/presidential-oral-histories/brent-scowcroft-oral-history-national-security-advisor.

Sparrow, Bartholomew. *The Strategist: Brent Scowcroft and the Call of National Security.* New York: Public Affairs, 2015.

NOTES

The author would like to thank Andrew Card, Brian DeVallance, Douglas Lute, Mulberger, Brent Scowcroft, Steven Weirich, and several anonymous reviewers for their assistance in preparing this manuscript. The views expressed in this chapter are solely those of the author and do not represent the official position of any organization or institution.

1. See, for example, Stephen J. Hadley, *The Role and Importance of the National Security Advisor*, address presented at the Scowcroft Legacy Conference, Texas A&M University, April 26, 2016; Richard Hooker, *The NSC Staff: New Choices for a New Administration* (Washington, DC: National Defense University Press, 2016); and Mark Wilcox, "The National Security Council Deputies Committee: Engine of the Policy Process," *Interagency Journal* 5, no. 1 (Winter 2014): 22–32.

2. John Tower, Edmund Muskie, and Brent Scowcroft, *The Tower Commission Report* (New York: Random House, 1987). See the bibliographic note at the end of this chapter for additional reading on the Iran-Contra affair.

3. The Iran-Contra affair also changed key internal security practices for succeeding administrations. As the Bush White House prepared to transition to the incoming Clinton administration in 1993, for example, security officials abruptly entered all of the NSC staff offices and swept up the internal hard drives and complete paper files of every member of the National Security Council staff. Not a single scrap of paper or electronic file was available to the handful of Bush appointees agreed by Scowcroft and incoming National Security Advisor, Tony Lake, to remain in place to assist the new president. More than inconvenient, it represented a severe blow to the patriotism and honor of those who continued to serve, and it hampered efficient policy making on key issues from the start. Asked by Lake to prepare the new president's first official national security directive to evaluate the raging war in Yugoslavia, the responsible staffer could only rely on residual knowledge, intuition, and memory to prepare PRD-1, as it became known, on the afternoon of January 20, 1993, to be ready for signature shortly following President Clinton's inauguration.

4. Presidential Order establishing the Tower Commission, December 1, 1986, instructed the panel to "get all the facts out."

5. See *The Tower Commission Report* and the numerous contemporaneous newspaper accounts in the *New York Times*, the *Washington Post*, and the *Los Angeles Times*.

6. Stephen J. Hadley, who would later serve in the George H. W. Bush administration as assistant secretary of defense for international security policy and subsequently as deputy national security advisor and as national security advisor to President George W. Bush, served as counsel to the Tower Commission and drafted signification portions of the report.

7. In contrast, President Reagan addressed the nation in a dramatic speech, taking full responsibility for what transpired. In one of his most memorable lines he noted: "A few months ago I told the American people I did not trade arms for hostages. My heart and my best intentions still tell me that is true, but the facts and the evidence tell me it is not." See "The Reagan White House; Transcript of Reagan's Speech: 'I take full responsibility for my actions,'" *New York Times*, March 5, 1987, https://www.nytimes.com/1987/03/05/us/reagan-white-house-transcript-reagan-s-speech-take-full-responsibilty-for-my.html.

8. For Scowcroft's recollections on shoddy performance of NSC in Iran-Contra, see "Brent Scowcroft Oral History," Philip Zelikow interview, *Presidential Oral Histories Project*, The Miller Center, University of Virginia 1999, https://millercenter.org/the-presidency/presidential-oral-histories/brent-scowcroft-oral-history-national-security-advisor.

9. *Tower Commission Report*, 88–93.

10. Ibid. on president's role.

11. For the text of the National Security Act of 1947, see https://www.dni.gov/index.php/ic-legal-reference-book/national-security-act-of-1947.

12. *Tower Commission Report*.

13. See, for example, Robert C. Toth, "*The Tower Commission Report*: NSC Staff is Faulted for Making Policy in Secret," *The Los Angeles Times*, 27 February, 1987, https://www.latimes.com/archives/la-xpm-1987-02-27-mn-4038-story.html.

14. The Iran-Contra scandal deeply affected everyone in the national security orbit of the Reagan presidency—including Vice President Bush, who did not escape criticism. For one critique of Vice President Bush and what role he might have played during the Iran-Contra affair, see David Johnston, "Years Later, Questions Remain about Bush's Role in the Iran Contra Affair," *New York Times*, October 4, 1992, https://www.nytimes.com/1992/10/04/us/years-later-questions-remain-about-bush-s-role-in-the-iran-contra-affair.html. As his own term of office was drawing to a close, Bush pardoned former secretary of defense Caspar Weinberger, former national security advisor Robert (Bud) McFarlane, and four others, an act for which he

received a good deal of criticism. See David Johnston, "The Pardons; Bush Pardons 6. In Iran Affair, Aborting a Weinberger Trial; Prosecutor Assails 'Cover-Up,'" *New York Times*, December 29, 1992, https://www.nytimes.com/1992/12/25/us/pardons-bush-pardons-6-iran-affair-aborting-weinberger-trial-prosecutor-assails.html?auth=login-email; and also Johnston, "The Iran-Contra Report: The Overview; Walsh Criticizes Reagan and Bush over Iran-Contra." *New York Times*, January 19, 1994, https://www.nytimes.com/1994/01/19/world/iran-contra-report-overview-walsh-criticizes-reagan-bush-over-iran-contra.html.

15. See George H. W. Bush and Brent Scowcroft, *A World Transformed* (New York: Random House 1998), 16–19.

16. All of the full-length treatments of the Bush presidency make this point. See the bibliographic note.

17. Bush and Scowcroft, *A World Transformed*. Citation for Scowcroft's Presidential Medal of Freedom.

18. See Bartholomew Sparrow, *The Strategist: Brent Scowcroft and the Call of National Security* (New York: Public Affairs, 2015).

19. "Brent Scowcroft Oral History."

20. Bush and Scowcroft, *A World Transformed*.

21. See "Brent Scowcroft Oral History."

22. Ibid.

23. Ibid.

24. Regular attendees at Deputies Committee meetings included Undersecretary of Defense for Policy Paul Wolfowitz, Vice Chairman of the Joint Chiefs of Staff Admiral David Jeremiah, Deputy Director of the CIA Richard (Dick) Kerr, and either Eagleburger from the State Department or Robert Kimmitt and later Arnold Kanter.

25. Scowcroft did not believe in using his access and relationship with Bush to "guide" the president. He knew that the way he formulated issues or framed decisions could strongly direct the kind of answer he hoped for. He avoided that practice, not only because he thought it was wrong, but also because he believed it contributed to the Iran-Contra outcome.

26. Of course, the staffer was never completely flying solo. Scowcroft protected his staff, especially with the political side of the White House. He would always be sure to alert the president's chief of staff or other necessary officials when the president engaged in an activity which fell under the NSC staff's purview.

27. See "Brent Scowcroft Oral History."

28. See Gates's reflection on paperwork in "Robert M. Gates Oral History," Tim Naftali et al. interviewers, *Presidential Oral Histories Project*, The Miller Center, University of Virginia 1999, https://millercenter.org/the-presidency/presidential-oral-histories/robert-m-gates-deputy-director-central.

29. See ibid., as well as "Brent Scowcroft Oral History."

30. "Brent Scowcroft Oral History."

31. One distinctive hallmark of individuals who served under Scowcroft during this period is that they never say they served on the NSC; it's always the NSC *staff*.

32. One of Scowcroft's most important mentors early in his career was George Lincoln, a giant in national security and defense circles for over three decades. Serving as General George C. Marshall's chief planner during World War II, Lincoln remained extremely influential and on a first-name basis with major figures in U.S. foreign policy over the years. He is credited with drawing the line at the 38th parallel that demarks North and South Korea and for designing the international security framework that gave rise to the North Atlantic Treaty Organiza-

tion. Lincoln declined promotion to general officer so that he could return to West Point to teach. He aggressively sought out promising young officers, sent them to Harvard, Stanford, Columbia, and other top universities to bring them to the faculty in the Social Sciences Department at West Point and then return to the Army. Generations of military officers made their way to the department, following in the footsteps of Goodpaster and Scowcroft. Senator Jack Reed of Rhode Island, Generals Wes Clark, Barry McCaffrey, David Petraeus, Peter Chiarelli, Daniel Christman, and Douglas Lute, among others, have all served as members of the "Lincoln Brigade." Les Gelb, former policy maker, journalist, and president emeritus of the Council on Foreign Relations credits "Sosh heroes" (as former members of the Social Sciences Department are known familiarly) with saving his academic career while in graduate school.

33. Virginia (Lampley) Mulberger, Arnold Kanter, Eric Melby, Daniel Poneman, and the indispensable Florence Gantt moved with Scowcroft to form the Scowcroft Group, a highly successful international consultancy.

34. The size of the NSC staff under successive administrations has grown significantly: From 1991 when it numbered approximately forty, to one hundred in 2000; two hundred in 2008; and approximately four hundred in 2016. See Mark F. Cancian, *Limiting Size of NSC Staff* (Washington, DC: Center for Strategic and International Studies, July 1, 2016), https://www.csis.org/analysis/limiting-size-nsc-staff.

35. Interestingly, nearly every other appointee in the early Obama national security deputies process had served in the first Clinton administration and worked closely with the outgoing Bush team, as noted above. Thus, when Obama administration deputies first sat down to meet in January 2009, they had already all known each other for nearly twenty years. These relationships greatly eased the transition of the new presidency.

36. Admiral Jonathan Howe, who succeeded Gates as deputy to Scowcroft, became a senior representative of the United Nations secretary-general and undersecretary-general—the senior-most operating rank in the United Nations. In the Latin American directorate, every individual went on to represent the United States abroad as U.S. ambassador. In the European and Soviet Affairs directorate, of the dozen or so individuals who served during the course of the Bush administration, one became national security advisor and secretary of state (Rice), five became U.S. ambassadors, two became deputies (directors of National Intelligence and the Department of Homeland Security), and two became deans of major public policy schools. From the Arms Control and Defense directorate, Heather Wilson served as a member of Congress and as secretary of the Air Force, Daniel Poneman became deputy secretary of the Department of Energy, and John A. Gordon, USAF, received his fourth star, became deputy at CIA and later Homeland Security advisor to President George W. Bush. Richard Haass went on to lead the premier U.S. think tank, the Council on Foreign Relations, and William J. Burns (who also served as deputy secretary of state) heads the Carnegie Endowment for International Peace. Peter Watson served as president of the Overseas Private Investment Corporation (OPIC) and as chairman of the International Trade Commission.

5

The End of the Cold War and German Reunification

Philip Zelikow and Condoleezza Rice

In September 1988, Henry Kissinger wrote a long and public "memo to the next president." Back then, there were not many Americans who could ask a national newsmagazine to clear the space for a nearly five-thousand-word "memo" about the fate of the world. Kissinger could.

"The postwar era in international relations is coming to an end," Kissinger began. This was much bigger than Gorbachev. "A new era cannot be based on ephemeral personalities," he explained. It would not be the first time that "the West deluded itself by basing its policies on favorable assessments of Soviet leaders," and Gorbachev "seems intent on weakening the Western Alliance" because the Soviet policy was "to diminish American influence, if not to expel us from Europe altogether." The real issue, the much bigger issue, was that Europe was about to be transformed. "The political structure of Europe—East and West—will thus emerge as the central issue of the '90s."

What Kissinger emphasized was the need "to create a *political* framework" to manage change, with a real political strategy behind it. He speculated about U.S.-Soviet arrangements that would give the Soviets "security guarantees (widely defined)." Kissinger put forward a radical idea. He suggested "a drastic reduction of all outside forces in Europe—including those of the United States—that might revolutionize present concepts of security." As "outside forces" left, Kissinger supported "rapid progress toward West European integration."

"The time has come," Kissinger concluded, "for the first comprehensive discussion about the political future of Europe since the outbreak of World War I." And not just Europe. He foresaw the development across the world of "a new international order." Weeks later, Reagan's vice president, George H. W. Bush, was elected as the new American president. Kissinger pressed his argument again, on Bush. "[E]mpires do not disintegrate without convulsions," he warned. Without a full political understanding, "the two sides are working themselves—in the name of peace and arms control—into a classical European crisis of the kind that produced World War I." Any sustainable solution for Europe "must either include both the Soviet Union and the United States or exclude both." At most, only small outside forces should remain in Europe, confined to their bases.

The "postwar" era was coming to an end. The whole political structure of Europe, West as well as East, was now back on the table, as it had not been for generations.

In Moscow, sitting with his Politburo colleagues as the year 1988 came to an end, Gorbachev expected conservatives in America and Europe to try to keep the Cold War going. They would either do nothing or take new steps that would "contribute to the arms race." More "liberal circles," he said, welcomed the Soviet efforts to rescue socialism. He analogized what he was doing as comparable to the way the American president, Franklin Roosevelt, had rescued capitalism with his New Deal program in the 1930s. Gorbachev thought the incoming Bush administration that would take office in January 1989 would be "centrist." It would probably not make matters worse. Nor would it do much to make them better. To Gorbachev, the new Bush group looked like "traditionalists" who "still do not have any foreign policy alternative to the traditional post-war course." They were still worried "that they might be on the losing side."

What exactly did the Soviets hope the Americans might do? This was less clear. In his December 1988 UN speech Gorbachev had stated three hopes. All had to do with arms control. He wanted the United States to move forward in the talks on strategic nuclear arms (START), chemical weapons, and conventional forces (CFE). Nothing had happened on either side that seemed likely to close the difficult gaps in the START talks. The discussions on banning chemical weapons were in an early stage and would depend on quite complex verification issues. The CFE negotiations were just about to get underway and were on an enormous scale, with all twenty-three NATO and Warsaw Pact states participating in talks that covered Europe from the Atlantic to the Urals. Meanwhile NATO was planning to move forward with new military moves on short-range nuclear missile forces, the SNF issue. None of this, though, directly addressed the broader vision for the future of Europe and the world.

The new Bush administration's "traditionalists" soon got their first test case about how they would react to Gorbachev. It was a very private test, and it was about Kissinger and his arguments. At the end of 1988, as Gorbachev was comparing notes with his Politburo colleagues, Bush and his newly designated secretary of state, James Baker, were musing about Kissinger's big ideas. Baker asked the State Department's European bureau and the aide who would be his new policy planning director, Dennis Ross, what they thought about Kissinger's arguments. The bureau counseled that the United States should just stay on course. Ross did not agree.

At the White House and in the election campaign, Ross had already worked with Bush. He had heard Bush say that it was time to "dream big dreams." Ross agreed.

"We're entering a period that is really unlike any we've seen throughout the whole post-war era," Ross wrote to Baker in December 1988, "and this is not the time to put our thinking in a straitjacket." He scorned the European bureau's advice as "more of the same." That would just "be content with the current trends, fostering them but not having to do much to fuel them." Ross argued instead that the full potential for change could be more radical, as radical as Kissinger imagined. It really was a crossroads in world history.

But Ross did not agree with Kissinger's recommendations. First, he thought Kissinger was too suspicious about Gorbachev, that he "probably exaggerates the dangers" of Gorbachev's initiatives. Nor did Ross like the idea of seeking a U.S.-Soviet understanding about how to handle change in Europe. "We certainly don't want to create a new Yalta."

The United States should have its own agenda for Europe's future, Ross argued. The future of Eastern Europe and the rest of Europe should be front and center. "[T]he division of Europe symbolizes the continuation of the Cold War. If we are entering a new era, and if there is a great new potential, we ought to be willing to deal with that key symbol—and we ought to tell Gorbachev this." Just because "we aren't prepared to accept or promote the 'Grand Design' in Europe as Kissinger has defined it, we ought not to be too constrained in our thinking and not simply reject new ideas. That's not the way to dream big dreams."

Kissinger offered to be an emissary to set up this U.S.-Soviet political dialogue. Since he was visiting Moscow in January for a previously scheduled conference, he suggested to Bush that, while there, he might meet with Gorbachev and explore ways to set up a channel for secret discussions. Bush, Baker, and Scowcroft went along with this. In his Moscow meetings, Kissinger repeated his argument that arms control was not so important. The key was a political understanding about the future of Europe, creating "conditions in which a political evolution could be possible but a political explosion would not be allowed." Kissinger did not repeat his idea of a mutual U.S. and Soviet withdrawal from Europe. To Alexander Yakovlev, a member of the Politburo, he said the U.S. presence was vital, if just as "a guarantee against the adventurism of Europeans themselves."

Gorbachev talked to Kissinger. On Europe, he said, "My view is that we should both keep an eye on Germany and by that I mean both Germanies. We must not do anything to unsettle Europe into a crisis." On Eastern Europe, Gorbachev was philosophical. Life brings certain changes that no one can stop. But both sides should be careful not to threaten the other's security.

Kissinger proposed a secret channel for U.S.-Soviet planning. In this channel, Bush's newly designated national security adviser (and former Kissinger aide), Brent Scowcroft, would represent Bush and the United States. Gorbachev designated former Soviet ambassador Anatoly Dobrynin as the likely Soviet representative in the channel. It would be like old times, when Kissinger-Dobrynin was President Richard Nixon's prime, secret channel, usually cutting out the secretary of state. Now it would be Scowcroft-Dobrynin. Gorbachev pledged secrecy. Only he, Yakovlev,

Dobrynin, and Soviet Minister of Foreign Affairs Eduard Shevardnadze would know about the channel. Dobrynin mentioned the Soviet desire to talk about China: "In 30 years they will be a nightmare." The plan was that the "political dialogue" in this channel could get going even before arms control efforts resumed in earnest. Perhaps it could get started as early as March 1989.

Two days after Bush received Kissinger's written report, Gorbachev phoned Bush to congratulate him on his inauguration. Bush promised to hear Kissinger's report in person. He added that we "would not necessarily believe everything [Kissinger said] because this was, after all, Henry Kissinger." Bush then brought up the issue of a channel for U.S.-Soviet discussions. There would indeed be a channel, but his spokesperson in it would be James Baker. Bush said he hoped Baker, after he finished his consultations in Europe with all of America's allies, would establish the kind of tight relationship with Shevardnadze that former secretary of state George Shultz had established. Bush stressed that "Jim Baker was very close to him."

That ended any notion of a special Scowcroft-Dobrynin channel. It also effectively ended Kissinger's role as a facilitator. The Baker-Shevardnadze discussions got underway on about the intended schedule; their first meeting was on March 7. Baker apparently took care to be sure that Bush established that he, Baker, would be the point person in the U.S.-Soviet relationship. The point was not just about reaffirming Baker's primacy. Baker and his team also wanted to stay in the lead because they regarded Scowcroft and Scowcroft's new deputy, Robert Gates, as too cautious and conservative. For Baker, as for Bush, it was time to "dream big dreams."

THE VECTORS OF CHANGE

During the next few months, between February and May of 1989, the new American leaders conferred intensively with their counterparts in Western Europe, Canada, and Japan. Among them, an agenda emerged for a new Europe and a different world. An operating partnership also began to emerge, a partnership between the U.S. leaders and key counterparts in Western Europe that actively planned together. Leaders cataloged key problems and systematically made choices about how to try and solve them. These choices would set vectors of change, providing a sense of direction and magnitude.

Gorbachev's leadership in the Soviet Union had done much to set the stage. So, in his first weeks in office in February 1989, before Baker set off on a whirl of trips to Europe and Asia and back to Europe, Bush met privately with Baker to go over their thinking about U.S.-Soviet relations. With help from Ross, Baker prepared in his usual careful way, noting key points he planned to make and boiling them down into core messages.

To Baker, the essential points were that the changes in the Soviet Union were real. Gorbachev really was different. The jury was still out about how it would turn out. Bush was struck by the public prediction from the Soviet dissident scientist,

Andrei Sakharov, that Gorbachev might soon be overthrown. Baker did not think the Soviet outcome depended on U.S. actions. But, Baker noted, even if the United States could only affect Gorbachev's prospects "on the margins," we did not want him to fail. The U.S. role then was to help frame the hard choices Gorbachev would have to make. It could do this with negative incentives, making it clear that military competition would not work. It could also do this with positive incentives, "offering him the hand of partnership and by challenging him to give his slogans real content." The United States, Baker thought, would soon have to muster its own initiatives, for instance on conventional arms control or on chemical weapons: "Let's honestly probe, and let's challenge him to be bold in actions, not only words."

On this point, as on almost all others, Bush and Baker's instincts were about the same. Although the media at the time and historians would later make much of a so-called "pause" early in the Bush administration, these commentaries misunderstand what was really going on. While there were a couple of doubting voices about Gorbachev in the new Bush administration, Bush and Baker were not among them. They agreed that they wished to find a way to help Gorbachev in a constructive way. What they wanted to do was put their own stamp on U.S. policies. Bush and Baker did not think the policy positions they had inherited from the Reagan administration on next steps with the Soviet Union or on Europe were very interesting or promising. They did not inherit any pending breakthroughs or novel ideas in arms control, for example.

One of Baker's earliest priorities was, in fact, to distance the new administration from the Reagan administration's stance in Central America. Baker tried to achieve an early win by persuading the Congress (with great difficulty) to fund nonlethal assistance to the resistance in Nicaragua, then use the emerging peace process there to press the Nicaraguan government toward a solution.

Less than three weeks in office, Bush offered a revealing outline of his thinking in a relaxed meeting, held in Ottawa, with his friend the Canadian prime minister, Brian Mulroney. Baker and Scowcroft were there too. Bush underscored to Mulroney that this was an important phase for all of Europe. His plan was to think, consult with allies, and then "take the offensive, to save the Alliance, not just be seen as reacting to yet another [Gorbachev] move." Baker was about to visit with every NATO ally. Maybe, Bush added, Eastern Europe was the key, "get in there in *his* end zone! Not stir up revolution." The United States was right on human rights, on democracy, and on freedom. "There is a big opportunity for us in dealing with Eastern Europe," Bush explained, "if we can get our act together. There is a potential for economic cooperation, but there is also the danger," he added, "of pushing too far in Eastern Europe and causing the situation to get out of control, at which point the tanks might come in."

In addition to Eastern Europe, what, Mulroney asked, were Bush's priorities for the Western alliance? Bush ticked off three. First, there was "Alliance solidarity," with particular concern about Germany. The urgent issue there was whether or how to go through with the 1988 NATO decision to modernize U.S. short-range nuclear forces in Europe, which above all meant in Germany. Next was "moving ahead with the USSR." Baker had already flagged the need to come up with initiatives, at least in arms control. Third, Bush added, the United States needed a policy to deal with West European integration, as the Single European Market was expected to take full effect in 1992.

Mulroney knew very well how strong protectionism had become in the United States, amid the general erosion of the Cold War trading system. He had just gone through the near-failure of the new U.S.-Canada trade agreement. Called in to save the deal by the Reagan White House, Baker (then the Treasury secretary) had rescued it in the waning months of the Reagan administration. It had been a very close call. Now the Europeans seemed, with the Single European Act, to be creating what could become a "Fortress Europe," the largest integrated market in the world. This could redouble protectionist pressures on both sides of the Atlantic. Bush said that he wanted to find a way to sustain an open economic system.

Baker brought the discussion back to Gorbachev. He stressed that the administration did not want Gorbachev to fail. This was the Bush administration's position, even if there were some people in the United States who might disagree. Perhaps feeling called out, Scowcroft added that he too wanted to "move forward" with the Soviet Union. But he wanted to think of ways to do it that could be reversed quickly if something happened to Gorbachev. He wondered what could be done to preempt Gorbachev strategically. "That's the big issue," Baker chimed in, "and what we're seeking but don't yet have." The Americans would work on this. But, echoing the point he had made to Bush, "we *do* think that it's what happens in the USSR that will determine his success or not—not what the U.S. or the alliance does." Mulroney had some advice that resonated with Baker: "Some smart politics by the president of the United States is in order—a trip, a statement, and an initiative in the near-term, at least by May or June."

Bush and Baker started off at the run, as Baker visited all the NATO allies then joined Bush in East Asia. Bush, the former World War II pilot who had flown missions against Japan, was attending the funeral of the emperor who had led wartime Japan, Hirohito, and then going from there to South Korea and China (a return to the country where he had been America's envoy in 1974–1975).

Scowcroft suggested organizing a series of formal policy reviews that might develop a distinctive Bush administration approach. Bush and Baker agreed. But they all, including Scowcroft, became disillusioned with that review process and quickly discarded it. Instead, beginning early in March 1989, Bush, Baker, and Scowcroft organized a different and more informal policy planning effort—centered among a few officials in the State Department and the National Security Council staff.

The informal policy planning still had the same goal—to come up with a distinctive, fresh approach by working through a series of issues. Bush took Mulroney's advice but multiplied it, with a series of trips, speeches, and initiatives. These were rolled out, one after another, from April through July 1989. Having done so, in July 1989 Bush invited Gorbachev for a substantial, informal summit meeting to be held as soon as possible. One decision Bush, Baker, and Scowcroft had made early on was that the wider future of Europe was in play. Many of the key issues first had to deal with Europe more generally, not just U.S. relations with the Soviet Union.

Bush is often portrayed as a cautious, prudent "realist." A less schematic but more accurate assessment would find something different. Bush was an intelligent and almost peripatetically restless man, a competitive college baseball player in his younger days now reduced to tennis, golf, fishing, horseshoes, or competing at anything else that came to hand. Unlike Reagan, a self-taught intellectual who loved thinking and writing about political ideas, Bush was more action-oriented than reflective.

Bush was never comfortable with prepared, public speeches. Here again he was unlike Reagan. Bush came across better in person than he did on television. Though conversant on the issues, Bush's judgments about basic direction were often intuitive. His conversation and his correspondence (he was a frequent and faithful note and letter writer) are full of expressions like "I thought I had a feel for his heartbeat" when explaining how he and Gorbachev came to be able to "go around the world on issues." Bush's characteristic way of operating was to read and listen and try to digest the essence of the tone or position he thought he should adopt. That done, he would then reach out to counterparts and talk it through with them in his own way. When it came to hammering out the details, Bush would often turn that over to "Jimmy." Few but George Bush would refer to James Baker that way. But, with the possible exception of Thomas Jefferson and James Madison, no president in American history had ever been this close to his secretary of state.

At the end of 1988, Bush and Baker had been close, almost brotherly, friends for more than thirty years. They had gone through a lot together, from personal tragedies to political campaigns. During the eight years of the Reagan administration, when Baker had been White House chief of staff and Treasury secretary while Bush was vice president, Baker's political power on a given day had often been greater than Bush's. At one level they regarded each other as peers, with an undercurrent of competitive rivalry that was part of their makeup. Yet Baker carefully separated two George Bushes in his mind, one the longtime friend and the other the person Baker would address even in small meetings as "Mr. President."

Like Bush, Baker was oriented toward action. Where Bush would look for an essential theme or stance, Baker would try to convert it into a practical strategy, mapping out and negotiating the details. Baker would frequently see Bush alone, discussing what they would do next. Scowcroft would often be invited to sit in. When Baker later made a move, he could count on Bush to back his play. To one former governor who later joined Bush's cabinet, Bush and Baker "seemed connected telepathically; each man appeared perennially aware of what the other was thinking and doing." Each was conscious of the other's strengths. Even when they had played tennis doubles together as winning club players, Baker remembered that Bush was "great at the net and I was great at ground strokes. We were both weak as servers."

When it came to foreign policy, Baker recalled simply that "there was no daylight between us. We really saw everything pretty much the same way." For their foreign policy team, they looked for strategists who could supply a conceptual framework and grasp the points of practical application. In the 1988 campaign these had been Robert Zoellick, the overall issues director, and Dennis Ross, the foreign policy lead. Zoellick had worked for Baker at Treasury. He was thirty-five, raised in the Midwest, near Chicago, and had earned joint degrees from Harvard's Law School and Kennedy School of Government before going into full-time government work. Ross, who in the mid-1980s had been at UC-Berkeley running a center on Soviet international behavior, was also a specialist on the Middle East. He had already served in government at State and Defense. In the Reagan White House at the NSC staff since 1986, Ross had worked closely with Bush. He knew Bush much better than he knew Baker.

After Bush chose Baker as his secretary of state and Scowcroft as his national security adviser, he invited the forty-year-old Ross to take his choice of jobs. He could either be deputy to Scowcroft or Baker. Ross chose to work with Baker. He knew he liked Baker's operating style and he wanted to be closer to the field work of diplomacy. Zoellick also turned down a top position on the White House staff in order to work on Baker's team. Baker's team, like Baker, also had good personal relationships with Bush. Zoellick and Ross then became Baker's two chief strategists at the State Department, Ross focusing on the Soviet Union and the Middle East and Zoellick on Europe and practically everything else. Baker relied heavily on them. Until he brought in a new team during the second half of 1989, Baker had little confidence in the leadership of State's European bureau, believing that they had no new ideas about future strategies.

Because Zoellick and Ross had worked in Bush's 1988 campaign, unlike Scowcroft or his staff, Scowcroft was thus, at least at first, a bit of an outlier in the Bush-Baker team. Bush and Baker had first worked with Scowcroft (and Cheney) nearly fifteen years previously in the Ford administration. Scowcroft was hardworking, discreet, and cautious, insisting that internal squabbles stay internal and not mar the conduct of American foreign policy. Scowcroft had served most recently as a member of the Tower Commission, investigating the role of the NSC in the Iran-Contra affair. The investigation had left him deeply uneasy about the way Reagan ran his White House. Scowcroft had a careful understanding of what he and his staff should and should not do, to ensure that Baker would be the face of U.S. foreign policy.

Scowcroft looked for top-quality staff—another deficiency he had observed in the Reagan White House. After Ross turned down the job as Scowcroft's deputy, that concern was a factor that drew Scowcroft to choose Bob Gates. Gates was a CIA career officer who had spent considerable time on the NSC staff. He was the CIA's deputy director during Reagan's second term. Gates was well organized, disciplined, and extremely skilled at the day-to-day operations of government. He ran the Deputies Committee of top subcabinet officials so efficiently that full meetings of the National Security Council were rarely needed to clarify issues before they were presented to President Bush. Gates had been relatively outspoken in voicing skepticism about Gorbachev. In October 1988, Gates gave a speech that so infuriated Secretary of State Shultz that Shultz directly confronted him about it and then tried to get him fired. Knowing this, during those early months in 1989, Baker and his staff kept a wary eye on Gates, to make sure the administration spoke with one voice.

The NSC staff office for Europe and the Soviet Union was led by Robert Blackwill. Blackwill was a career diplomat who had worked on Kissinger's staff in the 1970s (but did not share Kissinger's policy prescriptions for Europe). He was probably hired because Bob Gates remembered him well from their common service on the Carter administration's NSC staff. Scowcroft recalled Blackwill's "reputation for brilliance, laced with irascibility," and described him as a "forward-looking original thinker who reveled in finding ways to take advantage of the rapidly changing European scene." Some of the office's ideas turned out to appeal more to Bush (and Baker) than they did to Scowcroft.

Joining Blackwill as the expert on Soviet affairs was a young (thirty-four-year-old) Stanford professor, Condi Rice. Scowcroft and Gates were both acquainted with Rice. Rice also knew and got along with Ross; they had both been part of the Berkeley-Stanford center on Soviet international behavior. To help on Western Europe and European security, Blackwill brought in a thirty-four-year-old career diplomat and veteran of the conventional arms control talks (and former trial lawyer), Philip Zelikow.

On March 7, Baker and Shevardnadze opened their channel with direct talks in Vienna on the margins of a conference of foreign ministers of all thirty-five European nations participating in the "Helsinki process," the Conference on Security and Cooperation in Europe (CSCE) that had been founded in 1975 and had picked up momentum since 1985. They agreed on an agenda and exchanged their positions on the range of issues. Shevardnadze stressed Soviet readiness to move on conventional arms control. The Soviets pressed the United States to put aircraft, helicopters, and troop numbers on the table too.

On strategic nuclear arms control, the START talks, one of Bush's first acts had been to replace the Reagan administration's negotiator Edward Rowny with Richard Burt. Burt was transferred from his post as Reagan's ambassador to West Germany. The Burt pick was a loud signal (to those who remembered the battles over arms control in the Reagan era) that Bush was siding with those who wanted rapid progress in the START talks. The issues holding up progress were difficult and technically complex, mainly involving strategic defense systems and cruise missile questions. The important moves to break these logjams began later in 1989.

Back in Washington, Scowcroft had launched the formal policy reviews. Baker had gone along with his wish to have these reviews, but they made no difference for what Baker and his team were doing, which proceeded on schedule. "We treated that exercise as something to monitor and manage so it wouldn't bind us," Zoellick recalled, "but not to treat it in a serious way." Just before Baker met with Shevardnadze, Scowcroft sent Bush a memo on "Getting Ahead of Gorbachev." Scowcroft's tone was wary. He warned against "early and dramatic proposals." He instead argued for "a sound strategy," laying out a set of sensible, conservative principles. The

American ambassador in Moscow also had just sent back a set of modest, conservative policy suggestions.

Meanwhile, Scowcroft's staff, like Baker's team, had already given up on the formal reviews. Zelikow and Rice joined in a memo to Scowcroft telling him that the reviews "were not proceeding well." The Soviet analysis was fine but "the policy half . . . is largely a restatement of last year's agenda, vague and unfocused." It "lacks any clear guide as to how the future may differ from the past and what we can or should do to shape it." While the European bureau's work on Eastern Europe was more constructive, they thought the Western European work was even worse than the Soviet effort. Ross and his aides "fully shared [this] negative assessment."

Returning from his March 7 meeting with Shevardnadze, Baker also had a quite different sort of approach in mind. Finally preparing to set down to work in Washington, Baker met with Bush on March 8. Baker argued for just the sort of early and dramatic proposals on Europe and the Soviet Union that, a week earlier, Scowcroft had warned against. To Baker, all the debates about whether Gorbachev would succeed or fail seemed like "academic theology." Each side had their case. "What mattered to me were what actions we could take in the face of these two different possibilities." The Soviet "new thinking" was not well defined. The United States should suggest some of the "content." On the plan to modernize U.S. short-range nuclear forces (SNF), Baker had listened to the Europeans and wanted to reconsider the U.S. position. He knew the worries about nuclear deterrence were linked to the conventional force position in Europe. On that key subject, "I'm less convinced we have ideas, much less the analysis to support them." Baker wanted Bush to ready a major conventional arms control move for the historic NATO summit meeting, celebrating the alliance's fortieth anniversary, scheduled for the end of May.

Baker thought a "small, reliable group" had to come up with really big ideas about the future of U.S. forces in Europe. He warned Bush that the bureaucracy would probably hinder or leak any such bold effort. He stressed that the pace of "both political and economic" change in Eastern Europe seemed to be picking up, "and the U.S. also needed to step up the thinking about how to encourage those developments." Bush agreed with Baker's activist approach. Scowcroft too had to admit that his formal policy reviews did not seem to be producing any interesting ideas. The word went down to Baker's top advisers and Scowcroft's staff (who knew little of the private discussions among Bush, Baker, and Scowcroft) that it was time to disregard the formal reviews. They should go all-out to develop a menu of ideas on all fronts concerning the future of Europe.

Bush, Baker, and Scowcroft decided to create action-forcing events that would oblige the government to develop policies. The White House and State teams mapped out a plan for two major European trips by the president in 1989. The first, in the late spring, would be to Western Europe and would include the NATO summit. The second, in the summer, would concentrate on Eastern Europe and would culminate in the G-7 economic summit, to be held that year in Paris. The White House also decided to use a series of speeches in the spring to deploy ideas about the direction of policy. Because it would be months before Baker had a new team in place to run State's European bureau, Blackwill's NSC staff office became a critical engine room for churning out policy proposals in this early period. Along with Zoellick and Ross on Baker's team, they would effectively become the "small, reliable group" that Baker had thought would be necessary to come up with needed ideas.

Meanwhile, in Western European capitals in early 1989, the prevailing mood was similar to that in Washington. There was plenty of wondering about Gorbachev's future. Leaders waited to see how the negotiations about political reform might turn out in Eastern Europe. They debated about the emerging Single European Market and proposals to intensify an economic and monetary union. They worried about what it all meant for the Atlantic alliance. Baker never tried the Kissinger ploy of running a triangular game, playing off U.S.-Soviet deals to leverage U.S.-European bargaining, as the Europeans then worked on their own bargains with Moscow. He and Bush, already familiar with the European governments, preferred an orchestrated, coordinated partnership. Rather than working that partnership mainly through a British-American transatlantic bridge, Bush and Baker consulted broadly and deeply with West European counterparts, especially with the West Germans. A Washington-Bonn nexus began to supplant the traditional Washington-London nexus. This came naturally to Baker, from his experience in working on economic issues and the Bonn-centered European Monetary System.

Though it is an issue now practically forgotten, the SNF modernization debate was the great security issue in Europe in the first months of 1989. As part of the bargains surrounding the INF Treaty of 1987, NATO had formally agreed that it would plod ahead with refurbishing the only remaining U.S. nuclear missiles that would remain in Europe (in addition to the nuclear bombs that could be carried on aircraft). The SNF commitment had become one more token that, as tensions relaxed, America would not "decouple" its nuclear deterrent from European defense. British prime minister Thatcher had no doubts. She devoted her first call to Bush after his inauguration to advising him to move forward on the "urgent" need to modernize SNF. But, especially in West Germany, the prospect of another huge debate about putting in new American nuclear missiles was disheartening, especially with elections coming in 1990. These proposed new missiles would have so short a range that the most likely targets would be in places inhabited by Germans. Such a push seemed more and more bizarre in the age of Gorbachev. To Gorbachev, getting reports on the Western debates, it seemed that, "Baker traveled around Europe and he is in a panic: Europe is breaking away from their [American] control. Their society is reacting powerfully to our work."

FUTURE OF EASTERN EUROPE

During March, in Warsaw and Budapest, Poles and Hungarians were hammering out their "Roundtable" agreements. These would set up a process, rules for their own first moves toward an inclusive and more democratic government of some kind. Those agreements were to be implemented during the early summer. The Washington press had been diverted by talk about Kissinger's supposed "Yalta II" plan for U.S.-Soviet management of change in Eastern Europe. That idea had been quashed secretly months earlier and was now quashed publicly. Baker warned that no one should see some "signal that somehow we are getting together with the Soviet Union and carving up Eastern Europe."

Throughout the first half of April, Bush and his team deliberated on how best to welcome the imminent conclusion of the Roundtable agreements. Bush delivered the first in the planned series of policy statements, on Eastern Europe. Speaking to a Polish-American community in Hamtramck, Michigan, Bush quoted his inaugural address: "The day of the dictator is over. The totalitarian era is passing; its old ideas blown away like leaves from an ancient leafless tree." The West, he said, "can now be bold in proposing a vision of the European future." Arms, Bush added in a conscious echo of Czech dissident Vaclav Havel, "are a symptom, not a source of tension. The true source of tension is the imposed and unnatural division of Europe." The occasion was memorable for him, partly because it was his first foreign policy speech since his inaugural and partly because he later learned an assassin had been in the crowd hoping to kill him. Deterred that time by metal detectors, the would-be assassin tried to intercept Bush at two other locations before he was eventually arrested and jailed.

Bush was already planning to go to Poland and Hungary in the summer, after the Poles held their first free elections. He had gone to Poland in 1987, as vice president. This would be the first visit by an American president to Poland since 1977, and the first such visit ever to Hungary. Internally, the Bush administration was divided about what aid the United States might give. His administration felt its resources were quite constrained, that it was dealing with the hangover of unsustainable public and private debt incurred during the Reagan years. In April, Bush started with some moves on export credits and again rescheduling and writing down Polish public debt.

All the sanctions against Poland that had been imposed after the 1981 martial law crackdown had been lifted by the end of the Reagan administration. But no president had ever offered major economic assistance to a Warsaw Pact state and Soviet military ally. In his speech Bush held out hope that America and international financial institutions, like the IMF, could do much more. But "help from the West will come in concert with liberalization," he declared. "We're not going to offer aid without requiring sound economic practices in return." Bush, Baker, Scowcroft, and Secretary of the Treasury Nicholas Brady had begun arguing about the scope of possible aid to Eastern Europe on April 4. Brady stressed that Poland had already gotten itself in deep trouble because of borrowing and squandering money. "Baker and I argued that the policy this time was different. . . . The dispute was emotional and irreconcilable," Scowcroft remembered. Bush recalls that he finally "directed that I wanted to see aid proposals—I hoped that, in a pinch, [the budget director] could find money." Since that budget director, Richard Darman, had been Baker's long-time deputy, there was a good chance that Baker could find the money he wanted. What emerged was the American aid program that was developed with the Congress, turned into legislation, and passed into law during the next seven months.

The United States looked to Western Europe for help in developing a wider agenda for assistance to Eastern Europe. They jumped into that common planning during the late summer of 1989, as the election results in Poland and Hungary electrified the world. Poland's elections produced a stunning vote against the government and for Solidarity in the seats that were up for grabs. It seemed clear that some new government would probably have to be formed soon in Poland. Opposition groups in neither Poland nor Hungary pressed any sort of foreign policy agenda about the Cold War. They were preoccupied with conditions at home and the daily hardships people suffered. They believed that a drastic change in governance was the only path that offered hope for a better future. In his July visits to both countries, Bush welcomed the changes in Poland and Hungary. He was exhilarated by the crowds at his speeches and by the exciting changes underway. He was impressed by the emerging leaders in Hungary.

Polish leaders began coming up with aid numbers based on analogies to the scale of Marshall Plan aid for European recovery that the United States gave between 1948 and 1952. No one using the Marshall Plan analogies had looked hard at exactly how that program had worked. The truth was that in the summer of 1989 neither Bush nor any other Western leader was ready to tell the changing governments what, exactly, they should do. None of the Western governments had developed substantial plans that presumed to tell those countries how to go about transforming the whole economy of a communist country. None of the Western countries had identified large amounts of money they could offer as an incentive or a grant program that made sense. As to the existing Polish and Hungarian debt, American banks actually held little of it. Most of the debt, and most of the relevant experience with Eastern Europe finance, was in West European and Japanese institutions and in the IMF. In any case, no Western government could do much until they saw what kind of government might emerge and what economic program it was prepared to adopt. Since any such program was bound to be painful, at least in the short-term, Bush had been careful throughout his visit and the surrounding talks not to promise any "blank check" that would deflect the Poles from making hard choices.

Bush had scraped up some U.S. aid to offer in his visits, such as a $100 million fund to help businesses and help with more loans. Although the move included the novel idea of "Enterprise" funds to stimulate small business, which turned out to be productive, the scale of the move indicated it was more for symbolic encouragement. The U.S. government led the way in putting Eastern Europe at the top of the agenda for the G-7 summit in Paris in July. The Americans and the West Germans argued for two main steps. First, they pushed to relax and reschedule the foreign debt, especially Polish debt. This had been high on the Polish list of concerns. Eventually, in 1991, the arguments would get down to which banks and which countries would accept major losses, an issue that would be especially painful for the Germans. Second, the West Germans and the Americans pushed for a multilateral conference to develop a significant aid and reform program for Poland and Hungary. The idea appears to have originated in a proposal that West German Chancellor Helmut Kohl made in a secret, strong set of agenda-setting suggestions that he sent to Bush in June.

Kohl was especially focused on Poland, remembering this was the fiftieth anniversary of the outbreak of World War II with Germany's invasion of Poland and the Hitler-Stalin partition of Poland. Although the issues were partly economic, the West German Minister of Foreign Affairs Hans-Dietrich Genscher and Baker led negotiations for the West Germans and Americans. Everyone could begin to see that their various bilateral aid efforts had to be coordinated somehow. There were also debt discussions among government creditors (the Paris Club) and private creditors (the London Club). The governments also quickly realized that most of the experience with planning economic transition on this scale was in the international financial institutions, especially the World Bank and the IMF; they also grasped that most of the experience in setting new trade relationships with Eastern Europe was in the European Community (EC). The EC had already cautiously been developing some trade openings, especially with Hungary, since 1988. The leaders agreed to create a new ad hoc body to get all the concerned states and organizations together. This new Group of twenty-four (G-24) would move both on urgent matters like food aid and on longer-term transition plans and assistance. Baker wanted the West Germans to organize the G-24 work. The Germans preferred to give the job to the European Commission. The Americans agreed to this, a result that also pleased the French. The G-24 quickly got to work, holding its first meeting two weeks later, on August 1. In the rest of 1989 alone, Poland received 359,000 tons of food aid, most of it from Western Europe, amounting to about twenty pounds of food for every person in the country.

FUTURE OF THE SOVIET UNION

Scowcroft had agreed with his staff (and Baker) that the formal policy review on U.S.-Soviet policy "is going nowhere." Late one March evening, he told Blackwill and Rice, "See if you can write something that has more bite." Rice took the better part of a weekend to rough out a notional policy statement and worked on it with Blackwill and Ross. The thrust of the paper was to throw the switch guiding the United States away from the grand strategy of "containment" that had shaped overall U.S. and Allied policy toward the Soviet Bloc during the generations of the Cold War. That was how "for forty years" the United States "had committed its power and will," but "a new era may now be upon us. We may be able to move beyond containment to a U.S. policy that actively promotes the integration of the Soviet Union into the existing international system." The paper then listed military and political conditions "that will support a cooperative relationship between Moscow and the West." These included a "smaller and much less threatening" force posture, renunciation of the principle of permanent international class conflict, permission for self-determination in Eastern Europe, a more pluralist and humane domestic political life, and at least a willingness to cooperate on other issues.

That document became the centerpiece of the president's first speech on policy toward the Soviet Union, an address given at Texas A&M on May 12. "Beyond containment" became a catchphrase for Bush. The American position, which was broadly supported by allies, did not presume that the Soviet Union had already accomplished all the changes that would reassure neighbors and the world. Instead, the concept was that the Soviet leadership was clearly moving toward or considering such fundamental changes. Therefore, the American stance was to spell out a set of goals, or tests, that could set clear and reasonable benchmarks for a Soviet shift to a cooperative world system. Soviet interpretations of the American position were mixed. Some disliked the tone of the American rhetoric, with its mention of Cold War concerns about Soviet behavior and posture. Others liked the basic American assumption that an end to the Soviet Union's isolation from the international system was now possible. Bush also made it clear, both in the speech and through Baker (who had just returned from Moscow, where he had met with Gorbachev and Shevardnadze on May 10 and 11), that he hoped for Gorbachev's success.

Secretary of Defense Cheney sought to offer a more skeptical and hawkish view. The White House censored portions of a speech Cheney had prepared. Then Cheney gave a press interview indicating that Gorbachev could well fail. Baker felt great regard for Cheney from their work together in the Ford administration. But, as he later recalled, "I picked up the phone. I called the president, and said, 'You can't have this.'" Bush and Baker decided that the White House would put out a statement disavowing Cheney's comment. "And they [the White House press office] went out there and they cut the ground out from under Dick quicker than you could imagine." In October, when he thought Gates was trying to voice a distinct view about Gorbachev, Baker would step hard on that too and make a point of having done so. Bush and Scowcroft backed Baker up.

Bush proposed a test for Gorbachev's new openness, his commitment to glasnost, by reviving an idea called "Open Skies." He proposed that the United States, the Soviet Union, and their allies should be willing to open their skies to multinational teams that could fly over and surveille military sites. Eisenhower had first tried out this idea in 1955, hoping to head off an era of thermonuclear fear. Bush thought it was time to try again and include all NATO and Warsaw Pact states. Scowcroft thought the idea was old and "smacked of gimmickry," even though it had been developed by Blackwill and Zelikow, members of his own staff. This dismissive view was echoed by Bush's political opponents and the press.

Bush did not agree with Scowcroft or the critics. "I thought we had a lot to gain," he recalled about Open Skies. Although it was commonly believed that satellites already provided abundant information, there were many advantages to aerial imagery compared to satellite imagery, especially in that era. Also, Bush's proposal would open up access and transparency to at least twenty-three states, not just the superpowers. The initiative later led to a treaty. As this chapter is being written, Open Skies flights continue in the United States and across Europe. Bush agreed with Scowcroft that it was best to delay a summit with Gorbachev until there was something "concrete" to do or announce. The press would place such high expectations on what a summit might produce. In July, Bush decided the time was right for the summit with Gorbachev, as soon as possible.

PRINCIPLES FOR EUROPE'S FUTURE

In early spring of 1989, the leading West European governments were busy. Their views were similar to those in the United States on the question of what to do with or about Eastern Europe or the Soviet Union. The leading governments, above all West Germany, were especially preoccupied with the SNF problem. If there was a major alternative within the Atlantic alliance, it was from Prime Minister Thatcher. Her positions, which she regarded as continuity with the Reagan era, were in sync with the more cautious and conservative factions in the U.S. government. The most important vectors of change coming out of Western Europe were about the future of the European project. In the next stage of the European project, the driver of the action was in Brussels. The president of the European Commission, Jacques Delors, had already achieved the Single European Act that had been signed in 1986 but had not rested on these laurels. He and aides argued that a Single European Market had to deepen into some kind of economic and monetary union.

By spring of 1989, as the Americans and Soviets were developing their ideas for how to end the Cold War, the Delors Report was also being finished. At this interesting time in the development of the European project, Bush invited the president of France, François Mitterrand, to come to his family's retreat on the Maine coast, in Kennebunkport. Bush also offered to speak about Europe's future, together with Mitterrand, at Boston University. The American administration had played practically no part in the advancing European argument about an economic and monetary union. The Bush administration was finally awakening to the full significance of the way Europe was changing. Bush wanted to make a conscious effort to improve relations with Mitterrand and with France. Blackwill had pressed Bush to reach out to Mitterrand, and he had helped persuaded a reluctant Scowcroft to go along. In their meetings Bush and Mitterrand renewed their acquaintance. They had known each other since 1981. The atmosphere in Bush's home was warm.

But their friendliness could only go so far. Bush asked Mitterrand to go out with him for a ride on Bush's cigarette boat, a racing-style motor boat. "Mitterrand took one look at the boat and firmly said, '*Non.*'" Bush then asked Blackwill to go. Blackwill, a loyal civil servant, did not feel quite able to decline. The ride, he recalled, "scared the bejabbers out of landlubber me, as the president drove like a maniac." Safe on dry land, Bush and Mitterrand reassured each other about the future of

Western Europe. The two leaders found that their strategic outlook converged on other European issues too. Mitterrand called attention to the divide between Britain and West Germany, personalized in the estrangement of both Kohl and Genscher from Thatcher.

The American vision for Europe's future as a whole was that the Cold War might end as all of Europe converged on shared fundamental principles. The European Community had become a magnet and precedent for this approach. Looking to institutions that embraced all of Europe, the Bush administration soon proposed that the pan-European political organization, the Conference on Security and Cooperation in Europe (CSCE), could do more. It could promote pluralism by setting guidelines for how to hold free elections in Eastern Europe, as the Hungarian and Polish Round-table talks were agreeing on their own tentative democratic experiments. Mitterrand and Bush had agreed, as they looked at Eastern Europe, to seek a balance between encouraging change while not doing anything that might provoke a violent backlash. They agreed on the need to focus on the future of West Germany and Kohl, as well as on the need for dramatic moves on both SNF and conventional arms control.

In his policy address at Boston University with Mitterrand, on May 21, Bush focused on Western Europe's future and its relationship to the United States. The coming single European market was hugely important. But it fed protectionist fears in the United States, as the world trade system seemed to be falling apart and Europe was now forming into an economic superpower. From the start of the Bush administration, Baker had warned the rest of the cabinet that European integration was "a major challenge; we need to make sure the result is outward-looking, not inward." This would require a "well-coordinated, consistent, active effort" by the U.S. government.

In his Boston speech, the NSC staff also wanted Bush "to make the strategic case for not letting our economic agencies declare war on the [European Community] at this point in history." Part of that strategic case was that European integration was a powerful magnetic force "drawing Eastern Europe closer toward the commonwealth of free nations." Bush followed through. He told his audience that "the postwar order that began in 1945 is transforming into something very different." In language that was heard loud and clear on the other side of the Atlantic, the American president declared that, whatever others may say, "this administration is of one mind. We believe a strong, united Europe means a strong America."

During his visit to Western Europe, Bush met directly with Delors in Brussels. Baker, joining Bush, kept up to date on Delors's plans for a European central bank. Bush emphasized to Delors the Boston speech language welcoming European integration. The Americans expressed no concern about the Delors Report to advance economic and monetary union. Instead, what Bush and Baker were worried about was to head off the danger of an integrated European economy becoming an economic Fortress Europe. They wanted a hard linkage to condition completion of "EC 92"—a single European Market—on parallel completion of a new agreement on global trade, one that would take the place of the crumbling Cold War GATT system. The negotiations to create this global trading system were called the Uruguay Round in the framework of the old GATT system. This round of global trade talks, ultimately involving more than 120 country signatories, was the most ambitious ever launched since the original framework was created in 1947. It was called the "Uruguay Round" because, after four years of exploratory work, the "round" had been launched in 1986 at a meeting at Punta del Este, in Uruguay. The new global trade agreement was, in theory, supposed to conclude at the end of 1990. Delors agreed that EC 92 and a conclusion of the Uruguay Round had to run together.

SECURITY IN EUROPE

Sitting around the Oval Office, with an informal group of his top advisers, on March 30 President Bush chaired a meeting to brainstorm about the whole future of Europe. This meeting set a pattern of informal sessions held in the Oval Office among just a small group of principals. One of the big questions they took up was the vision for the future of U.S. and Soviet forces in Europe. Associated with that was the vision for what conventional arms control in Europe might achieve. Scowcroft had been intrigued by Kissinger's original idea of a mutual withdrawal, perhaps of all foreign forces at least in central Europe. He asked Blackwill about it, who was appalled. Undeterred, Scowcroft broached the idea in the Oval Office session on March 30. He recalled that "Dick Cheney looked stunned and replied that it was too early to consider such a fundamental move." Scowcroft liked the idea as a way of getting Soviet forces out of Eastern Europe. His staff warned that such Soviet forces would still be in the European USSR, while U.S. forces would be going back over the Atlantic, erasing that fundamental commitment. At the same March 30 meeting, Baker had tried a different tack. He wondered about just withdrawing all tanks, since they were so essential to an offensive military posture.

The United States and its allies kept going back and forth during April about how to address the European security issues. West German, British, and U.S. envoys crisscrossed the Atlantic searching for common ground. The Dutch foreign minister also played a helpful role. Back to Moscow in early May, where he met with Gorbachev and Shevardnadze, Baker encountered more Soviet gestures about what they were prepared to do about their short-range nuclear forces. He returned fed up, determined to find some way to pull back from the controversial and seemingly outmoded 1988 NATO decision to modernize the U.S. SNF. Baker's impatience was matched at the White House. Gorbachev would be making a triumphant visit to West Germany and France in June. Bush's staff had the sense that Gorbachev was the toast of Europe, while they fought over short-range nuclear missiles.

Blackwill and Zelikow had developed a plan for Scowcroft for a major move on conventional forces. Armed with these ideas, Scowcroft and Baker talked about how to move forward. Together, they arrived at a key insight. They agreed to fuse two problems, SNF and conventional forces in Europe, into one solution. A breakthrough on conventional arms control would help Gorbachev. It would enlarge and accelerate the withdrawal of Soviet tanks and troops out of East-Central Europe. It could also defuse the quarrel over the short-range nuclear forces. The SNF part of the idea was to put off *both* modernizing and negotiating about the shorter-range nuclear forces. U.S. nuclear forces were supposed to offset the Soviet advantage in conventional forces. Very well. Then first complete the CFE treaty. That would reduce and equalize conventional forces in all of Europe.

That strategy required a credible commitment to finish the CFE treaty very soon. To make that credible, the NSC staff proposed that the United States move toward the Soviet position on how to complete a fair framework for the talks. The Soviets and their allies had offered to go along with reductions to common ceilings in tanks, artillery, and armored fighting vehicles. These were potentially huge reductions, eliminating tens of thousands of weapon systems. In return, what Moscow insisted on was that the NATO side reciprocate and put its strengths on the table too. If the Soviets would reduce these key ground force weapons, the Soviets insisted on Western agreement to similar reductions in two categories of weaponry where the West had at least a qualitative edge: combat aircraft and helicopters.

This Soviet proposal was quite controversial in Western capitals. Bush decided he would agree to include the ceilings on aircraft and helicopters. He would lead the NATO alliance to agree to offer such a deal. Bush approved another U.S. move. The United States would offer to set a common ceiling on American and Soviet troop numbers on foreign soil in Europe. Bush personally pushed the Pentagon to come up with a manpower number that would represent a significant move by the United States. The final number they came up with was two hundred seventy-five thousand. This ceiling was about 15 percent below the existing U.S. number deployed in Europe, then about three hundred twenty thousand. Bush, Baker, and Scowcroft were not trying to implement Kissinger's idea of a withdrawal of both U.S. and Soviet forces out of Europe. They thought their proposal would greatly reduce the Soviet forward presence while retaining a strong anchor for the United States to stay coupled to Europe's defense.

Their core instincts were still traditional. "Forward defense" was an axiom of how to defend the United States while reassuring long-troubled Europe. They were not trying to abandon forward defense. Since the Soviets had so many more forward-deployed troops, this common ceiling would require a much larger drawdown of the Soviet troop presence in Eastern Europe than anything Gorbachev had proposed so far. Gorbachev's well-known proposal of December 1988 announced a unilateral plan to withdraw about 20 percent of Soviet divisions from Eastern Europe. The American (and NATO) proposal would require withdrawal of more than half of the Soviet forces stationed in their forward foreign bases in East Germany, Czechoslovakia, Poland, and Hungary.

The Defense Department opposed these CFE moves. Cheney argued that the proposal would "unhinge the Alliance" and that the "British and French would go crazy." The Joint Chiefs of Staff chairman, Admiral Crowe, joined the opposition.

He called the proposal "PR" moves that would put "forward defense" at risk. President Bush overruled the objections. He sided with Baker and Scowcroft. Those in the meetings remembered that Bush "was the most forward leaning of all." "I want this done," he said. "Don't keep telling me why it can't be done. Tell me how it can be done." Baker's deputy, Lawrence Eagleburger, and Scowcroft's deputy, Gates, were secretly dispatched to Europe to tell allies what the United States had in mind. Their trip was bracketed by presidential phone calls and more envoys exchanged with the Germans.

Thatcher did not care for the plan. Gates recalled that, "We both felt like schoolchildren called before the principal for committing some unspoken dastardly act." Kohl, on the other hand, was "ecstatic." All the Allied leaders ultimately went along. Baker and Zoellick hammered out a document at the NATO summit codifying the deal agreed to by sixteen Allied presidents and prime ministers. SNF decisions would be deferred to later negotiations with the Soviets, with a "zero" solution ruled out. The CFE proposal would be advanced. The British foreign secretary, Geoffrey Howe, pushed hard to toughen the commitment to stay with SNF. As the talks went on, Zoellick asked Baker why he kept going along with some of the hardline British suggestions. Baker replied, "At some point, either very late tonight or early this morning, George Bush, as the leader of the alliance, is going to have to get Margaret Thatcher to compromise. I want him to be able to say to her, 'Jim stayed with Geoffrey the whole way. . . . This is the best we can do.'"

The NATO leaders agreed to a nuclear stall, linked to the new push to reduce and cap conventional forces. As Bush privately explained at the time, "Some say we're cold warriors, that we don't want Gorbachev to succeed. I've made clear that's not the case." Gorbachev and Shevardnadze welcomed the NATO moves. They accepted the planned framework for the rapid conclusion of a CFE agreement. Such a treaty would drastically change the whole defense posture of the Soviet Union, in the context of a mutual agreement. If achieved, CFE would be the most ambitious arms control treaty ever concluded. The CFE talks took off and made rapid progress.

Bush's conventional arms control/SNF joint initiative came as a complete surprise to gathered journalists. The episode, along with the way the huge SNF shadow had suddenly dissipated, had a dramatic and positive effect on the perception of Bush within Europe and also on Bush and his team's confidence in themselves. Bush and his team tended to rely thereafter on the improvised and secretive policy-making processes they had used in the spring of 1989. A bit bemused by the acclaim that greeted the summit outcome, Bush reminded reporters three days later, "I'm the same guy I was four days ago."

FUTURE OF GERMANY

In mid-March 1989 Blackwill and Zelikow drafted a deliberately provocative memo about Europe's future. Their memo opened by declaring: "Today, the top priority for American foreign policy in Europe should be the fate of the Federal Republic of Germany." The Kohl government was expected to go to the polls the next year, in December 1990. It was then projected to be a very close election. Bush's advisers bluntly urged him to do what he appropriately could to "help keep Kohl in power." Kohl's "government is now lagging in the polls behind an opposition that, as currently constituted, has too little regard either for nuclear deterrence or for conventional defense."

The NSC staff argued that the broad goal of U.S. policy in Europe "should be to overcome the division of the continent through acceptance of common democratic values." Gorbachev was proposing a "Common European Home" divided into different rooms by social systems, alliance structures, and historical realities. Instead of that, the United States would propose a vision for a "commonwealth of free nations." In the same memo to Bush, Scowcroft signed off on a principle, though he was uneasy about it, that urged the United States to do more to highlight possibilities for movement on German unification. The United States should "send a clear signal to the Germans that we are ready to do more if the political climate allows it."

The State Department's European bureau, headed by a former ambassador to East Germany, had been scornful about ideas that would jeopardize the hard-won Cold War status quo. Zoellick later recalled that when, in early 1989, he had asked a visiting West German colonel about German attitudes toward unification, the bureau chief sharply observed that unification was "the subject that all Americans are interested in and no German cares about." Scowcroft himself shared some of these doubts. But Blackwill and Zelikow pushed the point about leaning forward to open up discussion of German unification. Bush marked up the memo and noted to Scowcroft that he had "read this with interest!" Bush liked the forward-looking tone. He regarded himself (in his words) as "less of a Europeanist, not dominated by [that] history." Bush noticed when Scowcroft flagged the issue of German unification at their March 30 brainstorming session. Baker too, urged on by Zoellick, was taking a forward-looking view about possible German futures.

In general, the value of the NSC staff advice was that it helped Bush, who was open-minded about how to think about unification, feel that it was okay for him to support it. During much of 1989, Scowcroft was more cautious, feeling closer, as he would later acknowledge, to the old guard State position than to the views of his own staff members like Blackwill and Zelikow.

Bush began openly expressing the view, as he put it in a May interview, that he would "love to see" Germany reunified. He added, "Anybody who looks back over his shoulder and then looks at the present and sees a country ripped asunder by division, a people ripped asunder by political division, should say: 'If you can get reunification on a proper basis, fine.'" When then vice president Bush had visited the German city of Krefeld in June 1983, at the height of the mass demonstrations against INF missile deployment, the new FRG chancellor, Helmut Kohl, had taken time to get to know the American. Bush recalled demonstrators slinging rocks at his car without any security counteraction ("Our Secret Service would have shot them!")

and sitting in a garage with Kohl waiting for a route to clear. West Germany, Bush remembered, was a society willing to pay the price for free speech. Though the first to admit he was not clairvoyant and "can't claim to have understood everything that would happen in Europe from Day One," Bush had concluded that West Germany was a solid democracy. It had done penance for its sins, and "at some point you should let a guy up."

When Bush met with Mitterrand, he asked the French president what he thought about the prospect of German reunification. "As long as the Soviet Union is strong, it will never happen," Mitterrand replied. Perhaps "after ten years" and a "disruption [*dislocation* in French] of the Soviet empire," but at this time the Soviets would oppose this "with force." They have other problems and "won't take a chance on reunification." Bush pressed. What was Mitterrand's own view?

"If the German people wished it, I would not oppose it," he answered. "But not enough has changed since World War II to permit it."

In any case, Mitterrand could not see how it would happen. The Soviets would not permit it and "Gorbachev is very happy that East Germany is the most reactionary [government in the Eastern Bloc]." This quizzing of Mitterrand about German unification set a pattern. In Europe, Bush kept asking leaders what they thought of the idea of German unification. None was quite as forthcoming about German wishes as Mitterrand had been. All were at least as cautious about any immediate moves.

Talking with the press after the NATO summit, Bush reaffirmed, "[O]ur overall aim is to overcome the division of Europe and to forge a unity based on Western values." Reporters talking to Bush on the final stop of his trip in London were struck by his emphasis on the potential for change in Eastern Europe. Although the region was relatively quiet at the moment—a week before the Polish parliamentary election and shortly before other states in the region would experience serious unrest—Bush called Eastern Europe "the most exciting area for change in the world." According to one journalist, he "came back to [Eastern Europe] time and again in response to questions on other subjects."

What did "beyond containment" mean, the reporters asked. Bush answered: "It means a united Europe. It means a Europe without as many artificial boundaries."

In a visit to West Germany, Bush gave a major speech at the Rheingoldhalle, in Mainz. Mainz was the capital of Rheinland-Pfalz, where Kohl had risen to political prominence. The West's goal now, Bush proclaimed, was to "let Europe be whole and free." He added, "To the founders of the Alliance, this aspiration was a distant dream, and now it's the new mission of NATO. The Cold War began with the division of Europe. It can only end when Europe is whole. Today it is this very concept of a divided Europe that is under siege." Alluding to Gorbachev, Bush observed that "there cannot be a common European home until all within it are free to move from room to room." He called for the Iron Curtain to come down: "Let Berlin be next."

Having introduced the volatile language of unity to his German audience, Bush's language was then carefully phrased. "We seek self-determination for all of Germany and all of Eastern Europe," he declared. This was more traditional boilerplate. The

drafts of the speech from Scowcroft's staff had suggested more radical phrases referring directly to German unification. Scowcroft did not want Bush to get ahead of
what Kohl was saying. He "was concerned about unnecessarily stimulating German
nationalism and took [such language] out." Bush's remarks nonetheless delighted
many Germans, who were quick to infer that Bush hoped the seemingly frozen German question would soon begin to thaw.

In his Mainz speech, Bush had also described the West Germans as "partners in
leadership." This was not an empty expression. One of the most important consequences of the spring 1989 diplomacy was that it cemented a true core partnership
between the U.S. and West German governments, in the sense of joint planning and
coordination of policy moves. Since the United States first began learning habits of
true coalition planning, in 1941–1942 and beyond under the pressure of war and
near-war, the default habits of core partnership were Anglo-American. Washington
and London also shared intelligence to an unusual degree, routines that were extended to Canada, Australia, and New Zealand as well. Sometimes in the early Cold
War other partners attained this sort of core status, of coordinated policy development, but the default usually was Washington-London. The Anglo-American core
had been the default pattern of the Reagan administration. Reagan and Shultz got
along well enough with Mitterrand or his ministers, or with Kohl and Genscher. But
the relationships were not close enough to become policy-making partnerships. In
the first half of 1989, Bush and Baker had changed this pattern. There is no evidence
that they deliberately set out to change it. It evolved that way as they worked to orchestrate common views about Europe's future. The American-German partnership
became central and remained so for years.

The routines of interaction with London remained strong, especially at the working level. But British diplomats, assigned to Washington and to Bonn, quickly sensed
"a shifting balance of power in the alliance as between US/UK/FRG." They reported
that "we are no longer regarded as necessarily the best interpreter between the US
and Europe." Bush's good relationship with Mitterrand complemented the strong
relationships with the West Germans. The Americans were therefore now linked
firmly with the Kohl-Mitterrand-Delors triumvirate shaping broader policies within
Europe and in the EC. By the middle of 1989 all these governments were therefore
unusually well positioned to pull together as they entered the rapids.

By the end of the summer of 1989, as the democratic revolutions in Eastern
Europe were beginning and the democratic revolution in China was put down, the
Bush administration had set fresh basic directions, and habits of work, that would
last. They did not foresee all that would come—the collapse of East Germany and
creation of a new, unified Germany in 1990, the collapse of the Soviet security system, and the disintegration of the Soviet Union itself in 1991. Nor should anyone
forget that the center of action was in Europe, with European governments playing
a central role in it. But Bush and his team reconceived and renewed an Atlantic
partnership to manage this epic transformation.

NOTE

For sources and further discussion of the scholarship relevant to this essay, see Philip Zelikow and Condoleezza Rice, *To Build a Better World: Choices to End the Cold War and Create a Global Commonwealth* (New York: Twelve, 2019).

6

President George H. W. Bush

A Stroke of Luck for Germany

Horst Teltschik

At the beginning of the 1980s, the Cold War between the East and the West had reached a new climax. General Secretary Leonid Brezhnev, leader of the Soviet Union, had begun developing and deploying nuclear intermediate-range ballistic missiles (SS-20s), despite having signed the KSZE—the Helsinki Final Act—in September 1975, which was celebrated by the West and the East as the beginning of a far-reaching policy of détente. Due to their range, they were not aimed at their "chief opponent" the United States, but rather at those European NATO partners who, like Chancellor Willy Brandt of the Federal Republic of Germany, had been the most determined supporters of the policy of détente between East and West.

In response to the Soviet arms buildup of the SS-20s, the Atlantic Alliance had passed a double resolution in December 1979. If the Soviet Union did not dismantle their missiles, NATO would deploy American intermediate-range missiles in Western Europe. At the same time, President Ronald Reagan had announced the Strategic Defense Initiative (SDI) in the Spring of 1983. However, the Geneva Disarmament Negotiations between the two world powers failed. Subsequently, Brezhnev's successor, General Secretary Yuri Andropov, threatened a third world war if the European NATO countries stationed American intermediate-range ballistic missiles (Pershings).

Mass demonstrations followed, especially in the Federal Republic of Germany, against the decision of the German government to station American intermediate-range ballistic missiles there. In Bonn, which was then the capital, and in many other places across Germany, over five hundred thousand citizens demonstrated against the government of Chancellor Helmut Kohl and Foreign Minister Hans Dietrich Genscher, who had been newly elected on October 1, 1982. Today we know that the secret service of the German Democratic Republic (GDR) supplied organizational and financial support to those responsible for the demonstrations.

West Germany received substantial support from the French president, François Mitterrand, who advocated strongly for the implementation of the NATO double resolution in a speech to the German parliament in January of 1983.

This collective steadfastness and determination of the countries in the Atlantic Alliance paid off. Mikhail Gorbachev, who at that time was only a member of the Politburo of the Communist Party of the Soviet Union (CPSU), the highest governing body of the USSR, once told me, after his time in office has ended, that two decisions in the West had led to a shift in thinking in the Politburo of the CPSU: First was the double resolution of NATO. The Soviet leadership had been aware that they could not financially afford another arms race. Second was Reagan's decision from the SDI. Moscow did not see itself as being up to that technological challenge from the United States. Therefore, summit diplomacy, as well as disarmament and arms control negotiations between the two superpowers, would resume in 1985. They were to begin between President Ronald Reagan and General Secretary Mikhail Gorbachev in 1985 and continue seamlessly with President George Bush.

During this time of heated atmosphere in Germany, Vice President George Bush arrived there in June 1983. It was his first encounter with Chancellor Helmut Kohl. Together with Kohl, he commemorated, in the city of Krefeld, the thirteen families who, as the first German emigrants, had moved to America in 1683. "Five hundred years of Germans in America" was for both a welcome occasion to celebrate the political and cultural connection between the two countries.

Those opposed to the NATO double resolution were greatly disturbing the celebration. The demonstrators threw rocks and paint bombs at the cars of the guests of the celebration and blocked the streets. However, Helmut Kohl and George Bush remained relaxed. George Bush's comment was unforgettable: "It's just like in Chicago. We are celebrated and have rocks thrown at us, here and there."

They also visited the wall in Berlin together. Richard von Weizsäcker, who was the governing mayor at the time, showed them where young Germans had been shot by East German border guards as they tried to reach freedom. Only six years later, in November 1989, President George Bush would see the images as the wall opened— as he once described it: "Freedom literally flooded over the wall."

This first meeting in 1983 became the foundation for the affection and friendship between President Bush and Chancellor Kohl, which would outlast their terms in office. Both were impressed by the determination, as well as the poise, of the other.

Their next meeting happened on September 30, 1987. Vice President Bush had just concluded his visit to Warsaw and, on a layover in Bonn, shared with the chancellor his impressions of the political dynamic that was starting to emerge in Poland. At this point, the two were still united in their skepticism over the beginnings of Gorbachev's reform policies. They still did not know enough about its foreign and domestic dimensions. However, that would soon change.

Helmut Kohl was the first foreign conversation partner who would congratulate George Bush in person only seven days after his election as the forty-first president of the United States on November 15, 1988, in Washington. The transition from

Ronald Reagan to George Bush was seamless. The conversations were marked by personal trust and the spirit of agreement from the start. President Bush was willing to continue summit diplomacy, which had already begun with success, and the disarmament and arms control negotiations with General Secretary Gorbachev.

The INF treaty with the double zero option, signed in December 1987 had already gone into effect. The first American intermediate-range ballistic missiles had already been dismantled in Europe. Further disarmament agreements were in the works. By the end of May in 1989, President Bush had already proposed a new initiative for conventional disarmament and arms control at the NATO summit in Brussels.

At the same time, President Gorbachev's reform course was already well underway in the USSR. It had effects beyond the Soviet Union. Profound political changes were especially noticeable in the Warsaw Pact countries of Poland and Hungary. It was against this backdrop that the NATO summit reiterated its joint obligation to Germany to "seek a state of peace in Europe" in which "the people of Germany achieve unity once again by free self-determination." Less than half a year later, the crucial test came for all participants. The Berlin Wall fell. In this situation, the close political accord and cooperation between President Bush and Chancellor Kohl would become a deciding factor.

Following the NATO summit, President Bush paid a visit to Germany. On May 31, he gave an extremely important speech in Mainz. It contained a forward-looking message, the meaning of which many observers did not recognize until later. Just like his predecessor Reagan, he demanded that the "wall must fall." Most important for the Soviet Union and for President Gorbachev was, above all, the promise the American president made that the Soviets should know that "our goal is not to undermine your legitimate security interests." The topic of security was the chief concern of the Soviet leadership, as it remains for the current leadership.

At the same time, President Bush's offer to the Germans of a "partnership in leadership" was completely unexpected. The German government and public reacted to this surprising statement by the American president with extreme caution, even insecurity. At that point, they could not yet quite grasp the meaning of this friendly offer.

Neither side was to come back to this announcement by President Bush right away. However, it would become reality after the fall of the Wall in November 1989. Chancellor Helmut Kohl knew that he could rely on his friend George Bush in all his decisions and measures without having to consult him constantly with single questions. His national security advisor, Brent Scowcroft, who would become a good friend, and who also had Chancellor Kohl's complete trust, said later that the U.S. administration would have had to hold their breath sometimes if they had followed the chancellor's every move. However, he had to admit that, while they had not always been consulted in advance, and their consent had not always been secured, they had always been informed about all decisions and measures as quickly as possible.

Admittedly, this was not always easy to manage. On the evening of November 23, 1989, Chancellor Helmut Kohl and the circle of his closest advisers decided he would use his annual budget speech at the German parliament in five days to announce officially that his government was now determined to seek a unified Germany. This meant that there were only four days left, including the weekend, to prepare the speech. The chancellor directed that nobody should be told in advance, including the four victorious powers—the United States, France, United Kingdom, and the USSR. After all, NATO had already publicly proclaimed its support for the German people to have the right of self-determination. In addition, it would have been expected that all state and government leaders would urge caution and ask to be consulted in advance. The chancellor would then have been in danger of losing valuable time, and possibly missing a historic opportunity.

However, a few years earlier, a secret telegraph connection between the White House and the Office of the Chancellor had been established. On the morning of the chancellor's speech, the connection was used to convey the speech to President Bush in advance. Thus, he would be able to say that he had received the speech before the chancellor delivered it. However, the speech was in German; there had not been enough time in Bonn, or in Washington, for a translation.

On December 2–3, 1989, President Bush and General Secretary Gorbachev convened for talks in Malta. The following day, there was a NATO summit in Brussels. Helmut Kohl had kept his declared friend Bush apprised of developments in the GDR and other Warsaw Pact countries such as Poland and Hungary in several phone calls and had always received unconditional support from President Bush.

One the eve of the NATO summit, the two leaders met for a personal conversation. Helmut Kohl reaffirmed that he would continue to pursue policies of European integration and that he would also continue to advocate for Germany to be part of the Alliance. Both were in agreement that President Gorbachev should not be put under pressure. They discussed the positions of other Western partners. When Helmut Kohl described British prime minister Margaret Thatcher's reaction as "reserved," Bush declared that this was the "understatement of the year."

During the NATO Council's session, Bush detailed his vision in an elaborate declaration for the "future configuration of a new Europe." With that, he took on a leadership role in the Atlantic Alliance, both personally and in content. Helmut Kohl agreed with him completely. Joint "partnership in leadership" proved itself during this crucial historic situation in Europe and in East-West relations and deepened the friendship between President Bush and Chancellor Kohl. In his memoirs, Helmut Kohl called President Bush the "most important ally on the way to German unity." And he added: "The two of us were not only bound by mutual political appreciation but also by deep human affection."

George Bush fascinated Helmut Kohl as "a man with healthy common sense, very devout, always very successful, but at the same time of a very humble lifestyle and capable of genuine friendship." In addition, he also made an impression on Kohl because "he had no reservations about the Germans."

At the NATO summit on December 4, 1989, President Bush contributed significantly to further clearing the path within the Alliance toward unification. It was still a condition for him that a unified Germany would also be a member of the Atlantic Alliance. This was never in doubt for Helmut Kohl, either. This new personal meeting on the eve of the NATO summit, and the unconditional support from President Bush at the summit itself, gave Helmut Kohl the certainty that he had the strongest support from President Bush for his continued path toward German unity. This strengthened his confidence and gave him the courage to be determined as he pursued the policy he had initiated.

This support from President George Bush in these early days was extremely important for Helmut Kohl, because his meeting with General Secretary Gorbachev was still ahead of him. The wall had fallen on November 9, 1989. Almost three months would pass before there was a personal meeting between Kohl and Gorbachev. Gorbachev had responded with an unequivocal "no" to Helmut Kohl's ten-point speech in the German parliament on November 28, in which Kohl had announced that he would actively pursue German unity.

Foreign Minister Eduard Shevardnadze once told me, after his time in office, that Soviet leadership was still discussing, even in January 1990, whether they should intervene militarily in the GDR and close the borders again. At this point, there were still three hundred eighty thousand Soviet soldiers in the GDR. Nobody in NATO would have been prepared for such military action from the USSR.

Before departing for Moscow, President Bush had written two letters to the chancellor—one official document and one private one. The official letter described, once again, the American position regarding matters of reunification. In his private communication, George Bush gave thanks for the support he had received from Helmut Kohl during his first year in office and for Kohl's willingness to deepen the relationship with the United States further. At the same time, he also thanked Helmut Kohl for the "terrific German wine and meat" and "for the wonderful German clock" as "a visible sign of our friendship." These were all presents from the Palatine home of the chancellor. There was an unforgettable picture of George Bush in the Oval Office with the lines: "Helmut, I am eating your Pfaelzer Sausage right now."

On February 10, 1990, Kohl and Gorbachev came together in the Kremlin in Moscow for a meeting that would have historic importance. The chancellor had received moral support from all three Western powers in advance. George Bush had assured him in a telegram that he would not allow Moscow to use the mechanism of the four powers as an instrument to force the chancellor to create a Germany that corresponded to Soviet interests both in manner and in speed. He showed particular satisfaction with Helmut Kohl's assurances that a unified Germany should remain in NATO and that he declined neutrality. To the contrary, he supported the idea that the GDR territory in the Alliance could receive a special military status. He added a crucial statement that NATO itself should change its mission and emphasize its political role more. In conclusion, he reaffirmed to Helmut Kohl his personal admiration over the way Kohl had handled his duties as a leader over the last few months.

On the day before the meeting between Kohl and Gorbachev, Secretary of State Jim Baker had convened with General Secretary Gorbachev and Foreign Minister

Shevardnadze for meetings. Jim Baker, as well as President Bush, had told the chancellor in confidence that Baker would report back to Kohl with the results of his conversations before Kohl's meetings with Gorbachev. This is exactly what happened. Immediately after landing in Moscow, I was handed a letter from Baker for the chancellor. In it, Baker reported that there had been marked progress in all areas of arms control, regional matters, bilateral relationships, human rights, and transnational matters. One tip from Baker was especially helpful and valuable: both Soviet conversation partners had expressed concern regarding German unity, but they considered it unavoidable. Their concern was that a unified Germany could lead to instability and new insecurity in Europe and that it was not clear enough that the Germans would be willing to accept the current borders in the future. There had been agreement on how to proceed further. They had agreed to separate the domestic and foreign aspects of the unification process. Therefore, Baker had suggested a two-plus-four arrangement as the only realistic path. In the matters of NATO membership and NATO's expansion, Gorbachev had behaved dismissively.

This process alone shows how closely and intensively the German government and the American administration worked together and supported each other. Their mutual agreement could not have been more complete, and this bipartisanship could not help but influence the Soviet government and especially General Secretary Gorbachev as well. He told me once, years later, that if he "hadn't trusted George Bush and Helmut Kohl, many things would have gone differently."

The result of the talks between Kohl and Gorbachev in February 1990 were sensational at the time. Gorbachev had unambiguously agreed that it was now the "sole right of the German people to make the decision whether it wanted to live together in one state, how quickly, and how." In the matter of membership in the Alliance, they would find a mutual solution.

A few days later, on February 24, Helmut Kohl flew to Washington, and from there, accompanied by Jim Baker, he flew in Marine One to Camp David. George Bush and his wife, Barbara, were expecting the Kohl and drove them in a golf cart to the guest house. Chancellor Kohl was the first German chancellor to ever be invited to Camp David. The atmosphere was extraordinarily friendly. Their joint lunch began with a prayer said by President Bush. Barbara Bush and Hannelore Kohl were especially responsible for this intimate atmosphere, because they had gotten along famously from the very beginning. Of their relationship, Kohl said, "they were the best of friends."

The policy talks proceeded in a relaxed manner and were very amicable. Chancellor Kohl affirmed the position that, for him, NATO membership of a unified Germany was an elementary condition for the security of Europe. At the same time, he repeated his statement that a unified Germany would, of course, respect the sacredness of existing borders. He knew that everything depended on giving the Poles certitude regarding their Western border. The final recognition of the Oder-Neisse border after the reunification of Germany was never in doubt for Helmut Kohl.

George Bush told the chancellor that he had spent a good hour on the phone with Prime Minister Margaret Thatcher before their meeting. By now, she had accepted the German reunification process. Only three months ago, she had still been against it. George Bush provided Helmut Kohl with crucial help in winning approval from Thatcher for the unification process.

The following morning began with an ecumenical church service for everyone, including some of the president's grandchildren. Afterward, the president and the chancellor fine-tuned their most important positions once more. There was complete agreement. At lunch, President Bush asked Jim Baker to say the prayer. After lunch, they went for a long walk. George Bush put a ballcap on the chancellor's head. He now looked like a baseball player. Bush himself grabbed a knobbed walking stick, and despite the stormy weather, they walked through the woods for almost two hours. These detailed conversations strengthened their mutual trust.

From then on, Helmut Kohl could count on unconditional support from President Bush, Secretary of State Jim Baker, and National Security Adviser Brent Scowcroft. All were in constant contact with the chancellor and his advisers and kept each other informed about their meetings and about political developments, whether in the Soviet Union, Warsaw, the GDR, or with the Western Alliance partners. President Bush met in April with Margaret Thatcher in Bermuda and with François Mitterrand in Key Largo in Florida.

President Bush's suggestion to hold a special NATO summit at the end of June or the beginning of July would be of crucial importance. It took place a few days before the party convention of the CPSU, which was fatefully important for General Secretary Gorbachev's political survival. NATO had sent an important message to address Moscow with the promise: "We are holding out our hand in friendship to the states of the Warsaw Pact."

On May 17, Helmut Kohl arrived in Washington once again to meet with President Bush. A few open questions remained. They were about the future of the of the American short-range ballistic missile systems in Europe, matters surrounding economic and financial support of Gorbachev's reform policy, and how to proceed with him. Bush and Kohl agreed: they should treat Gorbachev at eye level and not as the loser of the Cold War. Bush affirmed, in front of the gathered press, that the United States and Germany agreed on the path and the goals of German unification. He reminded them that, in his speech in Mainz in May 1989, he had offered Germany partnership in joint leadership of the West and that this had now come to pass. The chancellor could not have hoped for more moral support from President Bush. What a friend and partner!

On May 31, Gorbachev arrived in Washington. The day before, Bush and Kohl had fine-tuned their positions once more. After the first day of negotiations, the president called the chancellor the same evening to report on the progress of the talks.

In their joint closing press conference on June 3, it became clear that the summit had been one of the most successful meetings between the leaders of the two superpowers. The number of agreements, as well as the declarations of intent, underlined the willingness on both sides to further increase their cooperation. George Bush explained that the possibility to come to joint solutions had never been as great as on that day. On June 3, Pentecost Sunday, the talks concluded at Camp David. That same day, President Bush called the chancellor at his private residence in Ludwigshafen, to tell him that there had not yet been a breakthrough in the German matter, but that he thought it was possible. The next day, a telegraph from the president arrived, in which he summarized the results of the talks again. It would not have been possible for their mutual briefings and coordination of positions to be any closer.

When the chancellor arrived in Washington, once again, on the evening of June 8 for a personal meeting with President Bush, the latter suggested playfully that he should have a bed made up for Helmut Kohl in the White House, since he was be visiting so frequently.

The chain of meetings and bilateral, as well as multilateral, agreement processes continued with the NATO summit on July 5–6 in London and the World Economic Summit on July 9–10 in Houston. Helmut Kohl handed President Bush a cassette in Houston of an interview he had given after the NATO summit in London. It contained a "declaration of love for the president."

On July 14–16, the deciding talks between the chancellor and President Mikhail Gorbachev took place in Arkhyz in the Caucasus. The results were sensational. Gorbachev agreed to German unity and membership in NATO once and for all. After his return to Bonn, the chancellor telephoned President Bush, who congratulated him on excellent leadership and spectacular results. Kohl should be proud of his achievements.

President Bush was for Helmut Kohl the "most important ally" in the process of reunification. According to Kohl, "we were bound not only by mutual political admiration, but also by deep human affection."

Years after his time in office had passed, Secretary of State Jim Baker would respond to my statement that, in the era of President Bush, Jim Baker and Brent Scowcroft, the relationship between the two governments had been very good and filled with trust, by saying: "They were the best ever."

Finally, a personal memory: When President George H. W. Bush received an award from the American Academy in Berlin in 2008 for his service to German-American relations, he suddenly interrupted his acceptance speech, looked around the hall with several hundred guests and cried: "Where is Horst?" The academy had not placed me with the guests of honor. I was sitting in the middle of the hall, stood up, and waved to him. And I flew to Washington, of course, when Brent Scowcroft celebrated his ninetieth birthday. A friend forever.

7

President George H. W. Bush's China Policy

Douglas H. Paal

The focus of this chapter is China policy during the presidency of George H. W. Bush. But to understand his personal level of interest in and attention to China and its government, we should look back briefly at what preceded it.

George Bush's direct experience with China began with his assignment to Beijing as chief of the United States Liaison Office (USLO) in 1974–1975. The Bush and Scowcroft volume, *A World Transformed*, and Jon Meacham's biography of President Bush, *Destiny and Power: The American Odyssey of George Herbert Walker Bush*, recount well how Bush got to China and his awkward prior experience of trying but failing to keep Taiwan, known formally as the Republic of China, in the United Nations when he was ambassador there, as the People's Republic of China (PRC) sought to displace it.

President Bush later spoke and wrote frequently about his year in Beijing and his and Barbara's efforts to get to understand the lives of the Chinese people. China then was still suffering through the late years of the Cultural Revolution, 1966–1976. Mao Zedong remained the dominant and increasingly frail leader, but the party and government below him were bitterly divided. Industry was at a standstill. The army provided rough order after the chaos of the early years of the Cultural Revolution. Higher education was suspended. The relationship between Washington and Beijing, brought about by President Nixon and Henry Kissinger, was still unofficial in diplomatic terms and tenuous. President Bush served as President Ford's representative, and the Chinese suspected Ford of being insufficiently anti-Soviet to suit their taste and interests.

The secrecy and intrigue of Chinese politics, the relatively small size of USLO (a staff of about twenty-five), the limited diplomacy conducted in China's capital in those strange times, and China's prevailing underdevelopment left the Bushes with plenty of leisure to explore the surroundings with their usual energy. The honorifically titled "Ambassador" Bush tried to get to know China and some of its leaders on the back of a bicycle, like millions of other blue-clad ordinary Beijingers, and on the tennis courts of the International Club near the Bush residence.

One anecdote of that period was told to me by Jimmy Carter's ambassador to China, Leonard Woodcock, former head of the United Auto Workers. In his efforts to project the dignity of the United States, despite the lack of diplomatic recognition, Bush wanted to look like a normal ambassador to the extent possible.

At that time, USLO's office and residence were of a size and luxury befitting their former occupant, the small African country of Burkina Faso, which had derecognized Beijing in 1973 in favor of Taipei. The larger French, British, and even Russian embassies had better housing and cars than the representative of the American superpower.

It was time for USLO to get a new vehicle, and Bush requested a stretch Cadillac limousine, which most U.S. embassies had in that period. He was informed by State Department functionaries, however, that Beijing was not a class A embassy, and therefore he would have to accept a workhorse but comfortably sized Checker sedan, series A, used widely as taxis in American cities and as the official vehicle at lesser missions at that time. Bush cabled a reclama that turned into an extensive exchange of messages that ultimately failed. In his last cable, Bush raised a white flag of surrender to the relentless bureaucrats and said, "Send Checker. Remove meter." (Checker went out of the taxi business in 1982. Woodcock was still riding in USLO's when he negotiated the normalization of relations with Beijing in 1978 and departed in 1981.)

When Bush became Ronald Reagan's running mate in summer 1980, he was given a delicate foreign mission to travel to Tokyo and Beijing and reassure leaders there that, despite Reagan's campaign remarks about upgrading relations with Taiwan, the presidential candidate was realistic and would not, if elected, overturn the decisions of his predecessors. Unfortunately, as Bush departed for his August visit to Beijing, and twice during his stay there, Reagan repeated his concerns for Taiwan, leading in turn to intense haranguing of the Bushes from Chinese officials, and as they departed, an official characterization of their trip as a "failure." Bush characteristically explained publicly that airing the differences between the two sides would strengthen understanding in the end, as he hightailed it out of town.

During his time as vice president, Bush was again sent to Beijing in May 1982, at the end of a long swing through the Pacific. The core issue on this trip was again Taiwan, prompted by loud Chinese objections to Reagan administration plans to sell $60 million in military spare parts to the island. After the visit, U.S. ambassador to China Arthur Hummel explained that the two sides had agreed to pursue the issue at lower levels, and a joint communique on arms sales to Taiwan was announced on August 17. Reagan made his only trip to China, widely regarded as successful, in 1984.

During the Reagan administration, common opposition to the Soviet Union and a growing commercial relationship underpinned a rapidly expanding official relationship. The Carter administration had initiated ties between virtually every U.S. agency and its Chinese counterpart, and these expanded considerably under Reagan, despite his campaign rhetoric, including military and intelligence exchanges and cooperation.

As with all presidents, Reagan's time was his most precious asset, and foreign policy aides had to struggle for time on his agenda to keep doors open to American visitors to the countries for which they were responsible. For Bush, his personal stake in, and familiarity with, China made him a willing substitute where appropriate and possible in meeting visitors. This kept Bush in contact with people he had known during his thirteen months in China, as well as newcomers. He stayed abreast of events while conveying a sense of warmth and interest that was unmistakable to the Chinese guests, even if sometimes abused by them, knowing that his door was always open.

Once elected in his own right in 1988, Bush made clear to those staffing him that he wanted to make an early trip to China to meet with "the old man," Deng Xiaoping, before he stepped down. At that time, Deng was taking advantage of the thaw in relations with Moscow brought about by the rise of Mikhail Gorbachev to dismantle the long-standing Soviet encirclement of China. Deng declared that there were "three great obstacles" to normal Sino-Soviet relations: Soviet occupation of Afghanistan, its troops stationed in Mongolia, and its naval presence in and support for Vietnam and its occupation of Cambodia. By late 1988, Gorbachev withdrew those Soviet forces and cleared the way for his own travel to Beijing, the first by a Soviet leader since a brief stopover by Alexei Kosygin in 1969. Bush wanted to ensure that America's relations with China remained secure as China felt less threat from its former Soviet ally and longtime nemesis. It became apparent fairly quickly, however, that the threat to U.S.–China relations would come less from Moscow than from within China itself.

In the transition from Reagan to Bush, the president-elect chose Lt. Gen. Brent Scowcroft (Ret.) as his national security advisor, reprising the role he had under President Ford, and approved Robert M. Gates, former deputy director of Central Intelligence, as his deputy. The two cold warriors undertook a review of foreign policy generally and reshuffled the staff serving under them. The Asia directorate got a new senior director, Dr. Karl Jackson, a Southeast Asia expert at Berkeley and later deputy assistant secretary of defense for Asia and the Pacific, and a mix of new and old faces. I stayed on as director for Asian affairs, largely responsible for China, Taiwan, and the Pacific.

President Bush's strategic calculation and desire to make an early trip to China required a pretext. Traditionally, incoming chief executives visit allies, including Canada, first. That pretext presented itself when the long ailing Emperor Hirohito of Japan passed away in January. President Bush decided he would take his foreign policy presidency seriously and make a trip to Canada, Japan, and China in February 1989, to attend the funeral rites of the late emperor. Bob Gates informed our directorate that he wanted President Bush to get to know Karl Jackson in his new role, so

Jackson would supervise the preparation and accompany the president on the Asian portions of the trip. I was told to accompany the advance team that would visit the three capitals to prepare the logistics.

Since the stopover of forty hours in Beijing was not to be a formal state visit, President Bush was free to decide he wanted to host a Texas-style barbecue for his Chinese counterparts and a large number of people representing the American and Chinese communities. While discussing the arrangements with the U.S. Embassy over dinner during the advance trip, I asked Ambassador Winston Lord whether he intended to add the names of known dissidents to the list of invitees. I recall his wife, the author Bette Bao Lord, answered that the Chinese leaders "would not like that."

Shortly after that, I was invited to take a walk in the freezing gardens of the Di-aoyutai state guest house, where we were staying, by an old friend who held a junior position in the embassy. The friend did not want us to be overheard by the omni-present listening devices in our quarters. The embassy officer told me that in visits to factories and offices around the city of Beijing, there was a seething resentment building against the official corruption and inflation that accompanied the reforms under Deng Xiaoping. "This city is ready to blow up," I was told. I asked why this was not being reported in the embassy's cable traffic and heard that it was blocked by higher ups in the embassy.

Preparations for the visit continued under Karl Jackson's supervision after our advance team returned to Washington. During the visit itself, President Bush and paramount leader Deng were on the same page strategically. As Bush described it in *A World Transformed*, Deng Xiaoping went to lengths to describe lingering suspicions of the Russians arising from seizing "more than three million square kilometers" of Chinese territory. Looking forward to Gorbachev's scheduled visit to Beijing in May, Deng and President Yang Shangkun reassured Bush that there would be no return to the alliance with Moscow of the 1950s.

Behind the facade of strategic congruence being staged in meetings with the lead-ers of Communist China, however, divisions were emerging in Chinese society that the embassy officer had forecast for me during the advance trip. These would quickly come to dominate debate about the U.S.–China relationship due to events that were entirely domestic to the Chinese. They would ultimately amount to what became a watershed in the Bush legacy and American relations with China—the Tiananmen incident—despite the president's personal commitment to and contribution to building a strong strategic framework.

In keeping with his personal investment in good ties with the Chinese, the president looked forward to hosting his barbecue at a Beijing hotel. He ordered a custom pair of cowboy boots, emblazoned with the Chinese and American flags, to give to his formal host, Premier Li Peng. In assembling a guest list that would be representative, Ambassador Lord in the end invited a well-known Chinese dissident astrophysicist, Fang Lizhi, whom many journalists called China's Sakharov. As events unfolded during the president's visit, Chinese officials made it clear that their leaders would not sit down in the same room with dissident critics of their regime. They wanted the invitation to be withdrawn, something the president knew would be wrong after it was extended.

A Chinese game of cat and mouse ensued, with police creating traffic jams that prevented Fang Lizhi and his wife from reaching the hotel and the banquet. President Yang attended without further worry that night about having to be in the company of Chinese dissidents. But this was the beginning of what quickly became not a game but a deadly struggle for control of China and the ruling party.

The events that followed Bush's early visit to Beijing are set out in *A World Transformed*, so I will not repeat them here. In a coincidence of what would prove to be tragic dimensions, preparations for Gorbachev's mid-May rebuilding of relations with China proceeded apace. The world's media sent their star reporters and anchors to witness the events, and as they were gathering, former leader Hu Yaobang passed away. Hu had been dismissed as leader of the party in 1986, reportedly for being too soft on student protestors. With his death, students again had an opportunity to use their mourning as a platform to protest corruption, dictatorship, inflation, and difficult campus conditions. With the world watching, China's leaders under Deng Xiaoping exercised uncharacteristic restraint, and the mourning morphed into a large protest presence in the heart of the capital accompanied by a rising clamor for political reform as well.

During Gorbachev's calls on the leadership, which had to be arranged around the protests, nominal leader and Party General Secretary Zhao Ziyang referred to Deng Xiaoping as the real decision maker in China, a comment that in retrospect publicly revealed a gap or division among the leaders. Throughout Chinese history, emperors and subsequent leaders have known that allowing divisions to be seen publicly can invite dangerous instability.[1] Mao Zedong's own war with his bureaucracy led to the massively disruptive Cultural Revolution within the painful memory of every Chinese leader in Beijing in May 1989.

With massive protests in the capital and twenty-three other cities as Gorbachev departed, the world's media stayed on to report the story as, in the background, the Soviet empire in Eastern Europe was beginning to collapse, raising premature Western hopes for the same in China. Premier Li Peng met with some of the protest leaders in a famously unsuccessful effort to persuade them to stand down. Zhao Ziyang went to Tiananmen Square to speak directly to the protestors, who increasingly included workers as well as students, saying he had come too late. Zhao was deposed on May 19. Meanwhile Deng Xiaoping summoned troops from all over China (to display loyalty and spread responsibility) before he authorized a declaration of martial law in Beijing on May 20.

The embassy in Beijing, under newly arrived Ambassador James R. Lilley, a longtime friend and colleague of Bush, as well as an experienced CIA officer, tirelessly reported on the protest activities as well as what we could learn of the troop movements around the city. We in Washington followed the developments intently and President Bush stayed closely informed even as he completed an important trip to Europe.

As Chinese preparations to crush the protests mounted, and then People's Liberation Army (PLA) troops and tanks were authorized to fire, the domestic and international outcry was deafening. The concatenation of Sino-Soviet diplomacy, media access, domestic unrest, and the unexpected death of a former leader created a perfect storm that deeply undermined what President Bush and his predecessors had sought to build with China.

On the Sunday after the People's Liberation Army cleared Tiananmen Square of the protestors, June 4, we called an interagency meeting at the assistant secretary level to develop options for responses for the National Security Council to present to the president. Assistant Secretary of Defense Carl Ford suggested the principal initial action, and it received unanimous endorsement. He argued reasonably that since it was the PLA that carried out the violence, we must direct our sanctions there first. He proposed an option to suspend military-to-military relations and the various cooperative projects that had developed through the 1980s. Legal counsel also noted that various pieces of legislation had human rights clauses that would force suspension of other agencies' activities, and it was agreed to investigate what those would be. The president quickly agreed when he returned to Washington and undertook to persuade other governments to stand up for human rights in China and to join in sanctions.

As Bush described in *A World Transformed*, however, he wanted to communicate directly to Deng Xiaoping why he was taking the actions he announced, that he was forced to do this by internal Chinese events that had damaged the American domestic consensus regarding China. General Scowcroft called and asked me for a phone number to reach Deng so the president could make the call. I advised against it for three reasons: it was not Chinese practice to do diplomatic business over the phone; Deng was not the formal leader and in any event would have to keep up a façade of collective, not individual, leadership; and, Deng was nearly stone deaf, so the phone call could be embarrassingly awkward. As Bush has written, he nonetheless tried to call, but without success.

Frustrated, he subsequently wrote his own letter to Deng: "the actions I took as President of the United States could not be avoided. As you know, the clamor for stronger action remains intense. I have resisted that clamor, making clear that I did not want to see destroyed this relationship that you and I have worked hard to build." He asked Deng effectively to moderate Chinese government behavior toward the protestors so as not to worsen the situation. Bush asked Scowcroft to personally deliver the letter to Chinese Ambassador Han Xu at his embassy on June 23. In light of his frustration at being unable to speak with Deng personally, Bush also asked Scowcroft to propose sending a personal emissary in total privacy. With surprising speed, Han conveyed Deng's response and less than twenty-fours later agreed to receive an envoy.

Events did not stand still as Bush tried to construct a response to the crack-down in China that would retain domestic support, but not throw the baby of strategic cooperation out with the bathwater of legitimate horror and reaction. China continued to propagandize videos of the arrests and prosecutions of dissidents. Western cameras famously captured a brave sole protestor blocking the progress of tanks in Beijing. The astrophysicist Fang Lizhi and his wife appeared at the U.S. Embassy seeking refuge from arrest on June 10. Despite the risks involved in taking them in, the president agreed with Jim Baker that there was no choice but to protect them from much worse.

Secretary Baker was scheduled to appear before the Senate Foreign Relations Committee on June 20, amid the rising clamor from almost every quarter to do more to reverse the course of events in China. After a quick exchange between Bush and Baker, the secretary of state told the committee that the United States would also suspend senior-level exchanges with Beijing.

Bush had all along intended that his emissary to Deng would travel secretly, and Baker's approved announcement created awkwardness in selecting the emissary. As Bush wrote in *A World Transformed*, Baker could not go—too public. Richard Nixon or Henry Kissinger had stature and effectiveness, but leaks would be hard to avoid. Lower-level officials lacked the stature. He finally decided Scowcroft, who had met Deng before and knew him better than anyone else at his level, would be his choice. Scowcroft asked Deputy Secretary of State Lawrence Eagleburger to accompany him on the secret trip, in keeping with Scowcroft's strong views on not having the national security advisor appear to be an independent actor in foreign affairs.

As an NSC staffer, I was kept in the dark about the letters, meetings, and travel initiated by the president in the period immediately following Tiananmen. When Scowcroft and Eagleburger flew to Beijing, they flew in an unmarked C-141, refueled mid-air, accompanied only by the Air Force crew and Scowcroft's loyal and effective secretary, Florence Gantt, who kept the records of discussions despite little familiarity with China. But secrecy was going to be hard to maintain because someone from the embassy had to pay for refueling the aircraft in Beijing and China distributed information about the emissaries' visit widely within the PRC government, presumably to portray the leadership favorably during stressful times.

Both the United States and China, having aired their respective views in Beijing, proceeded to continue to disagree. Scowcroft was satisfied that channels of communication were kept open, and Bush thought the mission had done well. Briefed on Scowcroft's return on July 3, Bush then turned to East Europe.

Meanwhile, controversies percolated in Washington. Americans were successfully evacuated from China under Ambassador Jim Lilley. Concern grew over the fate of Chinese students abroad who had supported the protestors back home. Bush promised to protect those in the United States through an executive order. New member of Congress Nancy Pelosi took up the cause of legislating protection for them instead. There ensued a debate over whether an executive order was as good as legislation, which led to a successful veto defense by Bush early the next year, arguing that he needed to protect his executive flexibility to manage foreign affairs.

As agency and departmental budgets moved through the committees of Congress, money for programs involving China was steadily slashed or removed entirely. These included relatively invisible items, such as ending support from the Commerce Department for a graduate business school in Dalian. The substance of the U.S.–China relationship went from somewhat thick to very thin quite quickly. Diplomatic communication was minimized.

In China, the momentum of economic and social reform launched in 1978 by Deng was stopped by the forces of reaction to the events at Tiananmen, and to Deng's reforms in general. Opponents of change in the party and economy, and losers in previous power struggles, saw their opportunity to turn back the clock. The Chinese, of course, put a premium on not allowing more internal divisions within the party to be observed, lest it encourage more dissent in the streets. But no one could mistake the chill in the atmosphere. It was no longer business as usual.

Later in October 1989, former president Nixon, having watched Chinese events diminish his own legacy, decided to travel to Beijing and see whether he could reopen a channel. He asked former Carter NSC staffer Michel Oksenberg to help prepare his visit and accompany him, signaling a bipartisan intent. They kept Bush, Scowcroft, and me well-informed, but even Nixon was not told about the earlier Scowcroft-Eagleburger secret trip.

Unsurprisingly, the isolated Chinese gave Nixon a warm welcome. The former president nevertheless maintained a cool public demeanor, trying to stay in step with the American national mood. But in their private meeting with Deng Xiaoping, Nixon and Oksenberg were unexpectedly presented with a "road map" or "package solution" to reconstruction of U.S.–China relations. The core of the proposal was to exchange American gradual lifting of sanctions for steps China could do to meet American concerns, such as releasing student prisoners early or ceasing to jam the Voice of America (VOA), plus others. Deng's apparent prime goal was to restart the stalled engine of Chinese growth and reform.

Nixon briefed Bush on Deng's "package solution" over dinner at the White House in early November. Internal discussions followed about whether Deng's proposal merited further exploration and in what fashion. By early December, Bush decided to send Scowcroft and Eagleburger back to Beijing, but not in secret this time. A compilation was prepared of complaints and demands from the administration and Congress, as well as notional relief of many sanctions if China proved forthcoming. Beijing in particular wanted reassurance that the administration would continue to support, and fight for, continued most-favored nation (in other words, normal) trading status, which was reviewed annually by Congress. In Chinese eyes, the process should culminate in a formal state visit to the United States by Deng's recently handpicked new party leader, Jiang Zemin.

There were other items, such as the seemingly trivial return of Chinese military planes that were being refitted in the United States. The latter were entangled in legalities, such as demands that China first pay rent for the storage of the aircraft after the Tiananmen sanctions were placed on their return. China felt that was an American problem and would not pay. (It did eventually pay, but much later.)

The United States had its list of human rights concessions and action on other concerns to address that would be necessary before relations could start to thaw. Very prominent among them was safe passage out of China for Fang Lizhi and his wife from their closely guarded refuge in the U.S. Embassy.

Returning from an important meeting with Gorbachev in Malta in early December, Scowcroft and Eagleburger left quickly for Beijing to explore the "road map." The political atmosphere in the United States remained hostile to China. Scowcroft did not want to stir opposition to his trip before he even got there to test Deng's proposal, but he did not want to surprise the media and Congress. As he later put it, he "made a mess of it," by revealing the visit only at the last minute. The Chinese, eager to show a return to normal, compounded the situation by surprisingly inviting a CNN camera crew to the lunch hosted by Foreign Minister Qian.

Before landing in Beijing, Ambassador Lilley suggested some polite but frank words that Scowcroft might offer at the lunch in a ritual toast to acknowledge tough times in both our countries for relations. The toast was seen in Washington, however, as too friendly and was chewed over on the Sunday morning talk shows.

The ensuing talks were very tough, especially with Premier Li Peng, who seemed to enjoy playing the heavy. They are extensively related in *A World Transformed*. In sum, the Chinese agreed to begin a process of step-by-step mutual accommodation. The Chinese began to release some protestors, approved a VOA correspondent for Beijing, lifted martial law, agreed to stop missile sales to the Middle East, and accepted the Peace Corps. Meanwhile President Bush worked hard to sustain his veto of the Pelosi bill on Chinese students.

But shortly after Scowcroft's return to Washington, the momentum begun in Beijing lost its force quickly. Most importantly, the Chinese leadership watched the collapse of Nicolae Ceaușescu's regime in horror. Chinese officials told me later that the senior leadership had viewed videos of the brutal execution of Ceaușescu and his wife, and this revived their fears of suffering a similar fate. Even though Bush successfully sustained his veto in early January, by then bilateral communications came to an effective standstill. This silence lasted for months, as the rest of the world celebrated the collapse of the Soviet Union's eastern empire.

Shortly after their return to Washington, the first secret Scowcroft-Eagleburger trip was revealed to the public by a Chinese source, and this added to the sour public mood in the United States. Ruminating over this at the time, I became convinced that however much the first secret trip to China by Henry Kissinger in 1971 may have been rooted in necessity, the tendency to manage big events in relations with China closely in the White House and to engage in secret exchanges would not be sustainable for public policy in the long term.

Despite the prevailing bad tempers, China had agreed with Scowcroft to hold talks with Ambassador Lilley to arrange the departure of Fang Lizhi and his wife for the United Kingdom. Beijing evidently concluded, as later became almost customary with dissidents, that letting them go overseas rendered them more harmless than jailing or otherwise keeping them in China. The Fangs left the embassy for Britain by U.S. aircraft in June 1990, whereupon they violated their pledge not to criticize China abroad. They also complained somewhat ungraciously about Bush's policy toward their homeland, despite his actions to save them from prison or worse.

During this period, I manufactured an opportunity to discuss matters in private with China's ambassador to the United States, Zhu Qizhen, whose tenure was unlucky. Beijing's propaganda had been using the phrase that American actions "hurt the feelings" of a billion Chinese. I asked him just who were the people with hurt feelings? He replied without pausing, "eight old men in Beijing." Presumably, these were the same party elders who also huddled in fear with Deng on the eve of declaring martial law in May, and reacted in shock to the end of Ceauşescu. Their profound fears were beyond the capacity of the United States to allay.

The next significant development in U.S.-China relations was derived from another distant crisis. On August 2, 1990, Iraqi dictator Saddam Hussein invaded Kuwait and set in motion what became an emblematic episode in the Bush presidency, recounted elsewhere in this volume. The China angle emerged late in the year, after painstaking preparation by the White House, State, and Defense Departments to muster the necessary forces and international approval for the United States to oust Saddam from Kuwait. The foreign ministers of the fifteen member countries of the UN Security Council gathered in New York in late November for a vote to give the United States and other countries with forces arrayed against Iraq the most sweeping authorization to engage in warfare under UN sponsorship since the 1950 Korean War.

Prior to the vote, China was playing hard to get, unwilling to confirm that it would not use its veto to block Bush's diplomatic initiative. On November 6, Baker met with Qian in Cairo to lobby him for the vote. In those talks, Baker told Qian that any assistance Beijing gave for the American policy in the Persian Gulf "will not be forgotten and the meaning of that assistance will not be lost on the domestic audience in the United States," an administration official said.

Early in the morning of November 27, I received a phone call at home from Ambassador Zhu, asking me for a number to call Scowcroft. Zhu was in New York with his foreign minister preparing for the UNSC vote. It became clear quickly that China was using Bush's need for an international mandate before asking for a congressional vote on the use of force to break the embargo on high-level meetings in Washington prevailing since the Tiananmen crackdown.

I never believed that the Chinese would be willing to exercise their veto right in isolation on the Kuwait vote and believed they would never support it either. Therefore, I did not think it would be necessary to receive Qian at the White House to ensure his abstention. But President Bush wanted to leave no stone unturned in preparing the offensive against Saddam, and he was willing to take the heat of resuming receiving high-level visitors from China.

Hours after the Chinese Foreign Ministry announced in Beijing that Qian had been invited to Washington, Chinese diplomats at the United Nations, who had waivered on whether to support the proposed Security Council resolution authorizing the use of force against Iraq, signaled definitively that they would not oppose it. China abstained in the end. By a vote of twelve to two, foreign ministers of the fifteen-member council adopted a U.S.-sponsored resolution that gave Iraqi President Saddam Hussein what would be his last chance to withdraw peacefully from Kuwait, which he invaded August 2. The resolution stated that, unless Iraq, by January 15, fully complied with previous council resolutions calling for its unconditional withdrawal from Kuwait and release of foreigners, member states may "use all necessary means . . . to restore international peace and security in the area."

The following year was consumed with Kuwait and its aftermath, and the China relationship remained idle. By November 1991, the Asian diplomatic calendar called for Secretary of State Baker to attend the Asia Pacific Economic (APEC) forum, which he had helped Australia to initiate, plus visit Allied capitals. I wrote to President Bush suggesting that this trip, after so much time, would be an opportunity to resume exercising normal American leadership in the region, including in dealing with China.

Baker and his top aides were understandably concerned with how to manage the optics of a stop in Beijing. The Chinese were still in lockdown mode after Tiananmen. Baker had tried to keep a distance from Chinese matters generally and was genuinely busy with developments in the Middle East and Eastern Europe, but he acquiesced in making the trip.

On the way to Beijing, Baker's staff tried to arrange a meeting or encounter with dissidents, much like those of earlier years with Russian dissidents in Moscow. Beijing evidently overheard these discussions, and on landing, the security arrangements were tighter than any I had seen before. I ventured out from the state guest house to shop in the old-style central Dong Feng market. To my amazement, every beggar or peddler who got near me was hauled off by plain clothes police. China was taking no chances.

There was a long list of unfinished business for Baker to take up with the Chinese, including M-9 missiles to Syria, M-11 missiles to Pakistan, nuclear cooperation with Iran, signing the Nuclear Nonproliferation Treaty, human rights in general, and releasing more prisoners. A series of calls on China's leaders prepared for the key meeting with Premier Li Peng. None of the meetings were easy, but Chinese officials gave some encouragement that Beijing might meet us half-way on matters outside sensitive internal considerations, such as on adhering to the limits of the Missile Technology Control Regime (MTCR).

When the time came to meet with Li Peng, nothing prepared me for the belligerent and uncompromising show he put on. As Baker pressed for agreement on national security matters, lower-level officials would pop up to explain constructively what the premier said or did not say but that he himself did not want to utter. At one point, Baker signaled that it was time to start the engines of his plane and leave Beijing behind. Then Li began to repeat the assurances his staff were encouraging, even offering the sop of a "dialogue" on human rights with State's assistant secretary for human rights. The gains on international issues were in fact substantial, if small by today's standards, but the human rights dialogue remained unconvincing.

As Baker himself later said to the media, "unless we were to keep U.S.-China relations in the deep freeze forever, we had to start talking. I did not come here expecting a dramatic breakthrough. The gulf is too wide to accomplish that in one trip."

In January 1992, during an economic slowdown at home, after Bush concluded a long-delayed series of economically focused state visits through Asia that did not include China, the United Kingdom assumed the presidency of the UN Security Council. Prime Minister John Major, to whom Bush felt very close, wanted to convene a summit of the permanent UNSC members to discuss the impact of the dissolution of the Soviet Union and the potential for nuclear proliferation. China saw this as an opportunity to emerge from the global doghouse. Beijing indicated Premier Li Peng would go to New York to lead the Chinese delegation.

Given the international disfavor with which the world regarded Li Peng, I paid a lot of attention to the publicly visible circumstances of the necessary multilateral and bilateral meetings at the UN. We arranged the bilateral to be held deep inside the UN headquarters, with no press availability. But a friend tipped me off to plans for Li to include a photographer in his official delegation to grab a shot shaking hands with Bush. When we sat down at the conference table, there was one figure whose name I had never encountered—the photographer. I tipped off the Secret Service detail. When Bush politely shook hands with Li, out came the camera just as two burly agents crushed him with their shoulders from both sides. No pictures.

The year propelled itself into the election season, and there was little room remaining for doing much with China. Democratic candidate Bill Clinton spoke to his convention about the "butchers of Beijing," and after taking office he pronounced a policy of linking normal trading relations to substantial improvements in human rights in China. To my eyes, this was instantly recognizable as an unsustainable stance, and Clinton reversed himself in late 1994.

Meanwhile, invisible to us at first, the eighty-eight-year old Deng Xiaoping was trying to restart his economic reforms within China. Even he needed months to break into the Chinese media after touring China's south in early 1992 promoting reform, so intense and effective were the forces of reaction that, paradoxically, he had helped to release in the suppression at Tiananmen. In time, Deng prevailed and set China on a growth path seldom seen in history, and never by so large and self-referential a country. This development demonstrated again the need to be modest in assessing the role of outsiders in China. The insider's game is very hard to read.

NOTE

1. See Ray Huang, *1587, a Year of No Significance* (New Haven, CT: Yale University Press, 1981).

8

"This Will Not Stand"

The Liberation of Kuwait

Robert M. Kimmitt

George H. W. Bush ranks among the finest foreign policy presidents in American history. He was informed and instinctive; experienced and engaged; effective yet self-effacing. His formation and leadership of a global coalition during the Persian Gulf Crisis and War was perhaps his finest hour in a presidency marked by epochal change.

From his military background, President Bush understood the significance of a clear, concise mission statement. In the case of Germany, it was, "Unite within NATO" (previewed, interestingly, in a *New York Times* interview in October 1989, three weeks *before* the Berlin Wall fell). In the case of Saddam Hussein's brazen and brutal invasion of Kuwait in August 1990, it was "This will not stand, this aggression against Kuwait."

There have been many excellent pieces written on the Gulf Crisis and War, including chapters in books written by President Bush and Brent Scowcroft (jointly), Dick Cheney, Jim Baker, Colin Powell, Bob Gates, Norman Schwarzkopf, and Richard Haass. As undersecretary of state for political affairs, it was my honor to serve as a member of this outstanding team.

What follows below is a narrative based on my role as lead crisis manager at the State Department and architect of the UN strategy under the leadership and direction of President Bush and Secretary Baker. The narrative is weighted toward Desert Shield—that is, the diplomacy conducted until the counterattack to reverse Saddam's aggression was launched on January 16, 1991. However, I do offer views on Desert Storm and its aftermath. This narrative is my personal recollection of that historic period, and any errors of omission or commission are mine alone.

PROLOGUE

The lead-up to Desert Shield and Storm began five decades before, when President Franklin Roosevelt met on February 4, 1945, aboard the USS *Quincy* in the Suez Canal with King Abdul Aziz ibn Saud of Saudi Arabia. The vast oil reserves of the kingdom were already being viewed in strategic terms as World War II ground to its end.

At that time, Iraq was also ruled by a monarchy, which was overthrown in 1958. In 1963, the Ba'ath Party took control, leading eventually to Saddam Hussein taking power in July 1979.

The year 1979 was also fateful in neighboring Iran, with the Shah fleeing in January, and Ayatollah Khomeini returning from exile in France on February 1. On November 4, fifty-two American hostages began their 444 days of captivity in the U.S. Embassy in Tehran. And to close that eventful year, the Soviet Union invaded Afghanistan on Christmas Day.

Just before he left office, President Jimmy Carter, in Presidential Directive 63 of January 15, 1981, said that the United States would "defend our vital interests in the [Persian Gulf] region as a whole." The words *vital interests* were crucial, because use of that term indicated the United States was prepared to use military force, if necessary, to protect its interests in the region. In anticipation of this expanded military requirement, the Carter administration had earlier negotiated military access agreements with Oman, Kenya, and Somalia and established the Rapid Deployment Joint Task Force (RDJTF), the forerunner of U.S. Central Command (CENTCOM).

As the Carter administration ended, and during virtually the entire Reagan administration, Iraq and Iran were at war. Out of concern about Iran, but also about growing Soviet influence in the Persian Gulf, the United States sided with Iraq during the war, providing materiel and intelligence support and restoring diplomatic relations in 1984. The Iran-Iraq War ended on August 20, 1988, two days after George H. W. Bush was nominated at the Republican Convention in New Orleans as the party's candidate for president of the United States.

GEORGE H. W. BUSH TAKES OFFICE

On taking the oath of office on January 20, 1989, President Bush made clear his respect for President Reagan but also his intention to preside over his own agenda rather than lead a "third term" of Ronald Reagan. This was especially the case in the field of foreign policy, which was a particular, even unique, strength of the new president, who had served as a member of Congress, representative to China, ambassador to the United Nations, and director of Central Intelligence, and, as such, director of the CIA.

The year 1989 turned out to be a momentous one in global affairs, with the opening of the Iron Curtain between Hungary and Austria; the massacre in Tiananmen Square; the fall of the Berlin Wall; violent insurrections in the Philippines and El Salvador; the U.S. military operation in Panama that deposed Manuel Noriega; and signs of apartheid's imminent collapse in South Africa.

Throughout the year, even as these historic events unfolded, there was a broad-scale foreign policy review process being carried out under the leadership of National Security Advisor Brent Scowcroft and his Deputy Bob Gates. In general, this review process produced serviceable but not innovative approaches, with some commentators saying the process resulted in policies that were "status quo plus."

One reason the process was not as creative as it should have been was the courteous and practical nature of President Bush. He said early in the administration that Reagan-Bush appointees could remain in place until their successors were confirmed. Most successors were sworn in over the summer of 1989, so almost all the policy studies were conducted by policy coordination committees chaired by lame-duck assistant secretaries. These individuals had the natural human tendency to defend what they had done rather than develop new ideas, which could be interpreted as making their past work look less creative.

An exception was the policy study on Persian Gulf strategy. This issue was looked at later than other topics, producing vigorous debate, including on U.S. policy toward Iraq. It also benefited from the active steering and shaping role played by Richard Haass, special assistant to the president and National Security Council senior director for the Mideast.

The result of these deliberations was National Security Directive (NSD) 26 of October 2, 1989: "U.S. Policy toward the Persian Gulf." The opening paragraph of the directive was strong and laid the foundation for what was to come ten months later on August 2, 1990:

> Access to Persian Gulf oil and the security of key friendly states in the area are vital to U.S. national security. The United States remains committed to defend its vital interests in the region, if necessary and appropriate through the use of U.S. military force, against the Soviet Union or any other regional power with interests inimical to our own.

And the paragraph on Iraq was equally clear, if more controversial:

> Normal relations between the United States and Iraq would serve our longer-term interests and promote stability in both the Gulf and the Middle East. The United States Government should propose economic and political incentives for Iraq to moderate its behavior and to increase our influence with Iraq.[1]

At the NSC meeting on that subject, the president asked Deputy Director of the CIA Dick Kerr what he thought the chances were of moderating Saddam's behavior. Dick's response was, "It is worth a try, but a tiger cannot change its stripes."

Throughout the remainder of 1989, consistent with NSD 26, efforts were made to reach out to Iraq. This included approval of Commodity Credit Corporation credits for agricultural exports and the settlement of past legal disputes. (These and other steps taken were cited by Democrats after the Gulf War ended in 1991 as evidence that the United States had inappropriately aided Saddam in the prewar period.)

By January of 1990, however, it was clear that Iraq was not only not responding to U.S. overtures but also accelerating troublesome behaviors. Those included the import of steel tubes, ostensibly for construction projects but actually used for long-range artillery pieces. Iraq also increased their threats to Israel and executed a journalist, Farzad Barzoft, on rigged charges that he had spied for Israel. As a result, the United States began to reapply pressure on Iraq.

The escalation of U.S. pressure on Iraq was concerning to Iraq's neighbors. In the spring of 1990, the Kuwaiti ambassador to the United States hosted me at a luncheon with the Iraqi ambassador and other Arab ambassadors to urge a de-escalation of tension between Iraq and the United States. But Iraq had not yet become a major global priority, even as late as the G7 Summit hosted by the United States from July 8 to 11, 1990, in Houston. The Summit concluding documents made no mention of Iraq.

By late July 1990, however, Iraqi actions were becoming even more troublesome. There were attempts by Iraq to restrict air and sea navigation rights, and Republican Guard units were being moved south toward the Kuwaiti border. Arab neighbors of Saddam counseled the United States not to overact, based on the belief—which King Hussein of Jordan conveyed directly to President Bush—that Saddam could be talked into a solution that would not involve armed conflict. On July 25, Ambassador April Glaspie said in a meeting with Saddam Hussein that the United States took no position in Arab territorial disputes but wanted them settled peacefully.

THE FATEFUL DAY ARRIVES

On August 1, the CIA included for the first time in the President's Daily Brief a report saying that the Intelligence Community believed Saddam's battle formations were now "more likely than not" indicating an attack was forthcoming. I convened a meeting of the Deputies Committee in the Secretary's Conference Room at the State Department (Bob Gates was out of town, as was Secretary Jim Baker, so I was both acting secretary of state and acting chair of the Deputies Committee). The deputies reviewed all the available evidence, agreed that hostilities were imminent, and asked Richard Haass to suggest via Brent Scowcroft that the president call Saddam Hussein to warn against an attack. I called Secretary Baker in Irkutsk, where he was meeting with Soviet foreign minister Shevardnadze, to report on the CIA assessment.

I left the department around 6:30 p.m., only to be greeted at home by calls from both Ambassador Nat Howell in Kuwait City and Dick Clarke, director of Political-

Military Affairs at State, to say Kuwait was under attack from Iraq. I immediately called the White House and passed that word to Brent Scowcroft, who, with Richard Haass, was with the president discussing the idea of a phone call to Saddam. I also called Secretary Baker, who said Shevardnadze had assured him there would be no invasion (based on a report from the Soviets' Iraq/Saddam handler Yuri Primakov). That embarrassment for Shevardnadze, building on Secretary Baker's already good relationship with him, led to unprecedented Soviet-U.S. cooperation on Iraq immediately and in the months ahead. I then made three additional calls:

1. To Ambassador to the UN Tom Pickering, saying we needed a UN Security Council Resolution calling for unconditional withdrawal;
2. To Treasury Deputy Secretary John Robson, to put full-scope U.S. economic and financial sanctions in place against Iraq and asset freezes in place against Iraq and Kuwait (to prevent Kuwaiti assets from falling into Saddam's hands); and
3. To Deputy Attorney General Bill Barr to draft a report to Congress consistent with the War Powers Resolution.

On the latter two tasks, the counsel to the president, Boyden Gray, was an important and integral participant, since it was he who took such actions to the president for signature. I then returned to the State Operations Center, where we convened what became a six-hour Deputies Committee meeting by secure videoconference, chaired by Brent Scowcroft. Two memories stand out from that marathon session:

1. At around 11:00 p.m., Acting Assistant Secretary for International Organizations Jane Becker (Assistant Secretary John Bolton was out of town) brought me a draft UNSC Resolution. The draft essentially said "aggression is bad and can't we all just get along," but had no mention of "unconditional withdrawal." I told her to pass to Ambassador Pickering that the "unconditional withdrawal" phrase was essential and non-negotiable.
2. Shortly before midnight, a message came from the Kuwaiti ambassador in Washington, saying he had been authorized by his government to request U.S. assistance in countering the invasion. Even though their country was under actual attack, it still was a difficult decision to request U.S. help formally.

The following morning, the National Security Council met. Reports about that meeting have described it as unfocused, and indeed there was discussion that rambled. But, as I reported to the president, we had secured passage overnight of UN Security Council Resolution 660 calling for unconditional withdrawal (14-0-1, with the Soviet Union, China, and Cuba voting yes; and only Yemen abstaining); full scope U.S. economic and financial sanctions were in place against Saddam, as was a freeze of Iraqi and Kuwaiti assets; and a War Power Resolution report was ready to be sent to Congress if the president decided to begin troop deployments to the region.

But clear strategic direction was missing, as discussed among the president, Brent Scowcroft, and Richard Haass after the NSC meeting. Haass was tasked with preparing a memorandum summarizing what would be required to get Iraq out of Kuwait and discourage it from invading Saudi Arabia.

The president then flew to Aspen, Colorado, for a previously scheduled meeting with British prime minister Margaret Thatcher. He returned to Washington for a second NSC meeting on August 3, followed by a busy weekend at Camp David. There he met with his senior military advisors and decided to dispatch Defense Secretary Dick Cheney to Saudi Arabia to determine whether Saudi King Fahd would permit deployment of U.S. forces to the kingdom. The president also began his wide-ranging and persistent telephone diplomacy, speaking that weekend with Japanese prime minister Kaifu, Turkish president Özal, Kuwaiti emir Al Sabah (who had fled to Saudi Arabia), French president Mitterrand, Canadian prime minister Mulroney, and other world leaders.

THIS WILL NOT STAND

The president returned to the White House on Sunday afternoon, August 5. In remarks to reporters, after being updated by Richard Haass as he disembarked from Marine One, the president gave the American people and their government, our friends and allies, and Saddam Hussein a crystal-clear statement of his strategic objective: "This will not stand, this aggression against Kuwait."

The president's strategy was straightforward: use skillful diplomacy, backed up by strong economic sanctions and a credible threat of military action, to get Saddam to withdraw peacefully and unconditionally. To that end, two important steps were taken on Monday, August 6:

- First, Defense Secretary Cheney reported that King Fahd had given the go-ahead for deployment of U.S. forces to Saudi Arabia. Secretary Cheney had made clear the president's intent to send sizable, capable U.S. forces, not a symbolic gesture like the unarmed F-15's deployed to the kingdom by the Carter administration in January 1979.
- Second, agreement in principle was reached on what would become UN Security Council Resolution 661, establishing a global economic embargo and asset freeze to complement and enhance the unilateral sanctions measures taken by the United States four days before.

After receiving Secretary Cheney's report, the president decided to begin to deploy U.S. forces to the Gulf, starting with the Army's Eighty-Second Airborne Division as well as Air Force units. In announcing these deployments, the president noted that Iraq had invaded with one hundred twenty thousand troops and 850 tanks and was moving farther south to threaten Saudi Arabia.

That same Monday, Prime Minister Thatcher stopped in Washington on her way back to London from Aspen. She and the president held a joint press conference, which was curtailed somewhat by a summer thunderstorm that kept her from being able to helicopter to Andrews Air Force Base for her return flight home. The president and Mrs. Thatcher repaired to the Oval Office with several senior U.S. officials in attendance. Having met twice in three days, there was not much left for the two leaders to discuss, so the president asked Jim Baker, who then asked me, to give an update on activity at the United Nations.

I responded that we were about to pass UNSCR 661, putting global sanctions in place. Mrs. Thatcher asked to see the text and immediately concluded the language was "too soft" and "not at all acceptable." When neither the president nor Secretary Baker responded, I stepped in to say the language was what we needed legally and would garner strong support in the Security Council. Richard Haass thankfully was in the meeting and came to my support.

When the prime minister continued to object, I informed her that both the British Foreign and Commonwealth Office and her attorney general Michael Havers (with whom I had just spoken) had signed off on the language. She responded: "There is no way Michael Havers would have supported something this weak." But he had, and Britain joined later that day in a 13–0–2 UN vote in favor, with Cuba and Yemen abstaining.

In a call to the president the following day after returning to London (as relayed to me by Bob Gates), Mrs. Thatcher told the president to "tell Mr. Kimmitt he has prevailed on Resolution 661" but that she would be "watching him carefully" going forward. (Mrs. Thatcher and I already had a little history: when I was NSC executive secretary in October 1983, I had, at President Reagan's express direction, kept calls from her from getting through to the president during the early hours of the Grenada operation.)

Later in August, when tankers laden with oil from Iraq were steaming toward Yemen, Mrs. Thatcher took the position that Resolutions 660 and 661 gave Allied Forces the right to intercept and board the tankers. The president and Secretary Baker believed it better to propose another UN resolution giving the Allied Forces explicit authority to enforce the embargo with a naval quarantine or blockade. That was done on August 25 in Resolution 665, which passed 13–0–2, with Cuba and Yemen again abstaining.

And on September 25, the ability to enforce the embargo also in the air and in ports was codified in UNSCR 670, at a session of the Security Council with Soviet foreign minister Eduard Shevardnadze in the chair—one of the rare instances of foreign ministers attending UN Security Council sessions. Our belief was that we would be more likely to succeed on this second enforcement resolution by elevating the level of representation, as a mark of respect for the good working relationship that had developed on Iraq with the Soviet Union and Shevardnadze, and it resulted in a 14–1 vote in favor. (Only Cuba—not a fan of embargoes or quarantines—voted against.) By using these gradually more forceful resolutions, we were also preparing the Soviets, and others, for an ultimate vote on a use-of-force resolution if needed.

OCTOBER 1990: DESERT SHIELD EXPANDS

The fall of 1990 was busy on all fronts: diplomatic, economic, and military. U.S. forces flowing to the Gulf numbered two hundred fifty thousand by November 1, 1990. In addition, what became a coalition of thirty-four nations contributing forces, and many additional countries providing other support, continued to form.

At the direction of the president, Secretary Baker and Treasury Secretary Nick Brady embarked that fall on an effort to obtain financial support for the U.S. military effort. This "tin cup" exercise was extraordinarily effective, raising over $70 billion and covering the full cost of the U.S. deployment, positioning, and ultimately combat operations.

On the economic front, sanctions began to bite, not only for Saddam but also for regional states in coalition with the United States, especially Egypt, Jordan, and Turkey. The United States formed a multilateral Gulf Crisis Financial Coordination Group, cochaired by Treasury and State, to provide assistance to these three "frontline" states. Multilateral meetings at the Treasury Department in Washington and later at the Finance Ministry in Rome secured pledges in excess of $15 billion.

On the political front, additional resolutions continued to pass at the United Nations, all intended to make clear to Saddam that the international community was unified in its view that he needed to withdraw unconditionally. Regrettably, he seemed barely moved by this unprecedented international cooperation.

It was during October 1990 that the "battle rhythm" was set for the interagency process. After being briefed by my exceptionally able front office staff, led by Executive Assistant Ken Brill and Special Assistant for the Mideast Mike Malinowski, I would meet in my office each morning at 8:00 a.m. with representatives from each of State's bureaus, numbering around forty attendees. Thereafter, my core group—Assistant Secretaries John Kelly, John Bolton, Dick Clarke, and Doug Mulholland, together with members of my staff—would set our approach for the interagency Policy Coordination Committee (PCC) chaired by John Kelly at 9:30 a.m. At 10:45 a.m., John would report to me on the results and recommendations of the PCC, in time for an 11:00 a.m. Deputies Committee meeting chaired by Bob Gates and conducted via secure videoconference. Thereafter, at 12:30 p.m., the "Small Group" would meet in the White House Situation Room: Bob Gates (chair), myself, Defense Undersecretary Paul Wolfowitz, Deputy Director of the CIA Dick Kerr, Vice Chairman of the Joint Chiefs of Staff Dave Jeremiah, and Richard Haass.

After the Small Group meeting, the "Big Eight" would meet in the Oval Office: President Bush, Vice President Quayle, Secretary Jim Baker, Secretary Dick Cheney, General Colin Powell, White House Chief of Staff John Sununu, National Security

Advisor Brent Scowcroft, and Bob Gates, who would brief the group on recommendations from the interagency meetings that had preceded the Big Eight meeting.

Thereafter, Bob Gates would debrief and instruct the Deputies Committee, who would do the same for the Policy Coordination Committee. At around 7:00 p.m. each evening, the workday would conclude with an all-hands departmental meeting in my office at State, to ensure clarity and coordination on cables of instruction and other decisions to be conveyed to embassies throughout the world.

The three-part lesson learned was the importance of having: (1) a process in place both for policy formulation and decision execution; (2) a clear mandate from senior leadership for the process to perform both functions; and (3) representatives from all relevant agencies and offices to be part of the process. Too often, bureaucratic energy and time are dissipated sparring over who should lead or be part of a policy process and then working issues up the chain of command to the point of presidential decision, leaving little energy for implementing those decisions. In crises, and wars, policy formulation and execution are equally important to ultimate success—and both need to be informed, crisp, and collaborative.

And a good policy formulation group is also the best crisis management group. The United States was fortunate to have senior leaders who had worked together since the Nixon/Ford years: President Bush, Secretaries Baker and Cheney, and National Security Advisor Brent Scowcroft. In the Small Group, you had members like Bob Gates (an exceptionally able chair), Paul Wolfowitz, Richard Haass, and myself who had served together in previous administrations. In both cases, there was no appetite for the traditional bureaucratic game playing, leading to an unusually effective process throughout the Gulf Crisis and War.

NOVEMBER 1990: THE FATEFUL MONTH

By November, it was becoming clearer that Saddam was unlikely to withdraw voluntarily from Kuwait. And it seemed he discounted the possibility that the United States might decide to use force. Well before he invaded Kuwait, he had once taken the Baghdad diplomatic corps, including Ambassador Glaspie, to a major dam construction project in northern Iraq. Most of the laborers on site were Vietnamese, and he remarked scornfully to the diplomats present: "Can you believe these little people beat the Americans?"

Inside the administration, preparations for going to war—more precisely, for using military force to counterattack and reverse Saddam's aggression—were going full steam. One key question was: Under what authority would U.S. forces engage in combat operations? There were four possible bases of authority, two under international law and two under U.S. law: (1) Article 51 of the UN Charter, in response to Kuwait's request for self-defense assistance; (2) a UN Security Council Resolution, under Chapter VII of the UN Charter, authorizing the use of force; (3) the president's Article II powers, subject to the War Powers Resolution, which purports to place a sixty-day time limit on active combat operations; and (4) an explicit grant of authority by Congress under its Article I responsibilities.

It was decided, without diminishing in any way the president's authorities as commander in chief, to prepare for an eventual congressional vote. And it was decided, not without dissent, that the best way to do so was to get a UN Security Council Resolution authorizing the use of force and then ask Congress to approve the United States living up to its UN obligations under the use-of-force resolution.

Defense Secretary Cheney was reserved in his enthusiasm for the United Nations, and once told me directly: "Bob, don't let the UN limit our ability to succeed if in the end we need to use force against Saddam." I responded that our goal was to use the United Nations as a means to garner both domestic and international support for the use of force, and that we would not put up for a vote in the UN Security Council any resolution—including use of force—that would not pass, and pass handily.

A key element of our approach was to seek passage of the exceptional use-of-force resolution—something not seen in the United Nations since the Korean War—in November 1990, because the United States was that month in the rotating chair as president of the Security Council. In a meeting in my office, Richard Haass and I sketched out a resolution that was short and to the point ("all necessary means") and offered one last chance for Saddam to withdraw (only effective on or after January 15, 1991). We kept it simple to avoid extended negotiations and unhelpful qualifications.

In anticipation of his chairing a historic meeting of the Security Council to consider the use-of-force resolution, Secretary Baker decided to meet with the heads of state/government and/or foreign ministers of the other fourteen countries on the Security Council. Over the course of November, Secretary Baker traveled around the world for meetings in London, Paris, Moscow, Sanaa, and Bogota; Cairo (to meet Chinese Foreign Minister Qian); Geneva (to meet with the foreign ministers of Ethiopia, Ivory Coast, and Zaire); Bermuda (to meet with Canadian foreign minister Clark); and Los Angeles (to meet with the Malaysian foreign minister). The meetings in Moscow and Cairo were particularly interesting and important.

In Cairo—where we met to avoid a visit to Beijing seventeen months after Tiananmen Square—the participants were Secretary Baker and me and Chinese Foreign Minister Qian Qichen and his head of North American Affairs Yang Jiechi (later ambassador to the United States and foreign minister). Foreign Minister Qian opened by chiding Secretary Baker: "You fly over China to see others but do not stop to see us." Secretary Baker responded he would like to visit Beijing again, having been there with Ronald Reagan in April 1984 (as had I), but that depended in large part on whether China continued to support the UN effort against Saddam. Qian quickly said: "So you'll come to China if I vote with you later this month?" Secretary Baker replied it would be better for me to go to Beijing first, to which Qian assented. I, of course, also agreed, but said my visit should be preceded by assistant secretary–level meetings in Beijing to discuss human rights and nonproliferation. The Chinese agreed.

In Moscow, Secretary Baker met not only with Foreign Minister Shevardnadze but also General Secretary Gorbachev. These important conversations with the Soviet leadership were crucial to securing their continuing support for the UN strategy, including the use-of-force resolution. The day after we arrived in Moscow, President Bush announced he was doubling the number of U.S. forces in the Gulf. That would take our forces to five hundred thousand, largely via addition of the VII Corps based in Germany, something only possible with the end of the Cold War. At a dacha outside Moscow, he asked LTG Howard Graves, assistant to the chairman of the Joint Chiefs of Staff, to brief the Soviet leadership on how the coalition intended to eject Saddam's forces from Kuwait.

The president's decision to increase significantly the number of U.S. troops was intended to make clear that we would defeat Saddam decisively and quickly if the use of force were required. But the hope remained that the assembly of this large, capable military coalition, undergirded by continuing UN solidarity, would get him to leave peacefully.

A week later, the president embarked on travel that took him to Czechoslovakia, Germany, France, Saudi Arabia, Egypt, and Switzerland. He met a wide range of world leaders, including Security Council leaders Mikhail Gorbachev, Margaret Thatcher, and François Mitterrand, and critical Gulf leaders King Fahd of Saudi Arabia and (in Jeddah) the emir of Kuwait. He also met with two senior Arab leaders of coalition countries, President Mubarak of Egypt and President Hafez al-Assad of Syria (in Geneva).

In one month alone, the president and secretary of state had met face to face with almost fifty leaders and foreign ministers, each of whom was either a member of the Security Council or a provider of troops, materiel, or financial support to the coalition. The scope of the global effort led by the president to seek Saddam's peaceful withdrawal is breathtaking.

The final step in the November strategy played out in the Security Council Chamber of the United Nations on November 29, 1990. Secretary Baker, in the chairman's role, laid out the resolution, which stated that it: "Authorizes Member States cooperating with Kuwait, unless Iraq on or before 15 January 1991 [withdraws unconditionally], to use all necessary means to uphold and implement Resolution 660." The measure—UN Security Council Resolution 678—passed 12–2–1, with China abstaining and Cuba and Yemen voting "no."[2]

We did not know until the moment of the vote what China would do, and still hoped for them to vote in favor, as they had done for all previous resolutions. In the end, they abstained, avoiding defeat of the resolution but maintaining their stance on "peaceful coexistence." Secretary Baker instructed me to tell the Chinese that he would meet Foreign Minister Qian in Washington the following day, but that a meeting with the president was not possible because China had not voted in favor of the resolution.

As I got on the last Delta shuttle of the evening to fly back to Washington, Senator Bill Bradley of New Jersey also boarded. He said, "Kimmitt, you had a good day in New York today." I responded: "Senator, it was the United States that had a good day, since you and colleagues in your party have said consistently that you could support the use of force if authorized by the UN." His retort was jovial, but he knew how difficult it would be for internationalists like him in his party not to vote for upholding a UN Resolution.

Back at home, I received a call shortly after midnight from the State Operations Center. It was the Chinese ambassador to Washington, Zhu Qizhen, who had on the line with him Yang Jiechi, who had been with Foreign Minister Qian in Cairo and also acted as interpreter for Qian when Secretary Baker spoke by phone with Qian from Paris after the meeting in Cairo. Yang read from his notes to say that Secretary Baker had agreed to a Qian meeting with the president "unless China voted no on the use-of-force resolution." I called Secretary Baker to relay this conversation, and the secretary spoke to his wife Susan, who was with him in his hotel room in November in Paris when he took the Qian phone call. Susan Baker's recollection matched the Chinese notes, and I was authorized to tell the Chinese the presidential meeting was on. So Qian Qichen, almost eighteen months after Tiananmen Square, on November 30 met with both Secretary Baker at the State Department and President Bush Oval Office.

Shortly after the Qian meeting, and in an effort to make clear his preference to have Saddam withdraw peacefully, President Bush announced he was willing to "go the extra mile for peace" by sending Secretary Baker to Baghdad before the January 15 deadline to meet with Saddam. The president also invited Iraqi foreign minister Tariq Aziz to meet him in mid-December in Washington.

THE SHIELD STRENGTHENS

December 1990 was perhaps not as historic as November, but it was eventful nonetheless.

Throughout the month, President Bush continued his face-to-face and telephone contacts with world leaders, as well as his public diplomacy for domestic and international audiences. His message was clear and consistent: (1) this aggression will not stand; (2) Saddam must withdraw unconditionally; and (3) use of force was on the table.

The reactions to the president's steadfastness varied widely. For his part, Saddam was not prepared to receive Secretary Baker in Baghdad nor to allow Tariq Aziz to travel to Washington. So preparations began for a Baker-Aziz meeting in January 1991 in Geneva.

Even with the overwhelming international support for the use-of-force resolution, and the formation of an international coalition not seen in five decades, voices of opposition and alarm started to arise in Washington. Leading voices like former chairman of the Joint Chiefs of Staff Bill Crowe (later Bill Clinton's ambassador to London) questioned the wisdom of the United States using military force, believing it better to allow economic sanctions eventually to topple Saddam. Others predicted American casualties could run as high as thirty thousand; in fact, there were 147

U.S. deaths and 347 wounded as a result of combat operations. Later, Representative Henry Gonzalez (D-TX) even introduced a resolution to impeach President Bush for his actions during Desert Shield.

The work of the Small Group began to intensify throughout December. Even while dealing with the day-to-day coordination of the diplomatic, military, economic, and intelligence dimensions of the crisis, the Group began to prepare for the increasing likelihood of war. As directed by the president after his consultations with the Big Eight, the Small Group began to prepare a very detailed paper on war aims. This process ran in parallel with the operational coordination effort largely conducted among Defense, Joint Chiefs of Staff (JCS), and the CIA.

The most controversial element of the war aims paper—and the subject of debate for the decade to follow—was whether U.S. and coalition forces should "go to Baghdad" by continuing military operations even after Saddam had been forcibly evicted from Kuwait. In the end, the paper recommended, and the president agreed, not to proceed further once Iraqi forces were driven from Kuwait and no longer presented a challenge to regional peace and security. Chief among the reasons for this decision was that proceeding further could very well have splintered the coalition that had fought the war, leaving the United States in charge of the entire country and needing to remain for an extended period to address postwar instability.

Another topic that was looked at exceptionally closely was how to deter Saddam's use of his weapons of mass destruction. It was decided that Secretary Baker would carry to Geneva a letter on this topic from President Bush to Saddam Hussein. In short, the letter said that the U.S. and coalition war aim was to force Saddam's unconditional withdrawal from Kuwait under Resolution 660. But, if Saddam were to use any unconventional weapons against U.S. or coalition forces, our war aim would change from solely ejecting Saddam from Kuwait to also removing him from power.

DESERT STORM APPROACHES

As the new year began, military, diplomatic, and political activities began to accelerate as the January 15 deadline for Saddam's withdrawal drew closer. At the direction of President Bush, and under the leadership of Secretary Cheney, General Powell, and General Schwarzkopf, U.S. and coalition forces moved steadily to full combat readiness and battle stations.

January 6–8, 1991, Secretary Baker met with leaders in the UK, France, Germany, and Italy, en route to his meeting with Tariq Aziz in Geneva. In Paris, Secretary Baker met with President Mitterrand, with whom he had a good relationship going back to the Reagan years. (Baker and French foreign minister Dumas did not have the same good relationship.) Both Mitterrand and Baker understood well "The Politics of Diplomacy" (the title of Baker's later book on his State Department years). Secretary Baker opened the meeting by explaining his approach for the Aziz meeting and told President Mitterrand about the Bush-Saddam letter he intended to give to Aziz.

Baker handed Mitterrand a copy of the letter, saying that President Bush had asked it be shared with Mitterrand in advance of the meeting.

President Mitterrand read the letter carefully and pronounced it to be good, clear, and strong. He then said, however, that on one point—what the United States would do if Saddam used chemical weapons or other WMD—the letter was "perhaps too direct." "Dictators," he said, "live in fear of uncertainty." He suggested a slight edit to leave some doubt in Saddam's mind, not about *whether* but exactly *how* the United States would respond to the use of WMD. Baker liked the edit and asked me if it could be made. I said I could make edits on all but the president's signature page, so the Mitterrand edit was in.

Baker then turned to the principal reason for his visit to Paris. "Mr. President," he said, "we need to know if French forces, who are currently operating independently in Saudi Arabia, will be integrated into coalition forces and operate under General Schwarzkopf's command. President Bush will respect whatever decision you make, but we need a decision today." Mitterrand smiled slightly, waved his right arm, and said, "But of course, James, when the fighting begins, French troops will be with American forces under General Schwarzkopf's command. But to ensure a positive vote in the National Assembly in the days ahead, I have to maintain some independence for our forces for now."

GENEVA

When we arrived at the Intercontinental Hotel in Geneva on the evening of January 8, we were greeted by both the Swiss president and foreign minister for what was to have been a brief courtesy call. Instead, they excitedly told us that Iranian deputy foreign minister Mahmoud Vaezi was in the hotel and available to speak if we wished. We told the Swiss politely but firmly that we were there to meet with Tariq Aziz only and that they should avoid such freelancing in the future.

Some background: In October 1989, after President Bush signaled an openness to direct talks with Iran, I sent a series of messages to Iran, via the Swiss ambassador in Washington, Edouard Brunner. No agreement was reached on whether or where to meet. After Saddam invaded Kuwait in August 1990, I decided to send occasional messages via the Swiss to Iran, principally to make clear that U.S. forces were coming to the Gulf to eject Saddam from Kuwait, not to threaten Iran. Deputy Minister Vaezi was my counterpart and the person to whom the messages were delivered, but there had been no response from him to me, nor certainly any suggestion of a meeting by me. We were in Geneva for one reason only: to meet with Tariq Aziz.

Secretary Baker's meeting the following day with Tariq Aziz lasted seven hours in a conference room at the Intercontinental. An early sign that Aziz was unlikely to show flexibility was when he came in and sat flanked by Saddam's half-brother Barzan al-Tikriti and Saddam's personal interpreter. Secretary Baker handed Aziz the letter from President Bush to Saddam Hussein. Aziz read it (his English was excellent, though he spoke Arabic for the duration of the meeting), then placed it on the table between them. He said he could not transmit such a letter because it was "not befitting of correspondence between leaders of countries." Baker responded: "Just remember, Minister, that you have read the letter, so the responsibility of the message falls entirely on you."

Baker went on to lay out the U.S., UN, and coalition position seeking peaceful, but unconditional, withdrawal, noting that efforts had been made to reach out to Iraq even before the invasion. Aziz responded that may have been true, but since January of 1990, it was clear to Iraq that the United States had begun to take a series of actions designed to "force Iraq into a corner." Aziz said that was one of the reasons Iraq acted against Kuwait when it did, while it was still in a relatively strong position.

Secretary Baker asked General Howard Graves, as he had in Moscow in November, to describe the array of forces assembled by the coalition, to make clear that, if force were necessary, U.S. and coalition forces would move quickly, overwhelmingly, and decisively. Aziz responded: "We know the capability of your forces; we read *Aviation Week & Space Technology*. But your words do not frighten me, someone who has survived for decades in the dangerous political environment in Iraq." Secretary Baker reminded Aziz that he had read two critical sentences in the president's letter. If war came and Iraq used WMD: "The American people would demand the strongest possible response. You and your country will pay a terrible price if you order unconscionable acts of this sort."

When the meeting concluded in the late afternoon, Secretary Baker called the president to report that Aziz had offered nothing whatsoever on the fundamental point of unconditional withdrawal. The president and senior advisers with him in the Oval Office seemed relieved that Saddam had not proposed some diversion— perhaps a partial withdrawal—that would have made it more difficult to hold the coalition together.

In their separate press conferences to end the day, Secretary Baker and Tariq Aziz gave very different reports on the "discussions." Secretary Baker, a former practicing attorney, observed that Aziz had argued well a very poor brief. Aziz's comments and responses were largely bromides, until he was asked whether Iraq would attack Israel if the coalition attacked Iraq. He looked the questioner straight in the eye and said, "Yes, absolutely yes," his only categorical response to the press.

Secretary Baker went from Geneva to Saudi Arabia (for meetings with the Saudis and the Kuwaitis), the UAE, Egypt, Syria, Turkey, the UK, and Canada to debrief coalition leaders on his meeting with Aziz. He made clear we were now moving to a war footing. Back in Washington, the action moved to the Congress. On January 12, three days before the UN deadline, the Senate voted 52–47 and the House 250–183 to authorize the president "to use United States armed forces pursuant to United Nations Security Council Resolution 678." And that is exactly what the president did four days later.

DESERT STORM ARRIVES

In the early morning of January 16, just hours after the UN deadline had passed, coalition forces led by the United States launched a massive air campaign against Iraqi forces in both Kuwait and Iraq. The air campaign lasted forty-two consecutive days and nights. Iraqi air defenses were generally ineffective throughout this bombardment, but, in spite of the severe damage caused by the air campaign, Saddam evinced no signs of beginning a withdrawal.

As Tariq Aziz had promised, Iraq struck Israel with Scud missiles, with the hope of drawing Israel into the war and making it more difficult for Arab nations to remain in the coalition. It took personal diplomacy on the part of the President and Secretary Baker, including an important conversation with Israeli Prime Minister Yitzhak Shamir, to keep the Israeli Air Force from entering the fray. The president and Secretary Cheney made clear to Israel that General Schwarzkopf would dedicate forces to eliminating the Iraqi Scud threat, and the president dispatched Deputy Secretary of State Larry Eagleburger and Paul Wolfowitz to Tel Aviv to survey the damage and offer reassurances.

As the need for a ground phase drew nearer and clearer, there were multiple attempts at finding a "diplomatic" solution. The Soviets, French, and others began to suggest that if Saddam could be given an incentive—perhaps some new initiative toward Middle East peace—he might be willing to withdraw in the interests of peace in the broader region. The U.S. response was clear: unconditional means unconditional, and the last person who would get credit for any movement on Middle East peace was the aggressor Saddam Hussein. (French foreign minister Dumas called so frequently to plead for "flexibility" on the part of the United States that Secretary Baker instructed the State Operations Center to direct all Dumas calls to me.)

On February 15, as the air campaign was being waged, the president said in a speech at the Raytheon plant that produced the Patriot Air Defense System: "There is another way for the bloodshed to stop, and that is for the Iraqi military and the Iraqi people to take matters into their own hands and force Saddam Hussein, the dictator, to step aside."[3]

On February 24, the full ground operation was launched and lasted one hundred hours. The fighting was intense, including large tank battles with Republican Guard units in both Iraq and Kuwait. Iraq lost over three thousand tanks and over two thousand other combat vehicles at the hands of coalition forces.

On the evening of February 28, as Iraqi forces were retreating in a rout, President Bush was joined by senior advisers in the Oval Office (where the fireplace chose an awkward moment to spew smoke into the assembled group). After speaking with General Schwarzkopf and consulting Secretary Cheney and General Powell, the president ordered U.S. forces to stop their attack. He informed the public that he had declared a ceasefire and announced that Kuwait had been liberated.

Some commentators (many of whom ironically had opposed the use of force) subsequently questioned why U.S. and coalition forces did not pursue the retreating

Iraqi forces, perhaps all the way to Baghdad. President Bush was clear: (1) American soldiers did not shoot retreating enemy forces in the back; and (2) the coalition's goal of ejecting Iraq from Kuwait had been achieved. As a combat veteran himself, the president knew that the two most difficult decisions of the war were his alone: (1) when to order forces to attack; and (2) when to order them to stop, especially in the heat of a battle well fought.

POSTCONFLICT ACTIVITIES

On March 1, the day after fighting stopped, President Bush, echoing his remarks at Raytheon two weeks prior, said at a press conference that "the Iraqi people should put [Saddam] aside, and that would facilitate the resolution of all these problems that exist."[4]

Along the "Highway of Death," where retreating Iraqi forces were targeted until the president called a ceasefire, lies Safwan, the Iraqi town where General Schwarzkopf met with an Iraqi military delegation on March 3. Many matters, such as prisoner exchanges and returns, were discussed, but the controversial decision was to allow Iraq to use its helicopter fleet, provided it did not threaten U.S. and coalition forces. In fact, Iraq used these aircraft to suppress subsequent uprisings by Kurds in the north and Shia in the south. Some critics also tied these tragic results to the president's two calls for the Iraqi people to remove Saddam from power.

Soon after the fighting concluded, Secretary Baker and I flew to Kuwait City to meet with the Kuwaiti crown prince on his return to the capital. We could see from the air the Kuwaiti oil fields set ablaze by Saddam's retreating troops, and we flew over the "Highway of Death," littered with destroyed combat vehicles.

The secretary and I went from Kuwait City to Saudi Arabia, then I went to Europe to consult with the European Union. Secretary Baker, as promised, began visiting capitals to pursue progress on Mideast peace: from March 8–16, Secretary Baker was in Kuwait, Saudi Arabia, Egypt, Israel, the Palestinian territories, Syria, the Soviet Union, and Turkey. This travel launched a process that culminated in the Madrid Conference in October 1991.

The formal ceasefire Resolution 687 was passed by the Security Council on April 3, 1991, by a vote of 12–1–2 with Cuba voting against and two abstentions (Yemen and Ecuador). This very detailed resolution, drafted under the leadership of Assistant Secretary John Bolton, covered border issues and reparations between Iraq and Kuwait; returns of prisoners; and removal and destruction of chemical and biological weapons and ballistic missiles with a range greater than 150 kilometers.[5] Regrettably, Saddam was a reluctant, even obstinate, party to this ceasefire document, and his efforts to undercut the resolution, especially by refusing to give UN weapons inspectors access to suspected WMD sites, began almost immediately.

Secretary Baker returned to the region in early April and saw firsthand the plight of refugees, mostly Iraqi Kurds, who had fled into Turkey. On April 8, he called me (I was again acting secretary) and told me to accelerate U.S. efforts to aid the refugees. Led by the exceptionally able Andrew Natsios, director of Overseas Foreign Disaster Assistance, the U.S. government responded promptly to the developing humanitarian crisis. Subsequently, an even more consequential step was taken by President Bush: the United States established a no-fly zone and launched Operation Provide Comfort in the Kurdish north of Iraq. (A no-fly zone was not established over southern Iraq until August 1992.)

The swiftness, success, and bravery of U.S. and coalition actions against Iraq produced the most vivid memory of Desert Shield and Storm. On June 8, there was a "National Victory Celebration" in Washington, the largest American military parade since the end of World War II. Over eight thousand Desert Storm troops, led by General Schwarzkopf, paraded down Constitution Avenue and rendered to their commander in chief, George H. W. Bush, an exceptionally well-deserved salute.

On July 3, 1991, in the East Room of the White House, President Bush bestowed the Presidential Medal of Freedom on members of the Big Eight and the Presidential Citizens Medal on the Small Group, officially concluding a remarkable eleven-month effort of historic diplomatic and military activity.

POSTSCRIPT

It was an honor to serve under the leadership of President Bush and Secretary Baker during the Gulf Crisis and War, and an equal honor to serve in one of the finest interagency efforts since the creation of the National Security Council in 1947. Many valuable lessons were learned from Desert Shield and Storm and have been recounted above.

But it is also important to note that this effort took place in the midst of an epochal transformation in world affairs. When Saddam invaded Kuwait, Germany was still months from unifying, and the Soviet Union a year from dissolving. There were still Vietnamese troops in Cambodia, apartheid was just coming to an end in South Africa, and the aftershocks of Tiananmen Square were still being felt in Beijing and beyond. Indeed, Saddam's willingness to invade Kuwait without the backing of his longtime Soviet supporters showed how significantly the Cold War rules of the road had changed.

Some have asked if my service during Desert Shield and Storm was my proudest moment as undersecretary of state for political affairs. I was indeed proud of my role in the outstanding international and interagency effort under President Bush's superb leadership. But, while that effort was strenuous and sustained, it was relatively straightforward to get things done because President Bush had made the reversing of Iraq's aggression an absolute priority during that period.

I was actually somewhat prouder, then, of the fact that, during Desert Shield, we had also secured passage of Resolution 668 on September 20, 1990, bringing the Cambodian War to an end and opening the way for our Roadmap to Normalization with Vietnam.[6] That effort was led by an interagency team headed by Assistant Secretary of State Dick Solomon, a team far removed from the Gulf Crisis but who had remained steadfastly engaged in the practice of diplomacy and saw an opening to end yet another conflict that was a vestige of the just-concluded Cold War.

The meetings of the Small Group ended with the conclusion of the Gulf War, and we resumed the prewar operation of the Deputies Committee. We were quickly confronted with a rapidly deteriorating situation in Yugoslavia and significant moves by North Korea in its nuclear program, both critical issues that would have benefitted from additional senior-level attention during the Gulf Crisis and War.

The lesson, then, is to make time, even during a period of major crisis and conflict, also to advance and safeguard U.S. interests far from the crisis. Even as they deal with *urgent* situations, leaders must identify—and address—*important*, though longer-range, challenges. Success in such an endeavor requires the international and whole-of-U.S.-government effort that proved so essential to success in Desert Shield and Storm. President George H. W. Bush was uniquely qualified to lead that effort, and I hope his successors will draw lessons and inspiration from him as they address their own series of challenges that threaten our nation's security.

NOTES

1. For the text of National Security Directive 26, see https://fas.org/irp/offdocs/nsd/nsd26 .pdf.

2. For the text of Resolution 678, see http://unscr.com/en/resolutions/678.

3. George H. W. Bush, "Remarks to Raytheon Missile Systems Plant Employees in Andover, Massachusetts," February 15, 1991, Public Papers, George H. W. Bush Presidential Library and Museum, https://bush41library.tamu.edu/archives/public-papers/2711.

4. "The President's News Conference on the Persian Gulf Conflict," March 1, 1991, Public Papers, George H. W. Bush Presidential Library and Museum, https://bush41library.tamu .edu/archives/public-papers/2755.

5. For the text of Resolution 687, see http://unscr.com/en/resolutions/687.

6. For the text of Resolution 668, see http://unscr.com/en/resolutions/668.

9

George H. W. Bush

Politics and Realism in the Middle East

Dennis Ross

George H. W. Bush did not intend to make the Middle East the centerpiece of his foreign policy when he became president in 1989. As someone who played a prominent role in the transition on national security issues, first for the incoming administration broadly speaking and then with James Baker as he prepared to become the Secretary of State, I can say that Mikhail Gorbachev and East-West relations were the president-elect's main priority. He saw Gorbachev and glasnost and perestroika—openness and reconstruction—as creating both an opportunity and a challenge. Bush wanted to test what was possible with Gorbachev in redefining the U.S.-Soviet relationship. He did not assume the Cold War was going to disappear, but he realized that the winds of change were being felt in Europe and he wanted to know how real the change might be.

The Middle East was a region in which he had developed relationships with several of its leaders. He had close personal ties with King Hussein of Jordan; he saw in the king a thoughtful leader who was moderate, unfailingly polite, and even humble with him. He liked him, he believed he was decent—and I saw this up close in Bush's trip to the Middle East in 1986 when he was vice president. He also knew and liked Hosni Mubarak—the president of Egypt. He liked Mubarak's open and at times gruff style; he also saw him as a good friend of the United States. While he did not have the same relationship and familiarity with King Fahd of Saudi Arabia, he liked his ambassador to the United States, Bandar bin Sultan, and would see him often as president.

Interestingly, he was not close to Israel's prime minister, Yitzhak Shamir, but he respected Israel as a democracy and liked the Labor Party leaders Shimon Peres and Yitzhak Rabin, who were part of Israel's national unity government at the time. But Bush was not like Ronald Reagan. Reagan's views of Israel were heavily shaped by the Holocaust. As he would later write, "I've believed many things in my life, but no conviction I've ever held has been stronger than my belief that the United States must ensure the survival of Israel. The Holocaust, I believe, left America with a moral responsibility to ensure that what had happened to the Jews under Hitler never happens again."[1]

Reagan's connection to Israel was emotional. This was not Bush. He was not a sentimentalist when it came to foreign policy. He saw interests and commitments and personal relationships. He felt Reagan had tilted too far toward Israel in terms of our interests in the Middle East, agreeing with what Richard Nixon told Baker during the transition: "Reagan has been the most pro-Israeli President in history. It's time for some evenhandedness out there."[2]

But if Bush was a traditional "realist"—not idealist or sentimentalist—in foreign policy, he was, nonetheless, someone who believed deeply in the sanctity of America's word. His word was his bond. American commitments reflected America's word and must be fulfilled. And, here, whatever might be his criticisms of Israeli policies, especially on settlements across the June 4, 1967, lines, the United States had made commitments to Israel's security and he would fully respect them. That was an essential part of the legacy that shaped Bush's view toward the region.

There were other legacies and lessons he had learned from the past and applied to the Middle East. Like many of his predecessors, he inherited a conceptual premise or assumption about the area: the core of the problems in the Middle East was the Arab-Israeli conflict and the Palestinian issue. Solve this and much of the instability in the region would go away. The conflict was exploited by radicals and extremists and put our more moderate Arab friends on the defensive. (The irony, of course, is that the region in the 1980s, especially after the Israeli debacle in Lebanon, came to be dominated by the Iraq-Iran War—a war that had nothing to do with the Palestinians and one that drew the United States into it with the reflagging and protection of oil tankers that had become threatened by Iran as it sought to deny Iraq of its main source of revenue.)

Bush's experiences in the Reagan administration also shaped his attitudes toward policy making in general and in the Middle East particular. He hated the in-fighting between first Alexander Haig and Caspar Weinberger and subsequently between George Shultz and Weinberger. Much, but not all, of their battling and leaks and counterleaks were over Israel, its war in Lebanon in the summer and fall of 1982, and later what to do about the Syrians in Lebanon as they acted to subvert the May 17 agreement brokered by Shultz between Israel and the Lebanese government in 1983—an agreement that Syria would subvert and force the president of Lebanon, Amin Gemayel, to rescind and recant.

Bush believed the Israeli war in Lebanon had been a huge mistake—and felt that Israel had made a strategic blunder by putting an Arab capital, Beirut, under siege and then entering part of it. I would often hear him say in the run-up to the Gulf War in 1991 that it was a terrible mistake to go into an Arab capital—a view that made him very reluctant to expand our war aims after Iraqi forces were expelled from Kuwait. He would not go to Baghdad and enter it the way the Israelis had gone into Beirut. Of course, that was not the only reason that he refused to expand our aims and authorize U.S. forces to move toward Baghdad: we had given our word in establishing the coalition of countries that would join us in the war against Saddam Hussein, and the goal was to expel Iraq from Kuwait; it was not to go and remove Saddam Hussein. He would not redefine our objectives and effectively walk away from what we had told our partners in forming the coalition. Again, he gave his word and settled the matter. The Middle East might be of interest to him but his attention would not be riveted on it until Saddam Hussein decided to invade and absorb Kuwait, very quickly calling it the nineteenth province of Iraq.

In looking back, there are only two real issues in the Middle East that produced deep and intensive involvement of the Bush administration. The first was the Arab-Israeli issue and the second was Iraq. The former would never greatly involve President Bush. The latter would do so—reflecting his belief of what was at stake and America's global responsibilities.

ISRAEL AND THE ARAB-ISRAELI CONFLICT

Arab-Israeli issues interested the president, but in reality, they involved him only sparingly. He might make an occasional phone call or see Arab and Israeli leaders or senior officials. He might go to Madrid to give a speech at the Madrid Peace Conference. But he would not be heavily engaged in Arab-Israeli diplomacy—that would become Jim Baker's responsibility and preoccupation, not his. His distance from the diplomacy reflected not a lack of interest; rather, this was the secretary of state's domain and he would involve himself when and if Baker felt he was needed. This is not to say that he did not make his views felt at certain points. Two examples stand out: the Baker speech to the American Israel Public Affairs Committee (AIPAC) in the spring of 1989 and the issue of loan guarantees to Israel. Both would affect the image of Bush's attitudes toward Israel. Both would reflect his readiness to adopt a position reflecting his belief that Israel should not take American support for granted—or believe it could adopt positions we opposed with no consequence.

In the case of the Baker speech to the American Israel Public Affairs Committee (AIPAC) in the spring of 1989, it was less what Bush actually did and more what Baker knew the president would not countenance. I was responsible for producing the draft, with Harvey Sicherman on my staff writing it. When Baker returned the draft to me with his edits, I saw he had edited out all the empathetic notes that conveyed warmth, understanding of Israel's predicament in the region, and the reasons for America's ties to Israel.

I told him it was a fundamental mistake to take these points out of the speech; he needed, I argued, to establish his credentials with the Israeli public so that they had reason to believe that his approach to Israel was grounded in genuine support for the country and an understanding of the hostility and threats it faced. Otherwise the public might simply believe his calls on Israel were a response to Arab pressure—and it would support an Israeli prime minister standing up and resisting us. This was especially important given the main message of his speech: one in which he was calling on Israel and the Arabs to do their part to promote peacemaking—and in the Israeli case to stop their settlement building and, in his words, "give up the dream of a greater Israel." While telling him this was a necessary message for Israelis to hear, I said it needed to be balanced by speaking about the deeper values that bound us together, as well as our recognition of what Israel continued to face in a region where too many still denied its right to exist.

Baker replied that the president would see this language as "pandering" and would never accept it. We worked for him and he would not say things in a speech that went against Bush's grain. The language came out and the speech came to be portrayed "as the toughest ever given to a Jewish audience."

Bush, however, was extremely happy with the speech and even with the reaction to it—expressing his pleasure to Baker as we flew with the president to Europe shortly after the AIPAC event. It was not just that he felt we were showing we would be more "evenhanded," it was that pandering in foreign policy was simply wrong. It went against his code of what was appropriate—just as he would not change the goal posts with our coalition partners and expand our objectives in Iraq after expelling the Iraqi army from Kuwait, because that would be wrong and go against his "code," so, too, would he not permit pandering.

Later when we were wrestling with getting to the Madrid Conference, he would also make clear to Baker that he did not want to do a deal on loan guarantees without Israel changing its policy on settlement building. In this case, Bush was determined that we should not subsidize Israel's policy of settlement building in the West Bank and Gaza. We were opposed to Israel's construction of settlements in the occupied territories and Bush was not prepared to provide the loan guarantees without specific assurances, lest they be used to accelerate Israel's settlement construction. In fact, he would only authorize the loan guarantees—guarantees that would greatly reduce the cost of borrowing for the Israelis as they tried to absorb the sudden torrent of Soviet Jews now emigrating to Israel—if the Israeli government froze settlement construction. Without that, he made clear to Baker and me there would be no loan guarantees.

Baker agreed with Bush on the policy, but wanted to avoid any public discussion of the settlement issue because of where we stood on our effort to launch a peace conference; we were close and Baker did not want the Arabs, who had not raised the settlement issue as a condition for the conference, to feel they must do so because we were suddenly giving it prominence. Similarly, he did not want Shamir to be backed into a corner domestically on the loan guarantee issue before we had nailed down agreement on the terms of reference for the conference; instead he preferred to defer any discussion on the issue for 120 days, well after the Madrid Conference would have taken place.

To that end, Baker engaged in discussions with Tom Dine, the executive director of AIPAC, and also sent me to Congress to meet key members, to work out an agreement on delaying the discussion of Israel's request for $10 billion in loan guarantees. To be fair, President Bush did not raise the issue. It was the Israeli embassy in Washington in August in anticipation of Congress coming back into session in September that was pushing AIPAC to press members of Congress to authorize the guarantees—and Baker prior to our leaving for a trip first to the Soviet Union and then to the Middle East was not able to persuade Shamir to give orders to his embassy to postpone the request.[3] Shamir did agree with Baker to discuss the issue of a delay when the secretary arrived in Israel. Baker and I thought at that point we might be able to work out an understanding once he met Shamir there. But events would take a different course.

While we were in Moscow in the chaotic environment created by the failed coup attempt against Gorbachev, Bush saw Senator Robert Kasten of Wisconsin who told him that I was trying to do a deal on the loan guarantees. I was not; I was simply following our plan of trying to defer the issue for 120 days, telling Kasten, as Baker had told Dine, that we hoped it would be possible to reach an understanding on the loan guarantees after the 120-day period. Bush, apparently worried that we might be so anxious to get to the peace conference that we would concede the loan guarantees, sent a handwritten note to Baker describing the Kasten comments and making clear he was not interested in a deal—and Baker with Shamir subsequently both publicly and privately adopted a tough posture on loan guarantees.

The Israeli government went ahead pushing to have Congress vote on them and Bush actively lobbied against it, describing himself in a press conference as "one lonely guy" up against thousands of lobbyists descending on the Hill trying to up-end our policies. Much like the Carter and Reagan administrations facing AIPAC's and Israeli opposition on the F-15 and AWACS arms sales, the Bush administration would succeed in gaining congressional support for its position of postponing the consideration of the loan guarantees.[4]

The AIPAC speech and the loan guarantee fight created an image that Bush was simply hostile to Israel. He was not. But there was no special attachment. Israel was an American friend. We had commitments to it and he would stand by it. He did not see it as especially beleaguered because he saw it as far stronger than its neighbors, but he understood it faced genuine threats and we would be there for it. One of the great ironies of the perception of Bush's posture toward Israel—one that would lead to his getting only 11 percent of the Jewish vote in 1992—is how it was belied by the reality of what he would do very practically for Israel. Consider the following extensive record of what the Bush administration did for Israel:

- It maintained assistance at $3 billion a year and in the aftermath of the Gulf War furnished an additional $650 million to compensate for damages caused by the Scud missile attacks, a figure well above the actual damages actually inflicted.
- It continued strategic cooperation begun under Reagan and augmented it with expanded Joint R&D ventures, exercises, training, prestocking of materials, and military contracts.

- It deployed two Patriot missile batteries on an emergency basis to Israel after Iraqi missiles struck early in the Gulf War, requiring the unprecedented deployment of seven hundred American troops to Israel to operate the Patriots.
- It established a direct communication link, Hammer RICK, for the first time between the offices of the U.S. secretary of defense and the Israeli minister of defense.
- Bush and Baker continued high-level efforts to get the Soviets to allow the Jews in the USSR to immigrate to Israel, and the floodgates on emigration literally opened.
- President Bush secretly arranged for Ethiopian Jews to be flown to Israel, and Secretary Baker persuaded Hafez al Assad to allow Syria's small Jewish community to leave.
- The administration mobilized and led the effort to repeal the odious "Zionism is Racism" resolution in the United Nations.
- The administration was, in Jim Baker's words, "instrumental in helping Israel establish diplomatic relations with forty-four countries, including the Soviet Union."
- It produced the Madrid Peace Conference, which ended an era of Arab state diplomacy through denial with Israel and effectively ended the taboo on direct talks between Israel and its Arab neighbors.
- The Bush administration destroyed the military capabilities of Iraq, Israel's most implacable Arab foe in the region at the time.

This is not the record of an administration hostile to Israel. Its tone was tough at times, but its support for Israel was also profound. Belying traditional assumptions, its support for Israel did not cost it anything with the Arab states in the region. In part, that resulted from the tough public posture it took toward Israel at times; however, the deeper reason is that the Bush administration showed it would use its power to stand by its friends and counter real threats. The Gulf War epitomized President Bush's readiness to use U.S. power decisively when called upon, which clearly impressed America's Arab friends in the region. It did not hurt that America now seemed to be the uber-power in what appeared to be a unipolar world. And it is on Iraq that President Bush was most deeply engaged in the Middle East during his administration.

IRAQ AND THE GULF WAR

Bush inherited one other legacy in the Middle East from Reagan: a tilt toward Iraq and Saddam Hussein. Even though Saddam had invaded Iran, the Reagan administration saw Iran as the bigger threat. Iran had a revolutionary ideology that it was seeking to export; it had seized and held American hostages, released the day Reagan became president. It was seeking to subvert the regional status quo; its Shia proxy in Lebanon, Hezbollah, was believed to be responsible for bombing both the U.S. Embassy and the Marine barracks in 1983, with the latter killing 241 American Marines. As if that were not enough, Iran appeared unalterably hostile to the United States. It was the hope of moderating that opposition that led Reagan to support an Israeli-inspired effort to connect to a supposedly "moderate" group in Iran that produced the Iran-Contra affair and what Reagan came to admit was the appearance of trading arms for hostages. The scandal surrounding Iran-Contra only added to the impulse to see Iraq as a balancer in the region against the Islamic Republic.

The tilt toward Iraq was remarkable given that Iraq had invaded its neighbor and later would use chemical weapons against Iran. And yet, given the perception of the Iranian threat in the region, the Reagan administration acted to take Iraq off the terrorism list in 1982; to restore relations in 1984; to begin providing intelligence and advanced TPQ radars that had a force-multiplying effect in the mid-1980s; and, in 1987, to reflag oil tankers to protect them from Iranian attacks as the Iranians sought to deny Iraq its oil revenue. Even before the end of the Iran-Iraq War, the administration was providing $500 million in agricultural credits to buy grains and produce from American farmers. The Bush administration continued the policy of warming to Iraq, increasing the credits to $1 billion conveyed in two tranches. Tareq Aziz, the Iraqi foreign minister, was invited to Washington, American delegations were going to Baghdad, and the trajectory of the relationship was on a continuing upward arc. Even early rumors of the Iraqi misuse of the credits did not bring them to a halt. It would take until 1990 for the relationship to begin to turn—and even then, it took Saddam making a threat to "burn half of Israel" to produce a pause. The second tranche of $500 million in agricultural credits was put on hold; that said, there was still a sense that the relationship had significant potential and the real threat in the region was Iran.

It is important to note that Iraq was not receiving the attention of the upper reaches of the Bush administration. The effort to produce German unification absorbed nearly all the attention of the president and the secretary of state. Baker was literally meeting his Soviet and European counterparts every two weeks, all over the globe. President Bush was constantly touching base to make sure that nothing fell through the cracks or to preempt potential problems.

Meanwhile, in May and June, at the height of the effort to work out understandings with the Soviets and the Germans on unification, Saddam was upping the ante and increasing his threats; he accused Kuwait of engaging in economic warfare against Iraq and demanded billions of dollars and territorial concessions; by July he was threatening both Kuwait and the United Arab Emirates. And yet all of America's Arab friends in the region were counseling the administration not to take the threats seriously—this was just Saddam posturing because of Iraq's economic problems. As late as July 25, when Iraq moved heavy concentrations of troops to the Kuwait border, and even the upper reaches of the administration were now becoming worried, President Mubarak declared after seeing the Iraqi president that "I believe he . . . has no intention of attacking Kuwait or any other party." Jordan's King Hussein told President Bush in a phone call on July 29, "Nothing will happen."[5]

Robert Gates, who was the deputy national security advisor at the time, would later say that the views of the Arab leaders had a great impact on the administration: "The truth of the matter is, people who knew it best, the leaders, who lived in the region, who knew the language, knew the culture, knew the history, were all . . . saying that nothing was going to happen."[6]

Clearly, what we were hearing from Mubarak, King Hussein, and others in the area had a big impact on the administration's views and helps to explain why it adopted a restrained posture as Saddam ratcheted up the pressure and moved forces toward Kuwait in late July. But, as Jim Baker later wrote, it was not just the reassuring statements of Arab leaders that led to our surprise about the Iraqi invasion. It was far more that he and the president—and those of us who were working closely with them on German unification and managing parallel negotiations with the Soviets, Germans, and other members of NATO—were quite simply distracted. In Baker's words, the administration was "grappling with one of the most revolutionary periods in world history." The great changes taking place in Europe—as well as unanticipated events like the Chinese killing dissidents in Tiananmen Square—created an environment in which Baker said, "None of us considered policy toward Iraq to be an urgent priority. And it was simply not prominent on my radar screen, or the President's."[7]

But suddenly Iraq was forced onto their radar screens. On August 2, four days after King Hussein had said nothing would happen, Saddam Hussein's forces rampaged through Kuwait and occupied the country. Even though we had no alliance with or commitment to Kuwait, and even though the administration had not begun to condition the public environment about Iraqi threats—in no small part because it actually still saw Saddam as a potential partner against Iran—President Bush declared on August 5: "This will not stand—this aggression against Kuwait."

At the time, I was sitting with Secretary Baker in his cabin as we were flying back from Turkey, as part of an initial flurry of diplomatic activity to isolate Iraq after the invasion. We saw the president's words and Baker said to me, "Dennis, you know what this means; if diplomacy does not work, we will go to war to force Saddam out of Kuwait."

Why? What stakes did President Bush see that led him to adopt this position so early into the crisis? The shock of the invasion and the misreading of Saddam no doubt played a part. The reality that Iraqi forces were now also on the Saudi border, with little separating them from Saudi oil fields in the northeast of the country, also played a part. It had been a vital national security interest of the United States to ensure that no hostile power could gain a stranglehold over the flow of oil from the Persian Gulf. Throughout the Cold War, the focus was on ensuring that the Soviets never achieve such a position of leverage, lest they be able manipulate the global economy and blackmail our allies in Europe and our friends in the Middle East. Now the president saw the threat could come from within the region—and if Saddam had such leverage over the flow of oil, he could use it to threaten our interests and threaten Israel in a way that would invoke our commitments.

However, as important as preventing Iraq, a power now seen as hostile, from politicizing the flow of oil for its purpose of regional dominance was, there was another critical factor that motivated President Bush. He believed that the fall of the Berlin Wall symbolized the end of the Cold War and meant we were ending one era and were entering a new one. He did not want this new era to be characterized by the law of the jungle—where there were no rules and aggression could take place without consequence. In his eyes, this new era must be shaped by order and not disorder. Jim Baker would later write that President Bush instinctively believed that "this was no ordinary crisis, that it truly would become a hinge point of history," and how we responded would have great influence on whether there would be "a new world order"—a slogan, a description, that Bush now began to use to explain the stakes.[8]

If one wanted to know why the Iraqi aggression could not stand, it was because the post–Cold War era was at stake. From Bush's standpoint, that was why it must be reversed. But "how" it was reversed was also critical in his eyes. It had to show that there were rules that were internationally accepted and that produced international responses. While he might be prepared to deal "with the crisis unilaterally if necessary," he fervently believed that this must be the world against Saddam Hussein, not the United States against Iraq. There must be a broad coalition that signaled the international community would not tolerate this kind of behavior. And, to produce such a response, President Bush would later explain that he "wanted the United Nations involved as part of our first response. . . . Decisive UN action would be important in rallying international opposition to the invasion and reversing it."[9]

It was one thing to say this and believe it, it was another to produce it. Moreover, generating this coalition did not take place in a vacuum: Saddam's forces were sitting on the Saudi border and he needed to be deterred from taking a run at the Saudi oil fields, or even, perhaps, at the Saudi capital of Riyadh, which was a mere 275 miles from the Kuwaiti border. As such, the administration had to take military steps to protect Saudi Arabia and deter further Iraqi military moves at the same time it was acting to forge an international coalition. It would do so by working through the UN Security Council and acting bilaterally with allies and others to join the coalition and help to sustain it.

The administration took a multiplicity of steps right from the outset of the crisis: President Bush telephoned our UN ambassador and instructed him to call for an emergency meeting of the UN Security Council—a step that would begin a process of adopting a series of resolutions that imposed draconian economic sanctions on Iraq unless it withdrew its forces from Kuwait; Secretary Baker a joint would issue statement in Moscow with Foreign Minister Shevardnadze that not only condemned the Iraqi invasion but also imposed an arms embargo as well—a significant step, given the Soviet military relationship with Iraq, and one that demonstrated U.S.-Soviet unity on the issue; tactical air squadrons were quickly deployed to Saudi Arabia and were followed in a month by larger forces to deter Saddam from a further adventure, or an attempt to create a fait accompli by seizing Saudi oil fields.

The initial flurry of activity was followed by an ongoing, intensive diplomatic effort that, as Baker would later observe, reflected the real challenge, not simply of putting together the coalition but of sustaining it. That was no simple task: for Egypt and Turkey to live up to the sanctions meant significant economic loss for each of them, with Egypt getting heavily discounted oil from Iraq and Turkey getting significant revenues from an oil pipeline that passed through Turkey from Iraq. Starting in September, Baker would initiate what we called a tin-cup exercise extracting commitments from the Saudis, Kuwaitis, Germans, and Japanese (the latter two depended on oil from the region, and yet their constitutions prevented them from contributing military forces). Baker made clear to all of them that we could not bear the cost both in blood and treasure of possibly going to war and sustaining the coalition without serious contributions from them, particularly when they all benefitted from what we would be doing. The administration would eventually succeed in collecting $53.7 billion from these four and other countries.[10]

President Bush's decision that the Iraqi aggression would not stand launched the administration on a process of first isolating Iraq politically; deterring further Iraqi aggression; imposing far-reaching economic sanctions; and, if none of this worked, using force to expel the Iraqis. At a certain point, that required switching from a defensive deployment to the region to an offensive one. Practically, we would have to project far more forces to the region. But even if U.S. forces would carry the brunt of the load and the fight, it was essential that this also be an international effort. It was especially important that regional forces participate in the fight, and Baker would elicit the commitment of Egyptian and Syrian forces to the coalition. It was also essential that the Soviets support the switch in mission from one of deterring to one of compelling the Iraqis to leave Kuwait.

With Soviet president Mikhail Gorbachev, this was a delicate matter. For him, new political thinking countenanced a different approach to international relations, not just domestic affairs. That was why he rejected what Saddam Hussein had done. Politically isolating and punishing with sanctions fit his model, but the use of force was a different matter. In addition, he knew that his entire foreign policy and security establishment was against treating a client state like Iraq this way, and for them, using force against that client was unthinkable.[11] Both for the need to bring the Soviets along and to ensure that the use of force had the stamp of international approval, Bush backed Baker's initiative to get a UN Security Council resolution supporting the use of force.

This was not without controversy in the administration. Brent Scowcroft and Dick Cheney each feared the consequence of going for a UNSC resolution on the use of force and failing. They understandably worried that if we failed in that, we would find it difficult to use force over seeming international opposition. (Margaret Thatcher, the British prime minister, agreed with them.) But Baker argued that he could pursue such a resolution discreetly and we would only present it at the UN Security Council if success was assured. Bush, in keeping with his instinctive desire to show that we were acting on the basis of broad international support, agreed with

Baker—and Baker over an eighteen-day, three-continent trip met with every leader or foreign minister of every country sitting on the UN Security Council and through a combination of cajolery and coercion succeeded in winning the necessary support.

With Gorbachev, in particular, Baker negotiated an approach that permitted the Soviet president to feel that his concerns were taken into account. Gorbachev did not want to use the words "use of force." Baker suggested instead the use of "all necessary means" to expel Iraq from Kuwait, and that was acceptable to Gorbachev. But the Soviet president did not want the resolution to automatically trigger the use of force immediately if Saddam Hussein did not comply. So he suggested a second resolution before force was actually used. Baker pointed out that such a posture would render this resolution meaningless but sought to address Gorbachev's concern by suggesting one resolution with a forty-five-day clock. That removed the sense of automaticity, gave space for diplomacy in the forty-five-day period and put Saddam on notice that he had a deadline for complying or his military would be forcibly removed from Kuwait. Gorbachev informed Bush that he accepted Baker's proposal, and force was used when the forty-five-day clock elapsed and Iraqi forces had not withdrawn.

Before that, however, President Bush felt it was necessary to address domestic public opinion. His decision to move from a defensive to an offensive posture in the fall, requiring sending many thousands more forces to the Gulf, triggered opposition in Congress. The focus of the administration had been on conducting diplomacy and garnering broad international support. It was almost as if the president believed that with international support, the American public would follow. But that was not necessarily the case. Senator Sam Nunn, an ardent internationalist, was, nonetheless, not supportive of using force over the Iraqi absorption of Kuwait; like many others, he felt that sanctions could work over time. He would hold hearings essentially to reinforce that point. One of the lead witnesses was the former chairman of the Joint Chiefs of Staff, Admiral William J. Crowe. He testified about the high cost of any such conflict, emphasizing that our casualties could be in the thousands.

With Bush and Baker belatedly believing that they must have a congressional resolution to support going to war, the president came up with the idea that he must show he had gone the extra mile for peace. That is what led to his developing with Baker and Scowcroft, the morning after the UN Security Council adopted the resolution authorizing the use of all necessary means, the idea that between December 15 and January 15—the day the forty-five-day clock ran out—the president would receive the Iraqi foreign minister in Washington and Secretary Baker would go see Saddam Hussein in Baghdad.[12] This offer would later be revised and the president would offer to send Baker to meet Tariq Aziz anywhere outside of the United States and Iraq, but not past January 12. The Iraqis accepted and the meeting took place in Geneva on January 9—a meeting that would go on for six and half hours, during which Aziz refused to offer any concessions; he would not entertain even the possibility of an Iraqi withdrawal, or accept to pass a letter from President Bush to Saddam. War was an inevitability after this meeting, but the president's willingness to go the extra mile for peace both enabled the administration to win congressional support—albeit in a relatively close vote in the Senate—and preempt other possible diplomatic intermediaries that Saddam Hussein might have been able to manipulate.

Two last points bear mention on the Gulf War. The first has to do with managing the Israeli response to Iraqi Scud missile strikes during the war. The second touches on the postwar period and what the administration did to try to stabilize the region.

On the question of Israeli retaliation, it is important to provide some background. Ten days after the Iraq invasion of Kuwait, Saddam, recognizing his isolation in the region with Arab states condemning his takeover of his neighbor, tried to transform the issue into an Arab-Israeli one by saying that in the context of Israel withdrawing from the Palestinian territories, he would consider a withdrawal. It was a transparent ploy, hoping to take an issue around which Arabs would mobilize and linking it to his invasion of Kuwait, a country he was now already referring to as the nineteenth province of Iraq. He gained no traction internationally with his ploy, but it cemented Bush and Baker's view that they must keep Israel at arm's length throughout the development of the coalition and the conduct of the war when it finally took place. Israel was never a stop on any of Baker's regional visits, but during his November trip to the Middle East, he would raise the possibility that Saddam could strike Israel in a war, and he sought to gain a commitment from the Saudis, Egyptians, and Syrians that they would not depart the coalition if Israel, having been struck by Saddam, retaliated. Every Arab leader committed to Baker that, as long as Israel did not initiate strikes, the coalition would remain intact.

Interestingly enough, President Bush did not trust these commitments; even if committed in good faith, he was convinced that if the fighting began, our Arab partners would come under enormous pressure from their respective "streets" if the United States was bombing Iraq while Iraq and Israel were exchanging military strikes. As a result, sent a team led by Deputy Secretary State Larry Eagleburger and Undersecretary of Defense Paul Wolfowitz to Israel shortly before the war. They made the case that Israel should not retaliate even if struck by Iraqi missiles, explaining that it was in neither U.S. nor Israeli interests to transform the conflict from the world against Saddam into an Arab-Israeli war; that the United States could bring more forces to bear on Iraqi weapons that might strike or threaten Israel; and that the United States would provide expedited delivery of the Patriot defensive missiles to Israel, including with U.S. forces to deploy and operate them until Israelis were up to speed and could operate them on their own. While the Israelis would initially say no to the Patriots, preferring self-reliance, they later accepted them, and the U.S. forces needed to operate them when Iraq did, in fact, hit Israel with Scud missiles a day and a half into the war. Israeli prime minister Yitzhak Shamir faced enormous pressure—from his military to retaliate lest Israel's deterrent be weakened, but also from the Bush administration not to strike back and allow Saddam to reframe what the war was about.

In this case, President Bush proved to be right—whatever the prior commitments made, none of the Arab leaders wanted the Israelis to retaliate against the Iraqi missile strikes once the war was underway. With Secretary Baker in frequent communication with Shamir, pressing him not to respond even as he would ask the prime minister to tell us what more we could be doing or targeting, the Israelis did not retaliate, even though they were hit by nearly forty Scud missiles. Baker would later say that it was not just what we were providing the Israelis to answer their needs, but also our unwillingness to furnish them the identification of friend from foe (IFF) codes that led Shamir to withstand the intense internal pressure he was under to strike back. Regardless, this was also an important part of the statecraft conducted during the war.

On the question of the postwar approach, planning on it was initiated well before the war itself began. Baker asked me after our trip in November to develop an approach for the postwar period. Our planning consisted of several parts, some of which would materialize and others would not. Because President Bush had committed to Gorbachev in their September meeting in Helsinki that we would make a serious effort on Arab-Israeli peace, Baker would initiate what would be eight trips to the region that ultimately resulted in the Madrid Peace Conference, cochaired by the United States and the Soviet Union.[13]

The Madrid Conference was only part of the "Madrid process." The conference initiated bilateral negotiations between Israel and Syria, Israel and Lebanon, and Israel and a joint Jordanian-Palestinian delegation. The process went beyond only bilateral negotiations and set in motion what would be multilateral talks, involving the wider orbit of Arab states and Israel organized around five working groups: arms control, economic development, water, environment, and refugees. We were looking to deal with the deeper sources of instability in the region and believed these working groups could address on a multilateral (regional and international) basis the sources of wider conflicts in the region. Many of these working groups operated for years with initially hopeful results; unfortunately, most were not sustainable over time without the political issues being resolved. Ironically, some did help to produce what is happening today between the Israelis and the UAE and Oman on environmental and water issues.

And, of course, part of the postwar planning focused exclusively on Iraq. We planned, developed, and implemented a postwar military infrastructure that allowed us to deploy forces more quickly to the area, with brigade-level equipment prepositioned in Kuwait. Even more importantly, because of genuine concern about what Saddam would do after the war on weapons of mass destruction, we planned for and then mobilized support for UN Security Council Resolution 687 that, among other things, established the UN Special Commission to conduct inspections to ensure Iraq did not have biological, chemical, or nuclear weapons and to prevent the lifting of sanctions until Iraq was fully in compliance with the conditions of the resolution.

CONCLUSION

George H. W. Bush believed in prudence in general. He was not a risk-taker, but he was also not risk averse when he felt America's interests were at stake. He believed in developing relations of trust with other leaders and wanted them to know that his word was good. In the Middle East, whatever he said he would do, he did. He might have had an edgy relationship with Israel's Prime Minister Yitzhak Shamir, but he would not be found wanting if Israel faced a threat. He would cross a threshold in the relationship, deploying American forces to Israel to assume on a short-term basis, an operational responsibility with the deployment of Patriot missiles. Yet, though he crossed that threshold in Israel, his relationship with the leading Arab states was very good. King Fahd of Saudi Arabia trusted his words and allowed U.S. forces to be deployed to Saudi Arabia after the Iraqi invasion of Kuwait, telling Secretary of Defense Dick Cheney that he would accept the deployment "because I trust George Bush and because I know when it's over with, you'll leave."[14]

Bush's legacy in the Middle East was remarkable. His administration broke the taboo on direct diplomacy between Arabs and Israelis, setting in motion the train of events that led to the Oslo process. He reversed Iraqi aggression, and the UN inspection regime that resulted from the administration's efforts did a far better job of destroying the Iraqi WMD programs than anyone realized. His word and his "prudence" led him not to go to Baghdad, but also not to come to the defense of Shia in the south and Kurds in the north after expulsion of Iraqi forces from Kuwait. For some in his administration who would serve later during the George W. Bush presidency, this left unfinished business. For Bush forty-one, he was not going to be drawn more into Iraq and was not going to leave Iraq open to Iranian aggression or penetration—something he feared would be the result if the United States destroyed the Iraqi military.

One can debate whether he could have, at least, prevented the Iraqi helicopter gunships from flying and decimating Shia in the south who rose up against Saddam after the ceasefire ended the conflict and after President Bush declared that Saddam's future was up to the Iraqi people to decide. Those who rose up may well have misread his intent with that statement.

For President Bush, the objective had been achieved. He would leave the Middle East in a state where American power and the United States were probably more respected than at any other point in the history of our involvement in the region. Then every country in the region looked to us—or knew it needed to be very careful in threatening the United States or its friends. Neither prior to the Bush administration nor since has the United States had such a posture or level of influence in the Middle East.

NOTES

1. Ronald Reagan, *An American Life: The Autobiography* (New York: Simon & Schuster, 1990), 410.

2. James A. Baker III, *The Politics of Diplomacy: Revolution, War and Peace, 1989–1992* (New York: Putnam, 1995), 116.

3. There was some basis for the Israelis acting at this time to try to get the loan guarantees; their finance minister, Yitzhak Moda'i, had called for the loan guarantees at the time that Sad-

dam Hussein was launching missiles against Israel during the Gulf War in January, and Baker not only persuaded Shamir not to retaliate, letting us take care of the Iraqi threat, but also to postpone the request until the Fall of 1991.

4. Bush would eventually agree to provide the guarantees but only after Shamir lost the election to Yitzhak Rabin in 1992. Even then, with Rabin, whom he saw very differently than Shamir, he required an understanding. While not requiring a settlement freeze, he did require a dollar-for-dollar reduction from the loan guarantees of the amount the Israelis spent on settlement construction.

5. Baker, *Politics of Diplomacy*, 260.

6. Robert M. Gates, interview by Timothy J. Naftali et al., July 23–24, 2000, p. 46, George H. W. Bush Oral History Project, Miller Center of Public Affairs, http://web1.miller-center.org/poh/transcripts/ohp_2000_0723_gates.pdf.

7. Baker, *Politics of Diplomacy*, 263.

8. Ibid., 276.

9. George Bush and Brent Scowcroft, *A World Transformed* (New York: Knopf, 1998), 303.

10. Michael Watkins and Susan Rosengrant, *Breakthrough International Negotiation: How Great Negotiators Transformed the World's Toughest Post–Cold War Conflicts* (San Francisco: Jossey-Bass, 2001), 194.

11. At the time that we were switching from defense to offense, the Politiburo pressed Gorbachev to send Yevgeny Primakov to Washington to try to persuade Bush and Baker to give Saddam face-savers to leave Iraq. Primakov, who would later serve as prime minister and head of the intelligence service in the post-Gorbachev period, was an Arabist and had a close relationship with Saddam. He was an integral part of the foreign policy/security establishment and someone I had previously known, given his Middle East expertise and quasi-academic status. Sergei Tarasenko, Shevardnadze's close aide sent me a highly delicate message telling me that the Primakov mission was forced on Gorbachev by the Politiburo and that if he succeeded, he would destroy everything we were now working to achieve not just in Iraq but more generally and Primakov would replace Shevardnadze as foreign minister. Gorbachev needed to be able to show the Politiburo that Primakov's way would fail, meaning we must show that we completely rejected what Primakov was suggesting. Needless to say, President Bush left no doubt in their meeting and then called Gorbachev to say that the Primakov approach amounted to rewarding Saddam Hussein for his aggression.

12. The president, Baker, and Scowcroft got together without any staff and announced this initiative; when Baker got back to the State Department after the announcement at the White House, I told him they had just let Saddam off the hook, explaining he would accept your coming on January 15 and, thereby, destroy the deadline. This led to the revision of the initiative; it, nonetheless, served its purpose

13. There was one very poignant moment in Helsinki that also revealed the personal weight of responsibility that President Bush felt as he contemplated the possibility of going to war. He had seen Gorbachev separately as Baker and I met with Shevardnadze; we had just flown directly from the region with warnings from Mubarak and Fahd ringing in our ears not to do anything on the Arab-Israeli peace issue now lest it look like Saddam is the one who forced us to address it. We had not had a chance to brief Bush before his meeting with Gorbachev. When Gorbachev said he wanted to have the joint statement at the end of their summit call not only for increasing pressure on Saddam Hussein but also for a peace conference on the Arab-Israeli conflict, Bush made clear to us afterward that he was fine with that. Baker would later write that I was "impassioned almost to the point of intemperance"

in telling the president why he could not agree to that, but when he insisted that he could, the secretary then interceded, saying, "You are wrong and Dennis is right." Bush answered by saying that he doubted Gorbachev would accept the statement without a reference to the conference, and Baker responded by saying we had an agreement with Shevardnadze on a draft without such a reference and added, "Don't worry about it." Bush emotionally responded: "Well, I've got to worry about it. I put all those kids out there. Nobody else did it—I did it. And I've gotta take every step to be sure that I don't put their lives at risk needlessly. If I can get them out of there without fighting, I'll do it." We did succeed in getting the joint statement issued without a reference to the conference, but that also produced the promise that we would deal with the peace issue when the aggression had been reversed in Kuwait (Baker, *Politics of Diplomacy*, 293).

14. Richard B. Cheney, interviewed by Richard Betts, May 16–17, 2000, George H. W. Bush Oral History Project, Miller Center of Public Affairs, 88. http://web1.millercenter.org/poh/transcripts/ohp_2000_0316_cheney.pdf.

10

Constructing the Alliance to Liberate Kuwait

Edward Djerejian

As an insider in President George H. W. Bush's administration, I can attest that Bush's clarity of thought and his strategic thinking are demonstrated throughout his foreign policy. Some of the key decision points in this realm include managing the fall of the Berlin Wall and the collapse of the Soviet Union; his very diligent, careful and strategic approach to the U.S.-China relationship, especially through his personal correspondence with Deng Xiaoping during the Tiananmen Square crisis; his coalition building during Operation Desert Storm; and transforming the Gulf coalition after we had reversed Saddam Hussein's aggression against Kuwait into a major political foreign policy coalition that led to the Madrid Conference which, for the first time ever, brought about direct negotiations between Israel and all of its Arab neighbors.

In this piece, I focus principally on the clear vision that Bush applied to the Middle East during his time in office. He exemplified this quality in what proved to be one of the most memorable experiences of my entire career: briefing the president aboard Air Force One before one of the most important summits between a U.S. and Middle Eastern leader in the latter part of the twentieth century.

When I was ambassador to Syria, the buildup to Desert Storm in 1991 made it crucial to strengthen U.S.-Syrian relations. President Bush and Secretary of State Baker wanted to build the widest possible coalition of Arab states so they could repel Saddam's offensive designs against Kuwait. I got word that the president and the secretary wished to have Syria join the coalition, if only by expressing Syria's support at the political level. In reality, the common denominator between the United States and Syrian president Hafez al-Assad was their enmity toward Saddam Hussein. Assad and Hussein were political rivals. Each one headed the Ba'ath regime in their respective countries. Thus encouraging Assad to push back on the harmful adventurism of his neighbor was not exactly pushing on a closed door.

137

At the same time, I knew this would be quite a diplomatic challenge given the history of adversarial relations between the United States and Syria. Even after all my dealings with Assad, I was unsure what his response would be. Calculating Syria's interests in the Arab world and the growing relationship with the United States, Assad ultimately agreed that Syria would join the Arab coalition against Saddam's invasion of Kuwait. Then, one day I got a call on the secure line in the embassy. It was Secretary Baker. He informed me that President Bush wanted Syria to go *beyond* just political support for the coalition and participate in the ground operations in and around Kuwait to repulse Saddam's military from the small Persian Gulf state. When Baker asked me what I thought, I replied, "Mr. Secretary, I think this is really going to be very difficult. Getting Assad to join politically is one thing, but to get him to commit his military forces is another."

"Well, you mean I have to come out to Damascus again?" Baker replied.

"Well, Mr. Secretary," I said as I bit my tongue, "with all due respect, it's certainly above my pay grade to ask Assad to do this . . . and I'm afraid it's above yours too. It really would require more than your coming out here." You never tell Baker that anything is above his pay grade, so I shuddered a bit wondering how my comment would be received. However, Baker, true to form and forever the realist, understood what I was implying.

"You're talking about a presidential summit meeting," he said.

"Yes, Mr. Secretary. The only way I think that Hafez al-Assad would say yes to this military commitment is if President Bush asked him directly."

Being very decisive, Baker said, "Okay, I'll talk to the president." With that subsequent affirmation, I got the green light to explore the idea with Syrian foreign minister Sharaa. Following our discussions, we arranged for what would be quite a historical feat: the George Herbert Walker Bush—Hafez al-Assad summit in Geneva in November 1990. It would be the first meeting between Assad and an American president in thirteen years since he met with Jimmy Carter (which likewise occurred in Geneva). It would also come as President Bush was returning from a trip to Asia, stopping in Cairo to meet with Egyptian president Hosni Mubarak before proceeding to Geneva.

As the date of the summit approached, I was preparing to travel directly to Geneva to join the presidential delegation. However, a call from Baker gave me a surprise and forced me to reconsider how my role in the summit preparation would play out. Baker announced that he was not going to be able to attend the Geneva summit, as his immediate task at hand was to go to Latin American capitals to drum up support for the UN Security Council resolution authorizing the use of force to repel the Iraqis from Kuwait. He said, "Ed, I want you to go to Cairo, get on Air Force One, and brief the president on the way to Geneva. Don't screw up, because you'll be representing me." To say that was a heavy burden was an understatement. At the same time, it was one of those moments in a Foreign Service officer's career where you realize that everything you have trained for and learned comes to a head at that moment when you brief the president of the United States directly. This was not to mention the highly consequential nature of this summit for the geopolitics of the Middle East and beyond. It was truly a challenging assignment.

To add another twist, the most difficult part of my adventure logistically would be getting on the plane in the first place! Secretaries of state and presidents sometimes forget that their ambassadors are not privy to government planes. This meant that I had to get from Damascus to Cairo in twenty-four hours, all on a commercial Egypt Air flight to Cairo. My timing to get aboard Air Force One was thus incredibly tight. Once I got on the airplane in Damascus, my heart almost stopped. The pilot came on the loudspeaker and said, "We will be delayed for takeoff. The air space over Cairo is closed because the American president is landing there." I said to myself, "Oh my God, *nobody* and certainly not Secretary Baker will understand why I didn't make it to Cairo."

At that moment, I did something just out of sheer desperation. I took out my diplomatic passport and said to the stewardess, "I'm the American ambassador to Syria and I have to see the pilot." I was ushered into the cockpit, showed the pilot my passport" and said: "I have to be on Air Force One after President Bush arrives. I am on a very important mission to accompany President Bush on his trip to Geneva to meet President Assad." It was public knowledge that there was going to be a summit in Geneva. To the pilot's credit, he contacted the airport in Cairo and they authorized him to depart immediately. We were the *last* plane to land in Cairo before the arrival of Air Force One. You can imagine my relief when we arrived.

Once we landed, I didn't have much time to get onto the presidential plane. I remember rushing and finally boarding Air Force One which took off no more than twenty minutes after that. When the president gets on Air Force One, it takes off instantly. While we were lifting off and the plane was at a sharp angle in its ascent, National Security Advisor Brent Scowcroft came down a ramp holding onto the handrail. He looked at me and gestured to me to come forward into the president's conference room. Fighting gravity, I pulled my way up the ramp. When I entered the room, my eyes immediately went to the president, sitting there in an Air Force jacket. I felt a great sense of intimidation and respect, knowing that I would be seated right next to the president and would have his ear for almost three hours. Accompanying the president on his trip in Air Force One and in the president's conference room were Brent Scowcroft, Marlin Fitzwater, John Sununu, Richard Haass, and Paul Wolfowitz.

Much of our initial discussion centered on Assad's personality. As ambassador to Syria, I had cultivated a close working relationship with Assad and met with him frequently. This was by no means an easy task. Earning Assad's confidence took patience and deliberation with some tense face-to-face encounters. He would often speak in analogies to get his point across, which meant you had to listen carefully to nuances in his position. Having been fortunate to have these numerous personal meetings with Assad, I was keenly aware of his modus operandi and wanted to ensure that President Bush knew exactly what to expect while sitting across from Syria's iron-fisted ruler. Bush consistently expressed curiosity over how Assad would approach the discussion, asking me about the types of political calculations he might make. The president's analytical mindset, wherein he sought not only to understand conflicts but also the people and motivations behind them, remains a deeply laudable quality of his.

A photograph of this scene on Air Force One hangs in my office at Rice University's Baker Institute for Public Policy. In it, Bush stares down inquisitively at a briefing paper as I carefully look on seated directly next to him. For the next few hours, the president continued to ask questions that ranged from Assad's personality to tactical and strategic issues. Concerning the pitch to Assad to commit his forces to the military operation, I made a suggestion. I said, "Mr. President, if you really want to underscore how important this is to you, personally, I would suggest that you ask to talk to him privately without us. You should have Brent Scowcroft with you, and he, I am sure, will bring Foreign Minister Farouk al-Sharaa with him." I assured him that this would leave Assad impressed and, thus, more primed to accept our proposal.

It is important to note that as a Foreign Service officer, briefing President Bush was substantively very gratifying. His extensive experience in foreign policy as ambassador to China and the United Nations, director of the CIA, and vice president gave him inherent knowledge of and insight into the geopolitical, historical, and cultural context behind his policy decisions. He displayed this attitude in our initial discussions about how to approach Saddam's aggression. Early on, the president emphasized to his national security team that the optics of American troops marching on Kuwait City, a small but geographically important Arab capital, would be highly detrimental to our mission of bringing stability to the Middle East. The United States was not a colonial power and should not present itself as such by leading this military charge; doing so could place the United States' important relationships with other Arab states at risk, he argued. With these remarks, Bush displayed his keen understanding of the history and politics of the Arab world, another quality for which I greatly admired him. Throughout my career, I had the honor of briefing many senior officials. Yet there was something truly enjoyable about briefing Bush in particular, for his grasp of Middle Eastern and other global cultures and issues made him uniquely receptive to and interactive with his advisors.

The subsequent fruitfulness of the Geneva summit would prove that Bush had carefully internalized the Air Force One briefing, developing a truly astute strategy for how to proceed. One touchstone of the president's strategic vision was that, once Saddam Hussein's forces were repelled from Kuwait, the United States would use the massive coalition he had assembled to launch a major Arab-Israeli peace initiative. We would want Syria to play a key role in that, and we knew that that would capture Assad's attention. He was a strategic thinker. It is remarkable to consider how all of this diplomatic ground was covered during this summit. During the one-on-one session, I was waiting anxiously outside the room with the other officials as Bush, Scowcroft, Assad, and Sharaa deliberated behind closed doors. The geopolitical weight of what was occurring on the other side of the door was not lost on me, and I desperately wanted to know if my advice had benefited the president. When the meeting finally adjourned, an unforgettable moment happened. President Bush walked up to me and said, "Ed, I did it." And the only words that could come out of my mouth were: "Well done, Mr. President!" That is the one time in my career that I had the opportunity to congratulate a president on his performance.

Assad did ultimately commit militarily. He was not willing to go so far as to place combat troops on the ground, but he did deploy Syrian military logistical units under the umbrella of Desert Storm. That compromise was certainly sufficient for us. And, as I said, that was one of the moments in a Foreign Service officer's life when everything you've learned about the region you're an expert on—your grasp of the policy and the people you're dealing with in the host country—comes to the fore to give your president and your secretary of state the best possible advice to help them succeed in their mission. Undoubtedly, the preparation for and result of the summit became one of the high points of my service in Damascus—and of my entire career.

Another demonstration of President Bush's strategic thinking was that he decided that once Saddam Hussein's forces were repelled from Kuwait, he would not direct the coalition to move on to Baghdad. Given his understanding of history and the Middle East, he did not want the United States to occupy an Arab capital, alienate Arab partners, and be perceived as a colonial or imperialistic power. Equally important, he did not want to waste the extraordinary international coalition that had been put together to just serve military ends. He knew that with the Arabs and the international community united under the aegis of Desert Storm, the political landscape of the Middle East had shifted and this coalition could be used to transition to Arab-Israeli peacemaking, which he and Secretary Baker achieved in the Madrid Peace Conference. Indeed, they succeeded in bringing Israel and all its immediate Arab neighbors to the negotiating table in direct, face-to-face negotiations for the first time.

In sum, George Herbert Walker Bush was a consequential foreign policy president with a strategic vision. He knew how to command a policy team with unparalleled cohesiveness and effectiveness. His national security advisor Brent Scowcroft is the model of what that key position requires. The tandem of Bush and Baker was unique. The two were inseparable and nobody could get in between them in terms of foreign policy formulation. This leadership team facilitated the task of those of us who were in the field. When I would have a meeting with Hafez al-Assad, he knew very well that I was representing the secretary of state and the president without any ambiguity. That was simply not the case under some other administrations in our nation's history. The channels of authority and communication were clear under Bush. He was also an excellent judge of character and knew how to instill trust among his staff and advisors. It was President Bush's unique ability to connect with, encourage, and inspire those who served him that made it a personal privilege to be in his administration.

President and Mrs. Bush greet troops and have Thanksgiving dinner at the First Marine Division Command Post in Saudi Arabia, November 22, 1990.

Senator Prescott Bush (R-Connecticut) and his family—three generations. Future President George H. W. Bush is standing in the top row on the left, and future President George W. Bush is standing to the left of his father. Senator Prescott Bush was identified by President Eisenhower as one of ten people who would make a good successor. George H. W. Bush Presidential Library and Museum.

President Bush stands with German Chancellor Helmut Kohl in Europe for the NATO summit in Brussels in 1989. George H. W. Bush Presidential Library and Museum.

President George H. W. Bush delivers a speech describing his vision of a new world order during the Persian Gulf crisis to a joint session of Congress on September 11, 1990. George H. W. Bush Presidential Library and Museum.

President Bush meets with National Security Advisor Brent Scowcroft and Secretary of State James Baker. George H. W. Bush Presidential Library and Museum.

President Bush, National Security Adviser Brent Scowcroft, Deputy Chief of Staff Andy Card, and British Prime Minister John Major at the Bush home in Kennebunkport, Maine. George H. W. Bush Presidential Library and Museum.

President Bush walks with his National Security team to a press conference. Included are National Security Advisor Brent Scowcroft, Vice President Dan Quayle, Secretary of State James Baker, Deputy National Security Adviser Robert Gates, and Chairman of the Joint Chiefs of Staff General Colin Powell. George H. W. Bush Presidential Library and Museum.

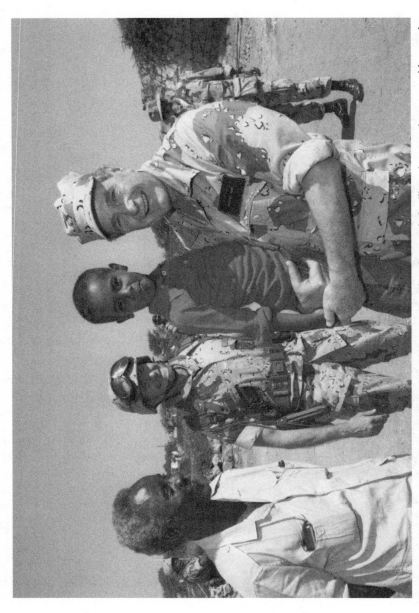

President Bush visits the Bonka Orphanage in Baidoa, Somalia, after the U.S.-led military intervention to provide security for the Somalia famine relief effort. George H. W. Bush Presidential Library and Museum.

11

Saving the Kurds

Humanitarian Intervention in Northern Iraq

Dayton Maxwell and Andrew S. Natsios

U.S. humanitarian relief to the Kurds fleeing Saddam Hussein's brutal repression after the liberation of Kuwait was one of the most successful humanitarian interventions in a refugee emergency in the post–Cold War era. Under the leadership of President Bush, the U.S.-led coalition intervention Operation Provide Comfort (OPC) broke several conventional practices of the Cold War period. John Major, prime minister of the UK, first recognized the need for action and encouraged Bush to act. U.S., British, and French military units led the campaign, with ten other countries participating, a force eventually totaling twenty thousand. The Kurdish crisis had profound historical consequences and changed the doctrine and practice of humanitarian invention for the post–Cold War era by

- defying national sovereignty to aid at-risk populations;
- deploying civilians and military simultaneously to address a forced migration crisis, including the first USAID Disaster Assistance Response Team (DART) to a complex humanitarian emergency;
- undertaking interagency coordination through the National Security Council process to resolve issues arising in field operations; and
- increasing USAID civilian humanitarian assistance funding and staffing for crisis response.

In all these respects, OPC established important new precedents that became accepted international norms in future complex humanitarian emergencies. These emergencies are characterized by macroeconomic decline, including hyperinflation; high unemployment and negative economic growth; large-scale population movements of people trying to find food or escape violence (sometimes 25–35 percent of the population); the collapse of political authority and public services outside the capital city; high mortality rates from starvation and disease; and civil conflict, human rights abuses, and violence against civilians. The number of these complex humanitarian emergencies quadrupled in the 1990s.[1] Many of these conditions were applicable to the Kurdish crisis of 1991.

Saddam Hussein's invasion of Kuwait in August 1990 prompted a phased response by the United States beginning with Desert Shield (the defense of Saudi Arabia from an Iraq attack and the preparation for the liberation of Kuwait), moving to Desert Storm (the combat phase of the liberation of Kuwait), and then to Operation Provide Comfort (the provision of assistance to the Kurds). Desert Storm was completed in March 1991 when the Allied armies drove Iraq out of Kuwait and the Iraqi army surrendered. OPC began a month later in early April 1991.

THE KURDS FLEE SADDAM HUSSEIN'S FORCES—U.S. AND INTERNATIONAL RESPONSE

Following Desert Storm in 1991, an uprising against Saddam Hussein among the Shiite and Kurdish populations of Iraq spread across the country. The Iraqi government responded by the random slaughter of civilian populations in which more than one hundred thousand died. Kurds feared Saddam Hussein would use the same brutal repression tactics against them that he had in the past. During the infamous Anfal campaign from 1987 through 1988, when the Kurds rose up against Bagdad, Saddam retaliated by bulldozing villages and using chemical weapons to kill civilians. As many as one hundred eighty-two thousand Kurds died during the atrocities. In March 1991, over eight hundred thousand Kurds fled to northern Iran, and four hundred thousand tried to flee to Turkey. While Iran permitted entry and provided assistance, Turkey refused entry, forcing the Kurds to find shelter on the mountainside as best they could. They lacked water, food, and sanitation; and the temperatures were below freezing, conditions that quickly caused a significant number of deaths. The media quickly communicated the Kurdish plight to the world.

In response to these desperate reports, the president ordered the National Security Council (NSC) to establish an interagency team in March 1991 to determine the U.S. response. Decisions would be coordinated through a series of Deputies Committee meetings. Ambassador Thomas R. Pickering initiated action at the United Nations on a Security Council Resolution (described in his essay in this book), the White House drafted a budget, and the U.S. military began planning an effort to provide humanitarian assistance to the Kurds.

April 5, 1991, saw UN Security Council Resolution 688 pass with Chapter VII authority to act to restore international peace and security. President Bush announced the same day that the United States would undertake airdrops of food, medicine, and other supplies for the Kurds in the mountains along the Iraq and Turkish border, which officially began Operation Provide Comfort.

On April 9, Secretary of State James Baker helicoptered into Cukurka, one of the five large Kurd refugee camps on the Turkey–Iraq border, and saw firsthand the difficult conditions under which the Kurds were living. Initial reports were that hundreds were dying each day. As soon as Baker left, he called President Bush, telling him "the need is immense, it is urgent, and action is needed now!"[2] On April 10, Bob Kimmitt, undersecretary of state for political affairs (the third-ranking official in the State Department) called Andrew Natsios, director of USAID's Office of U.S. Foreign Disaster Assistance (OFDA), to ask when the DART was deploying to Iraq. In fact, Kimmitt called Natsios three times on the same day asking the status of the DART, because Baker kept calling him to press for immediate deployment.

By April 10, the need for expanded airdrops was realized, authorized, and announced by White House Press Secretary Marlin Fitzwater. Fitzwater made clear that Iraqi military interference would not be tolerated, and a no-fly zone (for fixed wing and rotary aircraft) was clearly set by the JCS above the 36th parallel.

On April 16, a massive expansion of troops was announced by President Bush in concert with the United Kingdom and France to establish safe relief encampments in the mountains to encourage the Kurds to move to areas more conducive to effective relief efforts. The security provided allowed the Kurds to move down, with all but forty-one thousand brought down by the end of May.

The very successful OPC relief operation transitioned to the UN on June 9, UN guards were deployed for security, and the no-fly zone was maintained as the Allied teams prepared to leave.

To best understand the dynamics of organizational change during and after OPC, it is important to examine how individual institutions reacted to the crisis. Each government department tends to prioritize decision-making based on its institutional priorities and traditional practices. The post–Cold War period thrust new U.S. government priorities into each department, requiring interagency cooperation. We can look at OPC with more detail from the perspective of each U.S. department or agency—the Joint Chiefs of Staff in the Pentagon, the U.S. ground forces in Iraq, the State Department, and USAID—as well as looking at the United Nations.

DEPLOYMENT DECISIONS:
THE CIVILIAN PERSPECTIVE

Secretary Baker's message to President Bush accelerated the U.S. planning process to provide a much-expanded humanitarian relief effort for the Kurds. Kimmitt held coordination meetings of the State Department and U.S. Agency for International Development (USAID) to make sure all the offices in State and USAID were consistent in strategy, public messaging, and policy. Sometimes Deputy Secretary of State Larry Eagleburger led these morning coordination meetings. While Andrew Natsios, who served as the director of the Office of Foreign Disaster Assistance, was in Iraq (his reserve unit had been mobilized for the Gulf War, and he had deployed to Desert Storm), his deputy, Dayton Maxwell, served as the acting director. At one of the early coordination meetings, Maxwell offered to deploy a DART before Natsios's return, and Kimmitt immediately accepted. This, however, was before Secretary Baker's trip. The DART, a rapid-response humanitarian deployment team, was conceived of following the inadequate disaster response to the December 1988 Armenian earthquake. DART teams were staffed by experts in food aid, health, logistics, shelter, and water and sanitation. This new organizational structure within USAID's Office of Foreign Disaster Assistance was established at the start of President Bush's term. They had been previously deployed to Panama in December 1989 during the U.S. intervention to remove Manual Noriega from office and to Kuwait during the liberation of the country from Saddam Hussein's occupation. OPC was the first time a DART would be dispatched for a protracted and messy refugee crisis, rather than as a short-term response to a natural disaster or other short-term emergency.

Natsios added Fred Cuny—a widely known disaster expert, published scholar, raconteur, and field person—to the DART. Natsios had brought Cuny with him along with Joe Gettier, an experienced OFDA disaster operations officer, to the Gulf War to plan for humanitarian needs after the liberation of Kuwait. Cuny moved from Kuwait to Northern Iraq in mid-April. He proved an excellent choice.

The decisive April 5 Deputies Committee meeting (followed by a dozen more) illustrates the beginning of civil-military coordination of OPC. Bob Kimmitt represented State. Maxwell accompanied Mark Edelman, USAID deputy administrator. Paul Wolfowitz represented Defense, and Admiral David Jeremiah represented the Joint Chiefs of Staff. Other agency deputies were also present. Deputy National Security Advisor Bob Gates chaired the meeting. He came in, sat down, and immediately said, "We're going to do air drops!"

"We're with you all the way, Bob," responded Kimmitt. The meeting continued to discuss the DART deployment, the need for drop-zone assistance at the refugee sites to avoid injury from dropped supplies, and how soon the effort could commence.

DART deployment for OPC lasted nearly four months, with close civil-military cooperation. The OFDA's Kurdish Response After-Action Report describes the effort. DART's expertise was used "to select the refugee camp site near Zakho, design the camp layout (using principally OFDA's tents), organize the refugee reception and care procedures and facilities, develop a repatriation plan in consultation with Kurd representatives, suggest to U.S. military staff security measures that would overcome the Kurd reluctance to repatriate, design a transition program to turn the operation over to the UN, and mobilize NGO (nongovernmental organizations) efforts in northern Iraq."[3] Additionally, DART funds were used to purchase construction supplies locally to build the camp facilities, bulk food, and water, and to support nongovernmental organization (NGO) representatives to manage the camp. In all, USAID funding from OFDA and the Food for Peace Office for OPC totaled $68 million, and the State Department contribution from their Refugee Program Office totaled $53 million. The Pentagon's total contribution, including the cost of logistics and troops, was $328,320,000.[4]

The deployment indicated a shift in OFDA's mission, one that has continued into the third decade of the twenty-first century. OFDA's principal activity prior to the post–Cold War period was responding to natural disasters such as earthquakes, storms, and floods. As civil wars, political unrest, failed states, and famines began spreading across the globe in the late 1980s, the mission and operations of the office evolved to address these new challenges. Following OPC, long-term DARTs were subsequently deployed to Sudan, Ethiopia, the southern African drought, and Bosnia. The invention of the DART and their long-term deployments to refugee and displaced emergencies are specific examples of institutional changes during the Bush presidency.

INITIAL DEPLOYMENT DECISIONS:
THE MILITARY PERSPECTIVE

Desert Storm was managed under the authority of the U.S. military's Central Command (CENTCOM). OPC required deployment through and with the cooperation of Turkey, which is within the geography of the European Command (EUCOM). The Joint Chiefs of Staff issued EUCOM a warning order to begin response planning in late March, which EUCOM's chief of staff Lt. Gen. Robert Chelberg did. U.S. Air Force in Europe deployed Maj. Gen. James Jamerson to Incirlik, Turkey, to begin operations. The area north of the 36th parallel was transferred to EUCOM's responsibility, permitting it to conduct operations in northern Iraq. EUCOM developed a plan for the operation.

A small Civil Affairs detachment from the 353rd Civil Affairs Command was assigned to EUCOM and participated in the planning. Two of its members, including Lt. Col. Michael Hess, briefed the deputy director of operations, Brig. Gen. Anthony (Tony) Zinni, on the need to have civil affairs units involved in the operations. Zinni quickly understood that this would be a civil-military operation (CMO), and he convinced Lt. Gen. Chelberg that the CMO components needed to be added to the campaign plan. The change in plan and focus of the planning toward a CMO operation included the deployment of an initial civil affairs team of six members.

EUCOM completed the plan and forwarded it to the EUCOM/NATO commander, General Galvin, on April 9. Gen. Galvin approved the plan and sent it to the JCS that afternoon. Later that week, Brig. Gen. Zinni and the initial civil affairs team deployed to Turkey.

In the meantime, the JCS had issued the Execution Order that arrived April 7 to commence airdrops. This led to the first two airdrops executed on April 7, with 41 U.S. C-130 airdrop missions completed by April 11, and U.S and Allied nations flying 198 such missions by April 16.

INITIAL DEPLOYMENT DECISIONS:
THE UN PERSPECTIVE

Developing countries viewed attempts by Western NGOs and donor governments to protect at-risk populations in conflicts as a violation of their sovereignty and a form of neocolonialism. Thus, the approval of UN Security Council (UNSC) resolutions authorizing humanitarian action to help the Kurds was critically important to get developing country support for OPC. UNSC 688, passed on April 5, condemned Iraq in the harshest terms for its repression of the Kurd population and demanded cooperation in providing humanitarian assistance to the Kurds. The Iraqi government was not cooperative despite the resolution. It was the presence of U.S., British, and French troops that made the UNSC resolutions enforceable; without them, the resolutions would likely have been ignored by the Iraqis.

Under the UN Charter, refugee emergency response is the responsibility of the UN High Commissioner for Refugees (UNHCR). International humanitarian law defines *refugees* as people who fled their countries to neighboring countries because of legitimate fear of physical harm or persecution. Populations leaving their homes and collecting in camps within their national borders are categorized as internally displaced populations (IDPs), and historically they had not fallen under UNHCR's responsibility. The newly appointed High Commissioner for Refugees, Sadako Ogata, who had the lead for the UN, had not yet implemented the transformational changes in UNHCR which she became famous, particularly during the Bosnian civil war. Importantly, Ogata personally took responsibility for providing assistance to the Kurds remaining in Iraq; however, neither UNHCR's operational capacity nor its policies permitted the organization to provide assistance on the scale needed, at least not at the start of the crisis. It wasn't until later, after OPC, that UNHCR formally adopted policies that permitted it to respond to crises involving internally displaced people.

INTERNATIONAL IMPEDIMENTS
REQUIRING REFORM

The Bush administration initiated a series of institutional reforms within the U.S. government (and in USAID in particular) and in the UN system to respond on a much greater scale with logistical capacity and force to crises in the future, although many did not come to complete fruition until after President Bush left office. (The UN reforms are described by Nancy Bearg and Catherine Bertini in their chapters.) One example of this was the change in UNHCR's policies and practices, which the State Department actively supported. The criticism of UNHCR's response during OPC was so strong that it led to UNHCR revising its policies to include IDPs.

The success of OPC was a precedent-setting intervention that led to the debate over how to protect at-risk populations within their own countries, particularly during conflicts. The question hanging over all the preparations to assist the Kurds was how humanitarian assistance organizations could best gain access to the Kurd refugee sites given Iraqi government hostility. This presaged a major debate within the UN and the humanitarian aid communities over the next several years on the right to intervene for humanitarian purposes, which culminated in a 2001 landmark UN report, *The Responsibility to Protect (R2P)*. The conclusion of this report was that the international community has a *responsibility* to intervene in a country that abuses its own population to protect them from their own government. National sensitivities of sovereignty could and should be secondary to the need to protect populations at risk of suffering and death. While Chapter VII of the UN charter contains a provision to permit such interventions, it had not been used much because of the reluctance of UN member states to allow outside intervention. The responsibility to protect doctrine in international humanitarian law had not yet been embraced by the UN at the time of the Kurdish crisis, and so the legal justification for intervention to protect the Kurds was based on specific resolutions, which are described in Ambassador Pickering's essay.

INITIAL IN-COUNTRY COORDINATION

USAID's DART arrived in Ankara on April 11, and then moved on to Incirlik on April 13.[5] Its original mission was to assess the humanitarian assistance needs and recommend the level and nature of funding to NGOs—such as CARE, Doctors Without Borders, the International Rescue Committee, and the International Committee of the Red Cross—and to UN agencies providing assistance to the Kurds. It was composed of the team leader, Dayton Maxwell; two representatives from the U.S. Centers for Disease Control to assess health conditions; a relief assessment specialist; a food expert; a procurement technician; and a technical support group for communications and reporting. The team worked directly with the military to undertake planning for the effort, first at Incirlik, then from Silopi. Shortly after arriving in Incirlik, the DART was joined by Cuny who provided critical guidance in the continuous planning that was needed as the operation evolved.[6] The DART carried out the first field site assessment on April 16.

Immediately after arriving in Turkey on April 13, the First Battalion 10th Special Forces Group sent an A Team along with two civil affairs officers into the Kurd refugee camp, Iskveren. The team assisted in establishing drop zones and landing zones so the humanitarian supplies could be collected and distributed by the few NGOs that were working in the camp. Reports back to the military leadership in Incirlik led to a decision that a change in mission was needed from air drops to deploying U.S. forces into or near the refugee camps along the border because of the ground logistics needs to feed and shelter the Kurds. As a result of this decision, the military established a forward supply base in Silopi, Turkey, just across the border with Iraq. This allowed helicopters to have a base closer to the refugee sites to begin the delivery of much-needed clean water and medical supplies.

As the Kurdish rescue operation evolved, a major dispute arose between the field and the higher U.S. military command over strategy. This pitted the DART and military command on the ground in Iraq on one side and the European Command and Joint Staff on the other. Cuny and Maxwell convinced the senior military commanders on the ground that the only solution to the crisis was to move the Kurds down from the mountain and then move them back to their homes. This would require military protection for the Kurds, both while returning home and into the future, which may be why EUCOM and the Joint Staff resisted the plan. The U.S. military units providing assistance had no history of working in refugee and displaced emergencies and no experience with refugee camps. Military planners in EUCOM and the Pentagon saw the crisis as a logistical undertaking that involved feeding and providing shelter to the Kurds *where they were* and nothing more. Their plan was to turn over the refugee camps they intended to build on the side of the mountain to the UN as soon as possible.

Cuny, Maxwell, and the DART team members knew that providing services to hundreds of thousands of traumatized people on a mountain side would be a logistical nightmare. They also knew from past experience that displaced persons and refugee camps were often militarized and used as recruitment grounds by rebel militias, violence against women was a serious problem, families were often broken up, children were deprived of access to education, and diseases spread more easily in a new disease environment. Perhaps most seriously, some factions of Turkish Kurds had been in revolt against the central government in Ankara, putting any semipermanent Kurdish refugee and displaced camps at risk of future attack by the Turkish military. Thus, Cuny and Maxwell worked from the start to convince ground commanders that building semipermanent camps was a mistake, and the Kurds had to be moved back to their homes.

PRESIDENT BUSH ANNOUNCES
THE EXPANDED OPERATION

On April 16, 1991, President Bush resolved the simmering conflict between the DART and the U.S. military ground forces in Iraq, and the European Command and JCS, holding a news conference to announce "a greatly expanded and more ambitious relief effort." He explained, "If we cannot get adequate food, medicine, clothing, and shelter to the Kurds living in the mountains along the Turkish-Iraq border, we must encourage the Kurds to move to areas in northern Iraq where the geography facilitates rather than frustrates such a large-scale relief effort." In announcing this interim measure, he reassured the world that the safety of Kurdish refugees from Iraqi forces would be of top priority. He reassured the Kurds that "adequate security will be provided at these temporary sites by the United States, British, and French air and ground forces, again consistent with United Nations Security Council Resolution

688." He emphasized his commitment to pure humanitarian relief efforts, rather, than military intervention.

By mentioning his consultations with heads of state and UN Secretary-General Pérez de Cuéllar, Bush pointed out that there was international support for the short-term effort, which would be handed over to the UN at a later date. He closed with the following lines. "But we must do everything in our power to save innocent life. This is the American tradition, and we will continue to live up to that tradition."

The U.S. military and other allies entered Northern Iraq around the city of Zakho. The Joint Task Force (JTF) was composed of two main elements. The first was JTF Alpha comprised of Special Forces and civil affairs personnel that operated in the mountain camps under the command of Brig. Gen. Richard Potter. JTF Bravo, under Maj. Gen. Jay Garner, had three components. The first was a security element with a Marine Expeditionary Unit (MEU) under Col. James Jones. The other two were an engineer unit to assist in reconstruction and a civil affairs component to focus the civil military operations of the task force. Gen. Garner would command the operations inside the security zone in Northern Iraq.

On April 29, the UN representative assigned to set up a UN facility in Northern Iraq, Staffan de Mistura, came to the DART to ask for advice on where to establish it and was told to consult with Fred Cuny. Cuny advised him to set up the UN offices just downhill from the interim camp. By May 7, the UN assumed responsibility for management of the interim camp and the UN flag was raised. But it was torn down by the refugees right away due to their distrust of the UN. It was a few weeks later that UN management responsibility was finally established.

OVERCOMING THE CHALLENGES

The DART team, using Fred Cuny's expertise, began influencing and leading some of the planning of operations in Northern Iraq from the outset. One crucial case was when Cuny wanted to expand the boundary of the area of operation to include Duhok, which had taken place without approval from EUCOM. An Iraqi-held town south of Zakho. Under Cuny's counsel, the military commanders convinced the city's mayor to let them assess the area. When on the ground, they personally negotiated with the Iraqi forces, who quickly left the area. The Kurds were then able to enter the area, due to this "renegade" operation.[7]

The first joint decision was the location of the interim refugee camp near Zakho, the first town inside Northern Iraq from Turkey. By May 10, the Zakho camp held about twenty thousand people.[8] Some in the military wanted to place it by the river just inside the border. Cuny advised locating it right next to Zakho so the refugees would have access to the services available in the town. His advice was accepted.

An incident took place when the military invited the press to visit Zakho on April 22. DART had brought in rental Land Rovers and was asked to transport some of the members of the press. As they entered the main street in Zakho, they saw sixty to seventy policemen sent by Saddam Hussein to establish his authority in the town. This posed a significant obstacle to bringing the Kurds back home, as it reinforced their fear on how they would be governed if they returned. The MEU security escort avoided a hostile situation by walking forward to meet them and shake hands in a friendly gesture; however, they did not leave then.

Members of the Peshmerga—the military force of the Kurds—came to Gen. Garner to ask how they could help. Gen. Garner sent them to the DART. Maxwell and Cuny began talking with them to determine the possibilities. (They did not know that the State Department had issued instructions not to talk to the Peshmerga, which was regarded as a terrorist group by the Turkish government.) Kurdish leaders in the refugee camps on the Turkey border insisted they would not come back down into Iraq from the mountains as long as Saddam was in power. They feared what he could do to them. If the Kurd refugees would not return, despite the United States and allies establishing a secure zone for them, the US government effort faced a serious obstacle to the strategy the president had announced. Maxwell and Cuny hoped the Peshmerga would help them find a compromise.

Cuny devised a two-step plan. First, they invited a few Kurdish leaders among the refugees to visit Zakho to see the current security situation for themselves. Fortunately, the British military made Saddam's police so uncomfortable that they left before this visit. Maxwell drove one of these Kurdish leaders around town, including right by his own house. The second step was to invite one thousand Kurdish men to come to the interim campsite outside Zakho to build the camp. The DART procured the necessary food and equipment for these men to stay in the tents as they erected the campsites.

We noticed that many of the workers began to disappear from the camp. Of course, the idea behind this plan was that if enough of the Kurds saw how secure it was for them to come home, they would reverse their refusal to return. Sure enough, a few nights later the spontaneous return of the Kurds began. DART could look up at the mountains and watch headlights of vehicles coming down the mountains with the refugees returning. The interim camp expanded significantly for those who lived beyond Zakho and were not yet willing to return to their homes deeper into Iraq. The facilities quickly became overwhelmed. It was crucial to find ways to get the refugees back to their homes, wherever they were.

The DART team assessment specialist conducted a survey among the refugees in the mountain camps to learn where their homes were so their return could be planned. He learned that a significant number were from the city of Dohuk, which was outside the established secure zone. Given that the military could not provide security there, this stalled any effort to get a large population out of the interim camp in Zakho and back home to Dohuk. The U.S. military on the ground requested Dohuk from higher headquarters, the authority to extend operations to Dohuk, but this was vetoed.

Most communications between the field operations and Washington were conducted through military channels. The DART, however, had its own communications system with Andrew Natsios in Washington. In mid-April, Maxwell sent a handwritten fax to Natsios informing him that they would be unable to accomplish the humanitarian assistance objectives of returning the Kurds to their homes if DART could not help them return to Dohuk.

Natsios attended the previously mentioned morning staff meetings on the crisis held by either Deputy Secretary of State Larry Eagleburger or Bob Kimmitt on the seventh floor of the State Department. The day after Natsios received Maxwell's fax, he attended the morning staff meeting with Eagleburger and told him that the DART had set out a plan to get the Kurds back to their homes and had convinced the U.S. military commanders on the ground (specifically Garner, Zinni, and Jamerson) of the wisdom of this approach. However, each time they submitted the plan, EUCOM rejected it. EUCOM then substituted its own plan, which had the U.S. military setting up Kurdish refugee and displaced camps on the side of the mountains between Iraq and Turkey and provisioning them there.[9] Natsios argued that the U.S. military had little experience in these sorts of operations but that the OFDA, UN, and NGOs had run these operations many times around the world. Eagleburger told Natsios, "You and I are going to the Pentagon to see the Joint Staff to resolve this tomorrow." The two of them visited the Pentagon and met with Admiral Jeremiah, vice chairman of the Joint Chiefs of Staff. Natsios expected a blowup, but the opposite took place. He told Jeremiah that this was not a logistics operation to provision the Kurdish as they were presently situated (though that too had to be done in the short term), but an effort to get the Kurds off the mountainsides and back to their cities and villages. Jeremiah responded, "We don't know anything about these emergencies and your office and your staff do. What do you want us to do?" Natsios responded, "Let the DART team write the strategy and then work jointly with us to carry it out." Jeremiah replied, "You write the order and we will send it out."

A couple of days later a short paragraph in the form of an order signed by General Colin Powell, chairman of the Joint Chiefs of Staff (written by OFDA senior staff in Washington), went out to all levels of the military command structure. It stated that the OFDA DART was in charge of writing the operations strategy and the military would carry it out. Many mid-levels of the command, particularly in Europe, were furious with the order. It took a couple more weeks before the DART strategy Fred Cuny and Dayton Maxwell had designed was finally accepted through the U.S. military command structure.

COMPLETING THE MISSION

Military operations are designed to complete their objectives and terminate within a given time period. OPC was the first of its kind in recent military experience, so no one in the military calculated a time period for the operation. Cuny said early in the deployment, however, that it could be completed in about three months based on his extensive experience, and Maxwell repeated that to a *Washington Post* reporter.

The three-month completion date was on the front page of the *Washington Post* the next day, saying this was the first time a U.S. government official provided a time frame for the operation.

The principal challenge to completing the mission was resolving the dilemma on returning the significant number of refugees to Dohuk, which EUCOM and the JCS in Washington had rejected. Given the important coalition presence on the ground and the success of Desert Storm, the Iraqi government was not the principal constraint. It would not inhibit an Allied security presence in Dohuk. The U.S. decision on the extent of the secure zone, which did not include Dohuk, became the main constraining factor. U.S. presence in Dohuk was required to establish secure conditions before the refugees felt safe about returning. Later, a continued international presence after the U.S. military withdrawal was required to sustain that security so the repatriated refugees would remain in their homes. The Zakho refugee camp was designed to hold only about twenty thousand people—DART wanted it to be only a transit camp—but it quickly grew to fifty-eight thousand by late May. Facilities were overwhelmed and conditions were poor. Opening Dohuk was essential.

JTF Bravo and DART began looking at facilities that could be used to settle refugees on a more permanent basis, such as abandoned Iraqi military training facilities. The DART and the ground commanders kept making appeals to Washington on the cost of having to maintain a long-term refugee support operation with protection, but that failed to achieve any policy change.

A breakthrough came in an unexpected manner. JTF Bravo regularly communicated with Iraqi military authorities on operational matters. Col. Naab, the principal American in charge of the communications, stressed that the withdrawal of Allied Forces would be delayed until the return home of the refugees was resolved. That captured the Pentagon's attention. He asked the local Iraqi authorities for an invitation for a detachment of JTF to come to Dohuk to show the refugees that they could return home safely. The Iraqis provided him the invitation.

Gen. Garner took the invitation and began preparing a group to go to Dohuk. The Pentagon at first resisted, but finally relented and permitted JTF to proceed. On May 23, a detachment of approximately six dozen soldiers and civilians took a convoy of twenty vehicles toward Dohuk, and they were met there by the Iraqis. Their purpose was to survey Dohuk and develop a short-term program to help the Iraqis rebuild the community and resettle the refugees.

Negotiations with the UN to take responsibility for the long term in Dohuk took place simultaneously. Gen. Garner was then able to develop plans to withdraw U.S. forces. The date and manner of withdrawal was quite sensitive, as it had to be done in a way not to alarm the Kurds and to give them time to prepare their own protection.

Critical to establishing the adequate security conditions was the need to reassure the UN and NGOs that they would not be abandoned. The Civil Affairs team and DART explained how the hand off would occur and the steps they would take to ensure that the Iraqi forces would not take over the security zone after the U.S. and Allied security forces left Iraq. Building relationships with the NGOs had been challenging due to the limited cooperation between the U.S. military and the humanitarian assistance community prior to OPC. This was a major change in the relationship that the military continued to develop after the operations in Iraq. It became the foundation for future work together, leading to the civilian-military relationships that exist today.

On May 30, General Colin Powell visited the security zone for or the first time. General Garner, who had been criticized for expanding the security zone beyond Zakho and for engineering the invitation to Dohuk, had an opportunity to explain the tactical and humanitarian situation firsthand. By the end of the visit, Powell said that much of the guidance from Washington had been wrong.[10] He also said he was beginning to consider the post-withdrawal security framework that needed to be put in place to protect the Kurds. The post-withdrawal framework included clear directives to the Iraqis to permit the Kurds to manage themselves and exercises with Kurds called "Poised Hammer" that indicated Allied military forces would return if conditions warranted.

The relief operation was turned over to the UN on June 9. OPC was officially completed on July 24. It was judged to be a significant success by most scholars and analysts. A secondary measure of success might be how it contributed to the careers of those who played leadership roles in the operation. Lt. Gen. Shalikashvili, Brig. Gen. Zinni, Col. James Jones, and Col. Abizaid (who participated in support activities) were all promoted to become four-star generals. Col. Jones, after retirement, also became the National Security Advisor to President Obama. Andrew Natsios became the administrator of USAID under President George W. Bush and later U.S. Envoy to Sudan. Col. Mike Hess became the assistant administrator of USAID's humanitarian bureau during the George W. Bush administration.

OPERATION PROVIDE COMFORT II

Establishing and maintaining security for the Kurds following the completion of OPC was of critical importance. A repeat exodus of Kurds from their homeland would compromise any mission success. Thus Operation Provide Comfort II (OPC II) began the day following the termination of OPC. It was focused on deterring Iraqi attacks on the Kurds. U.S. fighters patrolled the skies over northern Iraq enforcing the no-fly zone. The USAF flew more than forty-two thousand sorties while the entire task force flew nearly twenty thousand additional sorties by the time that operation ended on December 31, 1996. This operation was followed by Operation Northern Watch.

Two additional factors ensured the long-term success of OPC. First, the Kurds built a sustainable government and economy in their autonomous zone. Second, the central Iraq government permitted the Kurds to manage the affairs in their zone without interference or repression. The "over the horizon" threat of further U.S. military intervention kept the Iraq government in check.

CONCLUSION

Operation Provide Comfort established much more robust norms for humanitarian intervention during the post–Cold War era when populations were threatened with mass atrocities by their own or other governments. As described at the beginning of this essay, the absolute sanctity of national sovereignty no longer protected governments who abused their own populations. The use of USAID DARTs working in an integrated campaign effort with U.S. military units to address a complex humanitarian crisis became an established response mechanism for future presidents. This model was later used in Somalia (1992–1993), the Rwandan Genocide (1994), Afghanistan (2001–2003), Iraq (2003), the Aceh Tsunami (2004–2005), the Pakistan earthquake (2005), the Haiti earthquake (2010), the Syrian civil war (2014) and the West African Ebola outbreak of 2014–2015 among others. Dozens of DARTs without U.S. military support became commonplace after the Kurdish crisis in 1991. OPC also established the use of the National Security Council decision-making process to resolve disputes among U.S. government departments and agencies as a regular practice in future ground operations. While this was a regular function between the Pentagon, State Department, and Treasury Department on broad policy issues, it had not been used before on complex humanitarian emergencies where USAID was involved in a major way on the ground.

One remarkable paradigm shift in the post–Cold War period was the rise in staffing, organizational complexity, and spending by USAID's Office of Foreign Disaster Assistance (OFDA) and Office of Food for Peace from the Kurdish crisis in 1991 through 2019. When George H. W. Bush was sworn in as president in January 1989, OFDA had a budget of $20 million and a staff of forty-five. By the time he left office, the budget (called the International Disaster Assistance Account) had grown to $200 million (through a supplemental budget) with a staff of sixty. Before the end of the Cold War, OFDA focused on natural disasters; by the time George Bush left office, most of its resources were being spent in failed states, famines, and civil wars as the world order destabilized and these crises became much more common. By 2018, OFDA's budget was $1.7 billion, with a staff of over seven hundred. Few international aid programs have more support in the U.S. Congress from both sides of the aisle than the International Disaster Assistance account. The increased funding, staffing, and organizational reforms had their roots in the success of the response to the Kurdish refugee crisis.

NOTES

1. Andrew Natsios, *U.S. Foreign Policy and the Four Horsemen of the Apocalypse* (Washington, DC: Center for Strategic and International Studies. Westport, CT: Praeger, 1997), 1–18.
2. James Baker III, *The Politics of Diplomacy: Revolution, War, and Peace, 1989–1992* (New York: Putnam, 1995), 433–35.

3. For a full description of what the OFDA DART accomplished during the Kurdish crisis, see *Kurdish Relief and Repatriation, DOD-AID/OFDA Partnership*, AID/OFDA Kurdish Response After-Action Report (Washington, DC: USAID Office of U.S. Foreign Disaster Assistance, December 1991), 1–2, https://pdf.usaid.gov/pdf_docs/PDABM963.pdf.

4. OFDA Situation Report No. 25, July 17, 1991.

5. *Kurdish Relief and Repatriation, DOD-AID/OFDA Partnership*, 4.

6. Fred Cuny disappeared and was presumably killed (his body was never recovered) in Chechnya during the civil war in 1994, where he was running humanitarian assistance programs. Scott Anderson's book *The Man Who Tried to Save the World* details Cuny's disappearance and reconstructed his work on the DART team in Northern Iraq among the Kurds. In writing this chapter, we used Anderson's research to reconstruct time lines and cross-check our memory of what happened.

7. Scott Anderson, *The Man Who Tried to Save the World* (New York: Anchor, 1999), 115–16.

8. *Kurdish Relief and Repatriation, DOD-AID/OFDA Partnership*, 7.

9. Ibid., 112.

10. Interview with Col. (Ret) Michael Hess who kept a detailed daily account of OPC, which this chapter relied on to confirm operational details of the campaign. General Powell's candid assessment of the Pentagon's misunderstanding of the situation on the ground was reported at a staff meeting of the U.S. military where DART representatives were present. Cuny wrote an unpublished manuscript on Operation Provide Comfort, which is in his archives at the Texas A&M University Library. See page 39 for a report on Powell's comments.

12

President George H. W. Bush's Historic Contributions to Open Trade

Carla A. Hills

President George Herbert Walker Bush's belief in the importance of opening global markets was strong and consistent. He had a vision about how nations of the world could and should work more constructively together. He understood that our economic growth and prosperity were increasingly tied to commercial opportunities beyond our borders and that our economic bonds enhanced our security. In his words, "We don't want an America that is closed to the world. What we want is a world that is open to America."[1]

That has been the position of the United States since the end of World War II. Whether under a Democratic or Republican administration, our government has been a leader seeking to open global markets in the belief that the free flow of goods and services, capital, and ideas would benefit all nations. America led in constructing the General Agreement and Tariffs and Trade (the GATT) signed by twenty-three nations in 1947. The steady opening of global markets over the next seventy years added substantially to our GDP. According to calculations done by the Peterson Institute for International Economics, the opening of global markets since 1950 has increased America's GDP by more than $2.1 trillion.[2] Our allies also benefited, and the expansion of trade helped create the economic bonds that have contributed to global stability.

The benefits flowed not only to industrialized nations. According to studies done by Dr. William Cline, an economist at the Peterson Institute, every percentage increase in a poor country's trade reduces its poverty by an equivalent percentage.[3] Helping poor countries advance economically through trade is not only an efficient development tool, but also creates customers for the future and enhances security, for too often countries mired in poverty cannot seal their borders or enforce their laws, and they become havens for international crime.

President Bush had an ambitious trade agenda that included the Uruguay Round of the GATT. His goal in the Uruguay Round was not only to further reduce tariffs, but also to create global rules to govern trade involving agriculture, services, investment, and intellectual property. He also strongly supported our efforts to pry open Japan's retail sector and to reduce its barriers covering procurement, telecommunications, semiconductors, construction, and computers using Sections 301 and Special 301 of the U.S. Trade Act of 1974. With the president's support, a new approach was initiated called the Structural Impediments Initiative, which sought and achieved the removal of oligopolistic measures in Japan that restricted outside parties from participating in a number of economic sectors.

In addition, several agreements covering investment, taxes, and specific sectors were negotiated with the newly independent states of the former Soviet Union as well as with Russia. An integral part of U.S. policy was to encourage command economic systems to adopt more market principles and to agree to a common set of trade rules that would increase the certainty required to enhance global trade and help to build investment relationships.

Most remembered today is President Bush's launch of negotiations of the North American Free Trade Agreement (NAFTA). He had a long-term vision of free trade from the tip of Alaska to the tip of Argentina, and he believed that President Carlos Salinas was courageously moving to improve Mexico's economy and could serve as a model for the rest of the hemisphere. Mexico had made substantial progress since joining the GATT in 1986. Serious conversations began in January 1990 at Davos when Jaime Serra Puche, Mexico's commerce minister, who was there with President Salinas, raised the possibility with me of initiating that spring formal negotiations of a bilateral free trade agreement. He said that his government's objective was to maintain the existing momentum for its economic reform. Puche wanted President Salinas to make a request to launch negotiations when the two presidents were scheduled to meet later that year on June 11.

In my weekly report to President Bush, I stated that in my view the only viable means for securing congressional approval of such an agreement was to use the "fast track" provisions contained in the 1988 Trade Act, which set forth procedures for securing congressional approval by means of an up or down vote without amendments. To use that process, we needed first to receive a formal request from Mexico to begin negotiations and second to notify Congress of our intent to move forward along with an outline of our objectives. The congressional notification triggered a period of sixty legislative days, during which either the Senate Finance or the House Ways and Means Committees, both with Democratic majorities, could deny the use of fast-track procedures by a simple majority vote.

Several groups, agriculture and labor among others, had already indicated opposition to a trade agreement with Mexico. Other groups worried that it would take our eye off the Uruguay Round of Multilateral Trade Negotiations, which were moving slowly. I believed that Congress would resist unless the president and members of his cabinet engaged in intensive consultations with congressional members and the private sector. My view was that we needed more time to consult and to lay the necessary groundwork for the negotiations. I suggested that in June when the two presidents met, they simply issue a joint statement that they believed that both nations would benefit from a comprehensive bilateral free trade agreement and had directed their trade ministers to initiate the preparatory work and report back before the two presidents met again in December. President Bush agreed.

In accordance with the plan, when the two presidents met June 10–11, 1990, they strongly endorsed a comprehensive bilateral free trade agreement between Mexico and the United States and directed their trade ministers to begin work. Jaime Serra and I met to talk about our "preparatory plans." I met with key members of Congress to discuss whether we might proceed in August. Chairman Rostenkowski and Representative Archer of the House Ways and Means Committee expressed concerns that an August notification would distract attention from the Uruguay Round Multilateral Negotiations during the crucial autumn months, but both said they would leave the decision on timing up to the administration. Senator Bentsen, chairman of the Senate Finance Committee, also said that he would leave the timing up to the administration, and Senator Packwood said he supported early initiation. All strongly agreed that notification of our intent to launch the negotiations should occur when both houses of Congress were back in session in September.

As soon as word started circulating regarding the possibilities of the potential negotiations, I was contacted by John Crosbie, then trade minister of Canada, stating that Canada wanted to join the negotiations. I was frankly surprised. Canada's Liberal Party and its New Democratic party had strongly opposed the U.S./Canada Free Trade Agreement that had been signed January 2, 1988, and their opposition almost brought down Prime Minister Mulroney's Progressive government. I said: "John, are you sure you want to go through that ordeal again?" He said "We do not want to be left out."

Over the Labor Day holiday, Prime Minister Mulroney, who was a house guest of President Bush at his Kennebunkport home, made it clear that he wanted Canada to join the negotiations. After discussions with President Bush, I talked with Jaime Serra about Canada participating in the negotiations. We were both concerned that politics could again erupt in Canada, forcing it to pull out, with the possibility of killing ongoing negotiations. To cover that possibility, in September 1990 we three trade ministers—John Crosbie, Jaime Serra, and I—arranged to have dinner in New York, after which we issued a press release acknowledging that the three governments were planning to move ahead with negotiations of a free trade agreement for North America and stating, without singling out Canada, that if any one of the three participants pulled out of the negotiations, the other two would proceed.

President Salinas, in accordance with the plan, delayed his formal letter proposing negotiations from June 11 until August 21, 1990. President Bush responded on September 25, noting that Canada had expressed a desire to participate.

That same day, President Bush sent a notice to the chairmen of the Senate Finance and the House Ways and Means Committees regarding President Salinas's request (at that time we did not have a formal request from Canada), which started the sixty-legislative-day fast-track clock ticking on the bilateral negotiation. We figured our September notification would not affect the timing of negotiations, since there were relatively few legislative days remaining in the year. Also, we believed it could be argued that the sixty-day clock needed to be restarted in January with the beginning of the new Congress. We did not want or need a debate on process. We knew we would face considerable debate on content. We used the time to consult with both members of Congress and the private sector.

On February 5, 1991, Presidents Bush and Salinas, along with Canadian Prime Minister Brian Mulroney, announced their joint intention to seek a North American Free Trade Agreement, and on that date President Bush officially advised the chairmen of the House Ways and Means and the Senate Finance Committees of his desire to begin trilateral negotiations with Mexico and Canada for a North American Free Trade Agreement (NAFTA). Both committees held public hearings on the proposed negotiations that February.

On March 1, 1991, President Bush requested a two-year extension of fast track procedures to cover the NAFTA negotiations. There was considerable debate, but the June 1, 1991, deadline for disapproval came and went, which guaranteed that fast track procedures would be available. Later that month, negotiations were formally launched in Toronto with a meeting of the three trade ministers, along with members of the nineteen working groups.

Subsequent ministerial meetings were held in Seattle, Zacatecas, Chantilly, Montreal, Mexico City, Toronto, and Washington, D.C. In addition, a number of public hearings were held across the country. I led a delegation of twenty-six private sector representatives and eleven members of Congress to Mexico to meet with President Salinas and Jaime Serra. We were anxious to complete negotiations before the November 1992 elections. I provided President Bush with regular updates on our progress, often focused on a key issue that he could raise with President Salinas when they met.

Negotiations were intense. The final session took place in Washington, D.C., with the three trade ministers, Jaime Serra, Michael Wilson (who had replaced John Crosbie), and me, along with our deputies and key members of the various negotiating teams. We all committed not to leave until negotiations were completed, and at times they were quite heated. At one point, Michael Wilson abruptly left the room upset about an issue, and from the window we watched as he walked around the hotel grounds. That persuaded me that we needed a break. I called my staff and asked whether it would be possible for me to buy tickets for that evening to whatever was playing at the Kennedy Center. The answer came back that "the Kennedy Center is dark this evening." I asked "What is available? We need to cool things off." The response was "Why don't you consider going to Camden Yards? There is a great baseball game, and I am sure that a member on one of our advisory committees will gladly donate their box."

The suggestion had little appeal to me, but I asked Michael and Jaime if they would like to take a break and drive up to Baltimore and see a baseball game. Michael was hugely enthusiastic; Jaime was willing. It turned out the Toronto Blue Jays, Michael's hometown team, were playing the Baltimore Orioles. We arranged to get the tickets. I drove up with Jaime. Michael came in a separate car. We arrived at the box, which offered an informal dinner as we watched the game. Around the fourth inning, Jaime, who was a great soccer fan but definitely not a baseball fan, said to me, "Have we seen enough?" I looked at Michael, who was transfixed. I said, "Jaime, absolutely not! We have not had dessert, and look, Michael is relaxed!" So, we had dessert. As the sixth inning was underway, Jaime again asked if it was time to leave. I said, "We will go after this inning." I said to Michael, "Jaime is anxious to leave; are you ready?" Reluctantly, he said he was. We thanked our host, left the box, and were in the hallway when the crowd roared. People rush out screaming: "Wow, a triple play! I have never seen one!" I thought Michael was going to cry. I was fearful that all the brownie points we had earned during "our break" had just then evaporated!

But we returned to the negotiating table, and very late on the night of August 12, following a total of fourteen days of continuous negotiations, we stood up, and shook hands having reached a deal! We followed the time-line procedures required for fast track approval, and President Bush signed the agreement on December 8, 1992. In 1993, in a more bipartisan environment than exists today, the implementing bill was passed by a Democrat-controlled Congress, and the agreement took effect on January 1, 1994.

NAFTA'S HISTORIC ACCOMPLISHMENTS

The North American Free Trade Agreement was a first in so many ways:

- It was the first comprehensive free trade agreement to join a developing economy with highly developed economies.
- By linking the economies of Canada, Mexico, and the United States, it created a huge market, today accounting for roughly $22 trillion and 493 million consumers.
- It eliminated tariffs on all industrial products and almost all agricultural produces, save for a few with Canada.
- It was the first trade agreement to open up a broad range of services, including financial services and banking, and provide national treatment for cross-border service providers.
- It opened up the automotive, textile, and apparel markets between Mexico and the United States.
- It removed significant investment barriers, provided basic protections for North American investors, and created an effective dispute settlement mechanism to

ensure investors had access to neutral, third-party arbitration in cases of disagreements with a host government.
- It was the first trade agreement to establish enforceable protection for copyright, patent, trademarks, and trade secrets.

This expanded coverage provided a template for our future regional and bilateral trade agreements. It also set a powerful example globally, giving much-needed momentum to the Uruguay Round, the eighth round of multilateral trade negotiations that had been launched in 1986 in an effort to upgrade the General Agreement on Tariffs and Trade (the GATT), which dealt primarily with tariffs. The Uruguay Round negotiations had virtually collapsed in 1991. On April 14, 1994, four months after NAFTA took effect, the trade ministers from all 123 nations participating in the Uruguay Round met in Marrakesh; adopted many of the of new market-opening provisions contained in the just-completed NAFTA; and, importantly, created the World Trade Organization to enforce the new rules-based system governing international trade.

NAFTA'S IMPACT ON NORTH AMERICA

After a quarter century, how has NAFTA impacted North America? Without question all three economies have benefited. Today, 80 percent of world trade is conducted through global supply chains, and NAFTA has created one of the most vibrant. Specialization among the three NAFTA partners has boosted the region's productivity, making North America the most competitive region in the world.

Intraregional trade is up sixfold since the agreement's implementation. Today one-third of America's global trade is with its two NAFTA partners. In 2017, Canada was our top export destination for goods and Mexico was our second. The United States sells more goods to Mexico than to all the rest of Latin America combined. Indeed, we sell more goods to Mexico than to Germany, France, the United Kingdom, and the Netherlands combined. Some fourteen million U.S. jobs depend on our commercial relationships with Canada and Mexico.

We do not simply sell to each other; we make things together. Roughly 40 percent of what the United States imports from Mexico consists of U.S. content, and 25 percent of imports from Canada consist of U.S. content. The equivalent figures for China and Japan are 4 percent and 2 percent respectively.

In addition, Mexico is not only a vibrant trading partner, but also an effective export agent for the United States. It has free trade agreements with forty-five nations, including the European Union, more than twice the number that the United States has. Since Mexico's exports have high U.S. content, its exports provide the U.S. producers of that content with preferential access to markets where we have no trade agreement. In Mexico, NAFTA accelerated and locked in its ongoing economic reforms that helped reduce its public debt, stabilize inflation, and build up its foreign reserves. Its economy is far stronger today as a result of NAFTA.

The agreement also incentivized new habits of cooperation that have enabled the three nations to take full advantage of the new economic opportunities. The economic bonds that it created strengthened trust, encouraging the three governments to work together on broader issues. They began to share intelligence, which helped to expedite the cross-border movement of legitimate products and travel, which enabled greater concentration on illegitimate traffic. Collaboration also has made us more effective in responding to natural disasters and in reducing the reach of organized crime.

President Bush forty-one will be remembered for his many outstanding contributions, foreign and domestic, but NAFTA will surely be high on the list.

THE NEW NAFTA

It is decidedly in our shared interests to build on the vibrant commercial and security ties that President Bush led in creating with our northern and southern neighbors. But much has changed economically and technologically since NAFTA took effect twenty-five years ago. To take full advantage of new twenty-first-century opportunities, the agreement needed to be modernized.

An effort to upgrade and modernize NAFTA commenced in May 2017 in the belief that all three nations would benefit from agreeing to new rules governing issues like cross-border data flows, digital products, and e-commerce that did not exist in the early 1990s. Today broader protection of intellectual property to cover the enormous technological innovation that has occurred and continues to occur is essential to a growing twenty-first-century economy. The three governments have sought to deal with these and some other issues in the negotiations of the United States, Mexico, Canada Agreement (USMCA). These negotiations concluded in September 2018 and consist of thirty-four chapters and twelve side letters.

The Congressional Research Service report describes the agreement as making "notable changes to market access provisions for autos and agriculture products, and to rules such as investment, government procurement, and intellectual property rights (IPR). New issues such as digital trade, state-owned enterprises, and currency misalignment are also addressed."[4]

Considerable controversy arose with respect to USMCA on a number of issues, including the stiffer rules of origin that are proscribed for automobiles, the sharply reduced commitments to Investor State Dispute Settlement and government procurement, the sunset provision, and enforcement particularly of labor and environment provisions. Without question the USMCA provides for more "managed trade" than the "open trade" that President Bush strongly supported in NAFTA. Critics of the USMCA point out that it will impose costly regulatory burdens on our tightly connected supply chains, making them less efficient, less profitable, and less competitive. They also point out that the new rules dealing with labor, environment, and e-commerce are similar to those provisions in the Trans-Pacific Partnership (TPP), from which we withdrew. However, Canada and Mexico remain as members of TPP and currently apply its rules in many of those areas in connection with their trade with us.

Supporters of the USMCA, even those who are critical of some of its changes, believe that its adoption reduces the uncertainty that over the past three years has severely disrupted business planning regarding investment and trade with our northern and southern neighbors. They welcome the clarity regarding the rules that in the future will govern our trade and investment with our two largest trading partners. Some six hundred business organizations have made their support of the agreement clear.

The current administration secured overwhelming support for the USMCA in both houses of Congress. On December 19, 2019, the House of Representatives voted 385 to 41 to approve, and on January 16, 2020 the Senate voted 89 to 10 to approve it.

CONCLUSION

Although the USMCA that replaces NAFTA provides for more managed trade than free and open trade, President Bush was strongly in favor of building and maintaining vibrant economic and strategic relationships with both Canada and Mexico. He provided the leadership that not only enhanced both of those relationships, but also set an example of sound economic and trade policy for rest of the world. The principles he followed in supporting open markets and building strong global economic and strategic relationships are principles we need to implement as we move forward. We have all benefited enormously from the wisdom, thoughtfulness, and experience of our forty-first president.

NOTES

1. Caroline Tanner, "Presidential and Relatable Quotes, Including the Broccoli Ban," *USA Today*, December 3 2018, https://www.usatoday.com/story/news/politics/onpolitics/2018/12/01/george-h-w-bush-his-most-presidential-and-relatable-quotes/547365002/.

2. The original calculation was made in Payoff to America from Global Integration (2005) by Bradford Scott, Paul Grieco, and Gary Clyde Hufbauer of the Peterson Institute for International Economics. It was updated and confirmed by Gary Clyde Hufbauer and Zhiyao (Lucy) Lu in 2017 in a Policy Brief (17-16) published by the Peterson Institute for International Economics in May 2017. The policy brief is available at https://www.piie.com/publications/policy-briefs/payoff-america-globalization-fresh-look-focus-costs-workers.

3. William R. Cline, *Trade Policy and Global Poverty* (Washington, DC: Peterson Institute for International Economics, 2004).

4. Congressional Research Service, "U.S.-Mexico-Canada (USMCA) Trade Agreement," Updated January 30, 2020, https://crsreports.congress.gov/product/pdf/IF/IF10997.

13

President George H. W. Bush and the United Nations

Thomas R. Pickering

The centerpiece of President Bush's leadership at the United Nations was the role he played in the First Gulf War (August 1990 to April 1991). He was key in the strategy and actions leading up to and ending the conflict. He understood the UN, having served as ambassador in New York (March 1, 1971–January 18, 1973). He was personally engaged, along with Secretary of State James Baker and National Security Advisor Lieutenant General Brent Scowcroft. Bush's own book (with Scowcroft) reserves nearly half the text for Gulf War I, in which the United Nations figures prominently.[1] The Security Council, mired in the stasis of the Cold War for forty years, finally played the role for which it was designed.

A host of other issues were also dealt with (see sections 2 to 8 below).

1. GULF WAR I: "MIRACLE ON 45TH STREET"

There are events where you never forget where you were and what you were doing when they happened. Two remain deeply engraved in my memory in connection with George H. W. Bush and the United Nations.

In late November 1988, shortly after Bush's election, I was camping in the Egyptian desert with my wife on a short break from Israel, where I was then ambassador. An early wake-up by an Egyptian policeman let me know I urgently had to call the U.S. Embassy in Cairo. Three hours later, when we could make the connection, I found that Vice President Bush wanted to speak with me that afternoon. At a Russian-built hotel at an aluminum plant on the Nile at Nag Hammadi, I made that call. After three consecutive short and disconnected conversations with the vice president, I was pleased to accept his request to serve as his ambassador to the UN.[2]

Nearly two years later, on the evening of August 1, 1990, at the Carlisle Hotel in New York, my wife and I joined former assistant secretary of state Tom Enders and his wife, Gaetana, at a farewell dinner for my UK colleague Sir Crispin Tickell and his wife, Penelope. As we were winding down, I was summoned to the phone in the pantry of the hotel. Robert Kimmitt, undersecretary of state, was on the line: Iraq has invaded and taken over Kuwait. Call an immediate meeting of the UN Security Council in order to pass a mandatory resolution to make Iraq withdraw.

I called Romanian ambassador Munteanu, who hours before had just begun his first term as president of the Security Council as well as the UN Secretariat, to request an urgent meeting that evening. The Security Council is supposed to meet on an hour's notice. I next located the Kuwaiti ambassador, an old friend, at the Russian Tea Room, with the help of the twelve-year-old daughter of the Bahrain ambassador, who was giving him dinner there. He was shocked at the news and promised full cooperation.[3]

We met in New York shortly after midnight with a text quickly agreed among the key parties. UN Security Council Resolution 660, calling on Iraq to withdraw and threatening sanctions if it did not, was passed in the early hours of the morning. This began a process of carefully coordinated action by the Security Council, ending at the close of November with Resolution 678 authorizing "all necessary means" to expel Iraq from Kuwait.

1a. The Strategy

The UN Security Council was designed to act on short notice to meet threats to international peace and security. It was central to President Bush's thinking that he both needed and wanted the council to be a partner in dealing with Iraq's aggression. Sanctions came first; there was valid skepticism they might not work. The Security Council can pass mandatory resolutions on all member states. The council in 1990 included Yemen, representing the Arab world; Cuba; Malaysia; and Colombia, all of which were skeptical about taking tough action to end Iraqi aggression. The Soviet Union, fast approaching the end of communism, was represented temporarily by a helpful deputy; Secretary Baker was in Russia, then working closely with Foreign Minister Shevardnadze on a host of issues.[4] China was against anything resembling authority to use force. The United Kingdom and France were strong allies with the United States. Nonaligned skepticism and potential vetoes remained a challenge. The president and Secretary Baker followed developments closely, ready to lead and assist—the "dream team" of any American ambassador in New York.

Our strategy was to use the Security Council to put continuous, escalating pressure on Iraq and Saddam Hussein. My goal was to not let a day pass without having council members consider the challenge of Iraqi aggression. They needed to believe they were members of the most important club in the world! If I had to invent a reason for a next resolution, I was ready to do so. Saddam was a perfect enemy and always gave us reason to further tighten the screws.

Working relationships with Sir David (now Lord) Hannay who replaced Tickell, and Pierre Louis Blanc and later Jean Bernard Merimee of France were strong and productive. Almost before the final vote on a resolution we three could agree on the next step. The three of us would meet and, working with Washington and their capitals, quickly iron out a draft text.[5] Our next step in the resolution assembly line was to go to Russia and China. We almost always were able to quickly resolve textual differences.

The sixth veto in the Council belonged to the Non-Aligned Movement, since their collective seven votes could prevent the necessary nine votes out of a total of fifteen required for passage of a resolution. The United States insisted on the next stage—a private meeting between at least four of the five permanent members and the seven Non-Aligned ambassadors to present and review the text. The Soviet Union always joined us, while China hung back—council members knew that China would be with the other five. Our allies in the council were kept fully and permanently briefed and involved. Changes and suggested improvements were often accepted on the spot and, if not, very quickly by referral to capitals. We never took a resolution to a vote if we were not confident of getting a minimum nine positive votes. Some votes were unanimous or included at least twelve positive votes. Losing a resolution could have been fatal to the continuation of the process of escalating pressure on Iraq.[6]

1b. Security Council Action

This approach served us well in the council—from the passage of the first resolution, 660, on August 2, 1990, through the acceptance of Resolution 678 on November 29, 1990.[7] The Security Council during this period was exceptionally and continuously used as the framers of the 1945 Charter had intended. It moved from sanctions to the use of force—unifying the international community around blocking Iraq's aggression, seeking relief for those under Iraqi military occupation in Kuwait, countering Iraqi measures to tighten control over Kuwait, and ending by authorizing "all necessary means" to expel Iraq by force from Kuwait. The process was important in emphasizing to council members their responsibilities and thereby helping preserve its cohesion. The resolutions represented a deliberate, step-by-step process moving carefully to validating the use of force. The process was important in emphasizing to council members their responsibilities and thereby helping preserve its cohesion. The resolutions were a strong reason why otherwise reluctant Democratic senators joined in supporting a congressional joint resolution authorizing President Bush to send in U.S. forces.

Resolution 660 on August 2, 1990, demanded Iraq's immediate and unconditional withdrawal. Iraq publicly rejected the demand and unwisely turned down the resolution's call for a negotiating process to resolve their differences with Kuwait. On August 6, the council passed a sanctions resolution blocking trade with Iraq and occupied Kuwait, as well as banning military supply and financial movements or assistance. Iraq then claimed to annex Kuwait and the council stopped all outside support for that step with Resolution 662 on August 9. Iraq's next offense was to use foreigners as hostages and human shields. Resolution 664, on August 18, called for all such individuals' safety, freedom of movement, and consular access. It once again declared the annexation illegal and required Iraq to rescind orders closing diplomatic and consular missions in Kuwait.

Iraq contested the sanctions on trade by sending tankers down the Gulf in late August.[8] Two mini-crises emerged. The Pentagon wanted to immediately board the tankers and block their movements. Others believed a Security Council resolution authorizing that step would be required, a view which prevailed. Simultaneously, it quickly became clear that China might veto the resolution as contrary to its "principled position" opposing council authorization of the use of force. In close consultations with the Chinese ambassador, Li Dao Yu, we organized a solution. The resolution draft strictly avoided direct "use-of-force" euphemisms and said instead to "use such measures commensurate to the specific circumstances" to halt inward and outward shipping.[9] Second, China agreed not to veto the resolution if they could make a statement that they did not believe the resolution authorized the use of force—and no one spoke at the council against that. We, with the help of the president of the Security Council, arranged for China to speak last after the vote. While seemingly a small effort, it helped to prepare the Chinese for their later abstention on the use-of-force resolution (678).[10]

Resolution 666 dealt with the growing humanitarian crisis in Kuwait brought on by the Iraqi occupation and covered steps to try (without success) to deliver food and medical relief. Resolution 669 on September 24 addressed (also without success) the interests of Turkey and other countries damaged as a result of sanctions against Iraq, as provided for in Article 50 of the UN Charter. Resolution 670 on September 25 tightened restrictions for all states on aircraft flights and overflights that were not being used for humanitarian relief to and from Iraq and occupied Kuwait. It also called on all states to detain Iraqi ships entering their ports.

Complications arose in October 1990, when Israeli police intervened in violence against Israeli worshippers at the Western Wall by Palestinians, leading to twenty Palestinians being killed and 150 injured.[11] Saddam claimed his occupation of Kuwait was only the first step to liberate Jerusalem. In this sensitive period leading up to the presentation of a use-of-force resolution at the end of November, a diversion over Israeli action would have severely threatened a successful outcome. The council members wanted to take some action as a result of the deaths. A carefully crafted resolution (672 of October 12) expressed alarm at the violence and condemned Israeli security forces for it, called on Israel as the occupying power to abide by its legal obligations, and requested the secretary-general to send a mission and to report the results. Supported unanimously, the resolution dodged the bullet but raised deep concerns among Israeli supporters in the U.S. public because of its criticism of Israel. The Israelis refused to accept the resolution.

A second resolution by the Security Council urged a changed Israeli position without success. But the issue simmered with further problems in mid- and late November in Jerusalem. With a council clearly churning with differences over whether again to consider the Israel issue, I, as president of the council, held an informal meeting to consider the question. We had run out of options. I told members of the council it was a make-or-break point in dealing with Iraq. Unsolicited and unexpectedly, my Soviet colleague, Ambassador Yuli Vorontsov, asked for the floor and strongly supported my view. A consensus quickly emerged; members of the council would not break ranks to relax pressures on Iraq despite serious differences over Israeli action,[12] which had opened the door to Saddam in his efforts to divide and defeat the work of the council over differences with Israel at the Temple Mount.

On October 29, the Security Council further attempted to oppose Iraqi hostage taking and harsh steps in occupied Kuwait. It again provided for humanitarian relief. Resolution 674 was the most extensive text on humanitarian issues. On November 28, a more technical resolution was passed covering Iraqi efforts to sequester and destroy civil records in Kuwait (677).

For several months, strenuous efforts led by the United States prepared a use-of-force resolution.[13] President Bush played a strong personal role through extensive personal telephone calls with foreign leaders, especially of member states of the Security Council, and Secretary Baker devoted an extraordinary amount of time, travel, and effort to craft a use-of-force resolution and ensure its success. He met every Security Council member state's foreign minister. He chaired the Security Council meeting on the subject on November 29, 1990, accompanied by many other foreign ministers. The resolution was simple and straightforward: "Acting under Chapter VII of the Charter" (a mandatory resolution) the council demanded that Iraq comply with all the existing, relevant resolutions and offered until January 15, 1991 for their full implementation. It authorized member states of the UN cooperating with Kuwait to use "all necessary means" to uphold and implement those resolutions and to restore international peace and security to the area.[14]

The resolution passed with thirteen favorable votes; Cuba and Yemen opposed it and China abstained.

After the vote, Secretary Baker announced he was open to meeting with Iraq before the January 15 deadline. A meeting between Baker and Tariq Aziz, the Iraqi foreign minister, took place in Geneva in mid-December without success. In parallel, Cuba, Colombia, Malaysia, and Yemen also sought a negotiating opening, which Iraq refused. UN Secretary-General Javier Pérez de Cuéllar traveled to meet Saddam in Baghdad in December, but without productive results. Since Iraq failed to comply with the resolutions, armed conflict began on the night of January 17, 1991, with air attacks. This was followed in March with a three-day ground offensive. These terminated with the United States and our allies' military contacts with Iraqi military representatives at Safwan airbase in southern Iraq at the beginning of April to arrange for a complete, unconditional Iraqi withdrawal from Kuwait.

1c. The UN and War Termination

War prosecution is an American forte; war termination has a mixed record. Strategically, President Bush and his team were correct in halting the fighting. Going on to Baghdad was seen by many as a losing proposition. Saddam had been expelled and paid a serious price for his invasion of Kuwait. Some, perhaps with less experience in the Middle East and with more a sense of hope than reality, expected him to be overthrown, killed, or expelled as a result of his failure in Kuwait. Others argued we should go on to Baghdad. There were good practical, political, and legal reasons why this would have been a bad choice.

First, a significant amount of Saddam's Republican Guard and other forces survived Kuwait and retreated with at least a portion of their arms in hand and intact.

Second, the problems we experienced in our 2003 invasion were sensed if not fully anticipated. In 1991, we expected stiffer opposition in Kuwait than we received. Were we then to go on to Baghdad, we expected nasty urban combat. In 2003, all this came true; we had not foreseen the demands on an American and Allied occupying force, the challenges of widespread urban guerilla warfare, and the increasing disaffection of a population under occupation with little to relieve their hunger and adversity and much to equip them to combat that occupation. In 2003, up to two hundred thousand Iraqi soldiers had been released into a country with few jobs, with weapons in their hands, and with training on how to use those weapons. Politically, we were not equipped to deal with the occupation or to construct a successful Iraqi governing structure. This was especially true against the backdrop of the complex divisions and antagonisms that were inherent in Iraq in both 1991 and 2003.

Finally, in 1990 and 1991, the Security Council mandate was to expel Iraq from Kuwait. Some farsighted international lawyers added in Resolution 678 the words: "to preserve peace and security in the area," but that was not what our friends and allies had then joined us to do.

What was possible, and unfortunately missed, was a more robust UN presence on the ground in western Iraq after the 1991 conflict. As early as December 1990, the U.S. Mission to the United Nations proposed, in connection with the potential for negotiations, the creation of a series of zones of limited armament in Iraq. This would begin with a two-hundred-plus-kilometer area in southwestern Iraq, bordering on the populated areas of Anbar Province, free of all Iraqi forces and monitored by the UN. Successive zones would include those limited in armor, artillery, air defense and, so on. A no-fly-zone would have been a clear advantage. These ideas were resurrected in April 1991, at the time of the first Safwan meeting, but came to naught because of U.S. military determination to cease further involvement and bring the troops home.[15] Meanwhile, consultations in New York had indicated a willingness on the part of France and the United Kingdom to consider keeping ground forces under UN auspices in the Iraqi evacuated zone.

In parallel, an unexpected French-sponsored initiative was successful in Resolution 688 (below) in providing a safe zone for the Kurds in northeastern Iraq. This move would have complemented and reinforced the proposed but rejected idea of a western zone. Instead, with Resolution 687 we ended up with an insufficient ten-kilometer UN zone in Iraq on the Kuwait border.

1d. The Mother of All Resolutions 687

Critically, the UN Security Council, for the first and only time in history, produced a mandatory resolution setting out the terms to end a conflict. Iraq was defeated. Turning that into a set of proposals required careful thought and extensive work both in capitals and in New York. A wide variety of issues had to be addressed. Although never publicly discussed, at the suggestion of the U.S. Mission to the UN, Secretary Baker authorized the establishment of a confidential diplomatic channel with Iraq using Ambassador al Anbari, the Iraqi permanent representative in New York, on the same day we began military-to-military conversations at Safwan. The United Kingdom and France participated in some of the meetings. The channel operated for half a year or more. During its lifetime, it allowed the delivery of very tough and demanding messages to Saddam, which were responded to rapidly and complied with. They included important support for the work of the UN Commission dealing with Iraqi weapons of mass destruction—UNSCOM.

Resolution 687, terminating the war, was adopted on April 3, 1991, after having been negotiated over the preceding days, in nine sections. It received twelve votes in favor, with Cuba voting against and China, Ecuador, and Yemen abstaining. It was a mandatory resolution. It included a long and complex set of nonbinding preambular considerations important for setting up its conclusions.[16] The substantive portion of the resolution began by reaffirming all thirteen previous resolutions applied to Iraq.

Section A of the resolution dealt with the recognized boundary between Iraq and Kuwait, calling on the UN secretary-general to assist in demarcating the frontier with the resolution guaranteeing its inviolability.

Section B set up a monitoring mechanism for the Kawr 'Abd Allah (the waterway between the Gulf and Basra, Iraq), established a demilitarized zone on the border, and requested a monitoring plan from the UN secretary-general.

Section C told Iraq unconditionally to destroy, remove, or render harmless all chemical and biological weapons and related facilities, and all ballistic missiles with a range over 150 kilometers. Iraq had to reveal the locations of those weapons and related facilities and open them to a commission of the UN for regular and continuing inspection. Iraq had to agree not to develop nuclear weapons or related manufacturing facilities, provide the location of any such facilities and remain open for nuclear inspections.

In section D Iraq was to facilitate the return of all seized Kuwaiti property.

Section E held Iraq financially responsible for all loss, damage, or injury to foreign governments and individuals as a result of its invasion of Kuwait—while setting up a UN-administered compensation fund using oil income to pay claims.

Section F provided for continuation of sanctions, except for humanitarian and medical items, with those restrictions to remain in force until Iraq complied fully with all related UNSC resolutions. In the meantime, restrictions on arms transfers and technology were to remain in place.

Section G provided for the repatriation of Kuwait nationals by the Red Cross and required Iraqi cooperation.

Section H required Iraq to refrain from any act of international terrorism.

When Iraq notified the UN secretary-general of its acceptance of all the provisions of Resolution 687, a formal cease-fire would be in effect.

Iraq had nothing to say about the peace arrangements. It formally accepted the resolution.

Strict constructionists might well argue that the UN Security Council in this instance went beyond its charter mandate to deal with threats to international peace and security. However, its champions argue that the requirement to end the conflict and keep it ended was part of an acceptable scope of work for the council. The Bush administration led the work to put in place a set of arrangements it had reason to believe would prevent the conflict from recurring. It was not a perfect arrangement. Over time, parts of it broke down. (The Security Council permanent member unity was badly frayed in 1998, when China, France, and Russia abstained in a vote about replacing the UN disarmament mission UNSCOM with a more capable successor UNMOVIC, an action that sent Saddam the message that the P-5, was no longer united over Iraq).

The final act of the immediate phase of the conflict was the Security Council's vote to accept Resolution 688 on the Kurdish situation in Iraq on April 5. It received ten positive votes, with Cuba, Yemen, and Zimbabwe opposed and China and India abstaining. Inspired in large measure by Danielle Mitterrand, the wife of French president François Mitterrand, and her close and continuing connection with the Kurdish population of northeastern Iraq, the resolution demanded an immediate end to Iraqi action against the Kurds and set up a mechanism to monitor the situation. It led to the end of Baghdad's presence in the region and the development of Kurdish autonomy at a time when Saddam was at his weakest. Iraq's Arab majority never recovered in terms of a presence and influence in northeastern Iraq. The long years of Kurdish de facto autonomy have not resolved differences with Iraqi Arabs or with Turkey. At the same time, the recruitment of Kurdish fighters played a salient role in opposing the Islamic state and its forces from 2015 to 2019. Fundamental internal differences among Kurdish leaders and groups have never been fully reconciled. Through U.S. and other presences, the Kurdish regional authority has become a key player and has influenced the outcome of postwar Iraq in significant ways.

1e. Conclusions

The Bush administration's action in the Security Council was a success.

A careful strategy of building cooperation and keeping a constant focus on Iraq in the Security Council maintained solidarity, despite rifts and differences. A strong team at the U.S. Mission to the UN made success possible, and the personal leadership of President Bush and Secretary Baker made a major difference on key Security Council actions, especially in gaining approval of Resolution 678 authorizing the use of force to liberate Kuwait. The Security Council action built U.S. congressional and public support, brought allies into the coalition, and helped raise international funds to finance the effort.

In addition, keeping the door specifically open to diplomacy before the commencement and after the termination of armed conflict added an important dimension. It helped to persuade the international community that support for the Security Council action was an acceptable and necessary approach. It made clear that efforts to exhaust all other methods were being made before turning to force (despite some differences over the timing of moving to this option). It illustrated the often-overlooked truth that armed conflicts end through political arrangements, which must be shaped by the parties concerned, whether by a diktat, negotiations, or in a Security Council decision.

The war achieved positive results with minimal U.S. personnel losses. Had the military conflict been more costly, as envisaged by many planners, the arguments for continuing sanctions and deferring combat would have been more prescient. The president accepted that risk and won. Clear Security Council objectives in Resolution 678 helped agreement to President Bush's decision for the United States not to go to Baghdad in 1991. The U.S. strategy on war termination suffered from failures to exploit more opportunities to confine Iraq and Saddam, and from too little advanced planning.

In the Iraq-Kuwait context, the Security Council came closest to achieving its 1945 specified role to deal with threats to international peace and security.

The Security Council will only be effective in U.S. foreign policy interests if we are prepared to convince its members, and especially the five permanent members of the Security Council (otherwise known as the "P-5": the United States, France, United Kingdom, Russia [formerly the Soviet Union], and China), of the common benefit of engaging it in the effort to deal with major challenges to international peace and security through sanctions and other pressures, up to and including the authorized use of force as a final resort. Personal relationships and common commitment help to define successful diplomacy within the Security Council and shape a common appreciation of shared state interests if carefully managed and led.

Coalitions of the willing, rather than established peacemaking and peacekeeping forces, may be a better way of dealing with international challenges involving the use of force by the Security Council.

The council's success in dealing with Iraq emboldened it but led it to forget the reasons for that success and thus to act in Somalia and in the breakup of Yugoslavia in ways that failed to understand or properly define either the end goals or the disadvantage of proceeding without a clear commitment by member states to support both sanctions and diplomacy and, as a last resort, the use of force.

2. REPEAL OF "ZIONISM IS RACISM" RESOLUTION

During the height of the Cold War, the Soviet Union singled out Zionism to seek friends and allies among the Muslim members of the nonaligned group, pressure

Israel, isolate the United States, and expand Soviet influence. Begun in the 1960s, this culminated on November 10, 1975, with the passage of UN General Assembly Resolution 3379 equating Zionism with racism. This was supported by seventy-two states, with thirty-five against and thirty-two abstaining. It was repeated frequently, with strong majorities, to the point where it had become seen as unstoppable. A speech by President George H. W. Bush to the UN General Assembly on September 23, 1991, calling for its repeal, sparked action by Israel in the U.S. Congress and helped to overturn the resolution.[17]

President Bush followed the speech by sending instructions to all U.S. ambassadors directing them to make a major effort to secure votes at the UN to undo the resolution. By September 1990, our New York UN polling indicated a fifty-fifty split among members. The strategy included hard work around the world and at the UN, and a strategic decision to introduce the revocation only when we had enough cosponsors to assure repeal. The resolution was a single brief sentence: "The General Assembly decides to revoke the determination contained in its resolution 3379 (1975) of 10 November 1975." The vote on the repeal resolution took place on December 16, 1991, and was supported by 111 states, including 90 cosponsors. Coming after the Gulf War and following the decline of communism (and almost on the eve the dissolution of the USSR on December 26, 1991), the vote represented a new way of thinking and acting at the UN.

Out of concern that Resolution 3379 itself had been damaging enough, we worked quietly with key Arab states to convince them not to make statements following the vote. A large number did not, and many were not present for the vote. We asked the then-foreign minister of Israel, David Levy, to exercise care to avoid further polarization in his speech (delivered in French), which he did.

Chaim Herzog, who had been the permanent representative in New York in 1975 at the time of passage of 3379, publicly tore the text in half at the podium of the General Assembly. In 1991, I had the pleasure of sending him the text with a short, handwritten note on the UN official paper saying: "Dear Mr. President: This one is not for tearing."[18]

3. NEGOTIATION OF AN EL SALVADOR PEACE AGREEMENT

President George H. W. Bush and Secretary Jim Baker made a decision at the beginning of the administration to end civil wars throughout Central America. The El Salvador conflict lasted through the eighties, pitting the Farabundo Marti Front for National Liberation (FMLN) against a series of governments appointed and elected after the military-led reforms of 1982.[19] An agreement ending the conflict was developed in 1990 and 1991 through UN mediation led by Alvaro De Soto, a deeply experienced Peruvian diplomat working closely for Secretary-General Javier

Pérez de Cuéllar. The agreement saw creation of a cease-fire, disarming of the FMLN and its integration into the democratic political process, demobilization of three government-armed police groups, and the establishment of UN training for a new police force. The negotiations were long and difficult. Their final stages took place in New York over the last half of 1991. The president of El Salvador, Freddie Christiani, led the government team's negotiations with leaders of the FMLN. The initialing of a final text took place in New York very early on New Year's Day 1992, with the secretary-general stopping the clock on his official departure from office to complete the process. After the initialing, the permanent representative of Mexico invited me to meet confidentially the FMLN leadership. It was an unusual talk, focusing wisely on the future of the country and their role in it.[20]

Normally, in UN-brokered negotiations, the U.S. Mission plays a logistical and process-related role. With El Salvador it was larger and more substantive. The United States had been involved in supporting anti-communist causes in Central America and the Bush administration had the leverage directly to end the civil war and bring about democratic elections. I had served for two years as ambassador to El Salvador, and my principal deputy, Alexander Watson, was a Latin American expert. Bernard Aronson, the assistant secretary for Inter-American Affairs, encouraged us to support directly the process. We focused on FMLN contacts and on the government and President Christiani.[21] During early 1991, the secretary-general appointed, with U.S. support, a group of "friends" to assist in the process. They included Spain, Mexico, Venezuela, and Colombia. De Soto and his team ably pulled together the complex portions of an intricate negotiation following the major outlines set out above. The initialing was followed on June 12, 1992, by a full signing of what became known as the Chapultepec Peace Accord at the Chapultepec Palace in Mexico.[22]

4. INDEPENDENCE FOR NAMIBIA

Two decades of conflict involving South Africa, Cuba, the Soviet Union, Angola, the United States, and the South West Africa People's Organization (SWAPO) had led to a parallel track of diplomatic negotiations to end the conflict and secure independence for Namibia. U.S. Assistant Secretary of State Chester Crocker played the most influential role in the diplomacy for the United States. By 1988, no party felt a military solution was assured. The central diplomatic formula was to tie the withdrawal of Cuban troops from Angola with South African removal from Namibia, leading to its full independence. Three days after the U.S. election of President Bush, a Tripartite Accord set the terms of military withdrawals on both sides, based on UN Security Council Resolution 435. On December 20, UN Security Council Resolution 626 created a UN verification mission to monitor withdrawals, which was followed in February 1989 by creation through the Council of a United Nations Transition Assistance Group (UNTAG) to oversee implementation of the peace.

A dispute over the size of UNTAG delayed its full deployment, leaving insufficient forces in place to monitor the movement of Namibian independence fighters and the South Africans who were to be confined to bases on April 1, 1989. The Namibians, many of whom were part-time fighters, returned under the cloak of being refugees. Significant Namibian forces were also gathering eight kilometers north of the border. On the morning of April 1, those forces crossed the border from Angola. The UN special representative, Martti Ahtisaari, and his military commander were informed and in the absence of the advance abating, Ahtisaari lifted restrictions on South African deployments. The advancing forces were pushed back over the border, with losses on both sides. The parties accepted a declaration by the UN that the fundamental agreements remained in effect. Namibian insurgents remaining across the border turned themselves in at UNTAG-supervised assembly points. The United States strongly supported these efforts both in the Security Council and on the ground. By the end of April, all advancing forces had been relocated north of the border.[23]

General elections were held in November of 1989, with 57 percent of the voters under general franchise supporting SWAPO, and Namibia formally became independent on March 21, 1990.

5. END OF THE COLD WAR

A meeting on December 26, 1991, marked the end of the Soviet Union. Organized by Boris Yeltsin, then president of the Russian Federation, it brought together the leaders of the other republics, except for the three Baltic States that had already become independent. The meeting led to each republic recognizing the demise of the USSR and assuming sovereignty, independence, and territorial integrity.

Two questions were raised for the United Nations: Would Russia succeed to the Soviet seat on the Security Council? And would the Russian Federation require readmission to the UN? Each of the other republics required separate admission, except Ukraine and Belarus, which had been original members of the United Nations in 1945. With the Yeltsin meeting looming before the traditional Christmas and New Year's break in New York, we organized quiet meetings with the Soviet Mission and U.S. international lawyers from the State Department.[24]

The Security Council membership issue was resolved by suggesting that the UN Secretariat remove the sign for the USSR and replace it with one reading Russian Federation. This was not opposed in the organization.

By that step, the Russian Federation's succession to the Soviet Union as a member of the UN was assured. All of the other constituent republics of the former Soviet Union who were not already part of the UN were approved as they applied as new members states (as required by the UN Charter both in the Security Council and the General Assembly) through the end of July 1992, again without objection.

6. CONFLICT IN PANAMA

Throughout 1989 and 1990, Panama and its president, Manuel Noriega, dominated previously quiet U.S.–Panama relations. Noriega, though a paid source for the CIA, also engaged in drug trafficking, effectively playing both sides of the street. Mistreatment of American citizens in Panama by both civilians and the military included severe beatings and several deaths. According to ballot counting in the precincts in an election early in 1990, the opposition candidate won by a 3-to-1 margin, but that was nullified in the final count. The United States had indicted Noriega for drug offenses in 1988. In return, Noriega threatened effective operation of the Panama Canal, guaranteed under the 1977 treaty.

In December 1989, President Bush, with the backing of the U.S. Congress, decided to invade using military plans prepared for the defense of the canal.[25]

The invasion lasted several weeks, with estimates of civilian casualties running from one hundred to three thousand, with a figure around five hundred generally accepted. Around twenty thousand Panamanians were dislocated as a result of urban fighting. U.S. losses were twenty-three killed and 325 wounded.

The seven nonaligned members of the Security Council supported a draft resolution calling for the immediate withdrawal of American forces. The United States opposed the text, claiming self-defense under Article 51 of the United Nations Charter to protect the thirty-five thousand Americans living in Panama. Several days of debate took place before a vote on the draft resolution. It garnered the necessary nine votes for passage but failed due to the negative votes of three permanent members of the Security Council—France, the United Kingdom, and the United States.

7. REPAIRING THE LAW OF THE SEA TREATY

Although the Law of the Sea Treaty was negotiated with full U.S. participation, it had been opposed by the Reagan administration because of perceived inadequacies in Part 11 of the treaty dealing with seabed mining.

A careful strategy was set out to open the door for change in close cooperation with the UN undersecretary-general charged with the issue, Satya Nandan. We began by signaling an interest in a modified treaty by abstaining on traditional Law of the Sea resolutions in the General Assembly, which we had previously opposed. The UN had meanwhile set up a "Friends of the Secretary-General Group" of Law of the Sea negotiators and senior officials from key countries to work with Nandan. Over time, the United States was welcomed into the discussions to negotiate a new protocol to the treaty covering the areas to which the Reagan administration had objected. Secretary Baker approved the approach and the renegotiated protocol was completed.[26]

Subsequently, the Clinton administration signed the protocol but was unable to convince enough Democrats on the Senate Foreign Relations Committee of the importance of the issue to obtain advice and consent to ratify the full, amended treaty. Despite being strongly favored by the Defense Department—especially the U.S. Navy—as well as mining and environmental groups, it remains unratified today.

8. PROMOTING UN REFORM

The Bush administration watched with interest the development by member states of ideas for improving UN governance. Retired undersecretary-general for political affairs, Sir Brian Urquhart, with an Irish colleague, produced a book in 1990–1991 covering the subject. Six permanent representatives—including the United States—joined in a luncheon to discuss the book, which created common interest in both further examining the ideas and seeing whether a group of like-minded states could help gain their acceptance.

Key reform ideas included the appointment of a deputy secretary-general, the creation of a more cabinet-like form of governance by convening the undersecretaries-general in regular meetings with the secretary-general, and efforts to hone and strengthen the UN budget and budget process.[27]

Successive meetings were arranged for informal discussion of the project, adding new members from among the states represented in New York. The original group asked Peter Wilenski, the highly capable Australian permanent representative, to chair the informal group. Some fifty-two states were participants when Boutros Boutros-Ghali, the newly elected secretary-general, arrived in New York in January 1992. Despite continuing and serious efforts by Wilenski and others, it was not possible to interest Boutros-Ghali in the ideas, and the reform effort did not prosper. However, Boutros-Ghali did propose two reform packages in 1992, and his successor, Kofi Annan, adopted many of the Wilenski group's ideas and incorporated them in a strong reform program which he instituted years later.[28]

NOTES

1. George Bush and Brent Scowcroft, *A World Transformed* (New York: Knopf, 1998), 345–518.
2. Personal recollection, Thomas R. Pickering, hereafter TRP.
3. Ibid.
4. Bush and Scowcroft, *A World Transformed*, 319.
5. TRP.
6. Ibid.
7. Bush and Scowcroft, *A World Transformed*, 314.
8. Ibid., 351.
9. For the full text of Resolution 665, see http://unscr.com/en/resolutions/665.
10. TRP.
11. Bush and Scowcroft, *A World Transformed*, 378.

12. TRP.

13. Bush and Scowcroft, *A World Transformed*, 400–404.

14. Ibid., 414–15. For the full text of Resolution 678, see http://unscr.com/en/resolu tions/678.

15. TRP.

16. For the full text of Resolution 687, see http://unscr.com/en/resolutions/687.

17. See Yohanon Manor, "The 1975 'Zionism Is Racism' Resolution: The Rise, Fall, and Resurgence of a Libel," *Jerusalem Center for Public Affairs*, May 2, 2010, https://jcpa.org/ article/the-1975-zionism-is-racism-resolution-the-rise-fall-and-resurgence-of-a-libel/.

18. TRP.

19. In December 1983, then Vice President Bush visited El Salvador at the request of the embassy to read the "riot act" to the military leadership to stop a wave of death squad killings in response to an FMLN offensive. He told the military leadership neither President Reagan nor he could stop the Congress from ending aid to El Salvador if they did not end the killings. It worked!

20. TRP.

21. TRP.

22. See Diana Villiers Negroponte, "Remembering El Salvador's Peace Accord: Why Was That Peace Elusive." The Brookings Institute, January 19, 2012, https://www.brookings.edu/ blog/up-front/2012/01/19/remembering-el-salvadors-peace-accord-why-was-that-peace-elu sive/.

23. See "The Namibian Struggle for Independence—1966–1990—a Historical Background," *South African History Online*, August 27, 2019, https://www.sahistory.org.za/article/ namibian-struggle-independence-1966-1990-historical-background.

24. TRP.

25. Paul Lewis, "Fighting in Panama: United Nations; Security Council Condemnation of Invasion Vetoed," *New York Times*, December 24, 1989, https://www.nytimes .com/1989/12/24/world/fighting-panama-united-nations-security-council-condemnation -invasion-vetoed.html.

26. TRP.

27. TRP.

28. TRP.

14

President George H. W. Bush and the Exercise of U.S. Power for Human Rights and Humanitarian Purposes

Nancy Bearg

There is but one just use of power, and it is to serve people.
—President George H. W. Bush Inaugural Address, January 20, 1989[1]

President George H. W. Bush's actions as leader of the free world were remarkable in many ways that have been recognized publicly, while many accomplishments have escaped public knowledge. His humanitarian and human rights record is little discussed but shines with purpose, leadership, innovation, and results. While much of the focus of his foreign policy concerned traditional diplomacy, human rights and humanitarian action became two building blocks for the new world order that the president and his administration sought to create as the old order was changing in the late 1980s and early '90s. True to form, President Bush did no chest beating, just steady work to strengthen the international system with U.S. leadership—and with great practicality and compassion.

As a former U.S. ambassador to the United Nations, President Bush well understood that human rights cuts across every category of human existence. His service in China and at the Central Intelligence Agency contributed to this knowledge and his instinct to protect human rights. Likewise, he knew that humanitarian issues, whether perpetrated by man or nature, demand attention and action. His deeply held American values further cemented his view that the United States had a leadership responsibility to guard against and respond to human rights and humanitarian violations in the international system. His extensive—and unique—knowledge of the United States' toolbox and the workings of the international system allowed him to act successfully many times during his presidency by lending U.S. leadership, prestige, resources, and sometimes troops to save lives, right wrongs, or strengthen the commitment of the world to give its citizens a fair shot.

Discussed here are eight situations illustrating that record. All of these provide much of the human-focused texture and deep understanding that shaped President Bush's approach to international relations and the international system at a time when events were moving on a large scale and dramatically. The situations herein are two crises involving Soviet and Vietnamese refugees, the UN World Summit for Children, revamping UN humanitarian relief coordination, U.S. ratification of a long-stalled human rights treaty, averting a bloodbath in Ethiopia and the rescue of Ethiopian Jews, and military-led humanitarian interventions for Iraqi Kurds and for Somalis. These events, plus signposts along the way, tell the story of U.S. policy development, support for existing and new institutions, and use of U.S. power for human rights and as humanitarian response, guided by Bush's steady hand and vision to build a different and new world order.

THE BEGINNING: U.S. POLICY TOWARD EASTERN EUROPE AND THE SOVIET UNION—LAYING THE GROUNDWORK

There is new ground to be broken and new action to be taken. . . . Great nations of the world are moving toward democracy through the door to freedom. . . . We know what works: Freedom works. We know what's right: Freedom is right. We know how to secure a more just and prosperous life for man on Earth: through free markets, free speech, free elections, and the exercise of free will unhampered by the state.

—President George H. W. Bush Inaugural Address, January 20, 1989[2]

In January 1989, change was fermenting in Eastern Europe, with some encouragement from Soviet leader Mikhail Gorbachev. In the Soviet Union, Gorbachev was undertaking fledgling reform efforts. To understand these winds of change and be ready with positive new policies, the newly sworn-in president ordered extensive policy reviews of key regions and issues. Through this effort and throughout the administration, Bush had the enormously competent Brent Scowcroft as his national security advisor to lead the interagency process.

In mid-April, the president started unveiling his foreign policy with a major speech in Hamtramck, Michigan, by welcoming and encouraging reform in Eastern and Central Europe and explicitly mentioning human rights: "While we want relations to improve, there are certain acts we will not condone or accept, behavior that can shift relations in the wrong direction—human rights abuses, technology theft, and hostile intelligence or foreign policy actions against us."[3] Though Hamtramck was mainly about Eastern Europe and a full speech would follow later on the Soviet Union, he said: "Let no one doubt the sincerity of the American people and their government in our desire to see reform succeed inside the Soviet Union. We welcome the changes that have taken place, and we will continue to encourage greater recognition of human rights, market incentives, and free elections."[4]

At Texas A&M in May, President Bush made human rights a key step in expectations for the Soviet Union to rejoin the community of nations. He spoke directly to Gorbachev, saying, "Dramatic events have already occurred in Moscow. We are impressed by limited but freely contested elections. We are impressed by a greater toleration of dissent. We are impressed by a new frankness about the Stalin era. Mr. Gorbachev, don't stop now!"[5]

In June 1989, as events galloped on, Hungary removed the barbed wire on its border with Austria. The world was beginning to see walls literally and figuratively crumble in Eastern Europe and freedom continue to grow. In November, the iconic symbol of repression in the Cold War—the Berlin Wall—came down, and people rushed through to their freedom and a better chance at human rights and the exercise of free will that Bush had referenced in his inaugural address. The Cold War would continue to wind down over the next two years. Also, during 1989, as the Bush administration shaped its policies for a new era, two major refugee crises played out that required human rights and humanitarian responses, with new policies and processes.

CASE 1: SOVIET EMIGRATION

Everyone has the right to leave any country, including his own, and to return to his country. Everyone has the right to seek and to enjoy in other countries asylum from persecution.

—Articles 13 and 14, *Universal Declaration of Human Rights*,
UN, December 1948[6]

Prophetically, George H. W. Bush had raised human rights the first time he met Gorbachev, in 1985 when Bush was vice president. Gorbachev's response, after a pithy comment on U.S. human rights, had been to suggest that the two sides be prepared to "think it over" and appoint rapporteurs to discuss it.[7] Bush had seen this as a harbinger of openness to discussion. Their relationship had developed well from there, and promise was in the air. Now, in 1989, one of the signs of change in the Soviet Union was a positive human rights move. Gorbachev had liberalized restrictions on emigration of Jews, Pentecostals, Armenians, and ethnic Germans, causing thousands to seek refuge in the United States and Israel. The process had gotten messy logistically, and the Bush administration needed to respond in ways that encouraged Gorbachev to continue the new policy and allow as many people as possible to take advantage of the rare opening to freedom.

In May, at Texas A&M, Bush addressed this issue publicly: "Why not, then, let this spirit of openness grow, let more barriers come down. Open emigration, open debate, open airwaves. . . . Let the 19,000 Soviet Jews who emigrated last year be followed by any number who wish to emigrate this year. And when people apply for exit visas, let there be no harassment against them. Let openness come to mean nothing less than the free exchange of people and books and ideas between East and West."[8]

The problem, though, required more than exhortation to the Soviet leader. The process from Moscow required departees to declare Israel as the destination but did not allow direct flights to Israel. En route to Israel through Europe, many would "drop out" in Vienna or Italy to apply for entry to the United States, as that was the preferred destination. The United States accepted all the Soviets who wanted to come; but as the numbers of those allowed to emigrate grew, the broad definition of "refugee" began to tighten, and some were refused and instead offered public interest parole status to enter. Many, however, did not want parole because it meant less resource support in the United States. In March 1989, a refugee supplemental had been requested due to the increased numbers, and the intention was set to raise the refugee ceiling.[9]

By July 1989, seventeen thousand Soviets (Jews and Pentecostals) had piled up in Italy in chaotic conditions. With the numbers growing (thirty thousand in the pipeline by late fall and more later), the Italians complained vociferously. Large backlogs existed in Moscow (forty thousand by October) and Vienna as well. Pressure mounted from Italy, the American Jewish community, and the U.S. Congress for a faster process and larger numbers that could come into the United States under the cap, as well as an orderly process to get people to Israel.

The Bush administration responded with extensive planning, creativity, and consultations led by the State Department and White House. The administration reached consensus with the congressional committees and the Jewish community. The major change was that Soviets would no longer qualify automatically as refugees with the right to enter the United States. To accommodate the expected increased outflow of the Cold War thaw, more would have to go to Israel rather than have the freedom of choice to go to the United States.

The new policy was multipronged, groundbreaking, humanitarian, and successful.

It is outlined in National Security Directive 27 with the summary: "The effect of these decisions is a larger program and a generous, humane policy that will more rationally manage the growing number of Soviet emigrants applying for admission to the United States. The number of Soviet citizens we are prepared to take into the United States will increase in FY 1990, the backlog of refugees to be processed through Rome will be eliminated, Soviet emigrants will be better able to decide whether to apply for admission to the United States or emigrate elsewhere, and refugee adjudications will be continued in Moscow after the Rome-Vienna pipeline closes, with emphasis on family reunification."[10]

Soviet admissions were to double and all Soviet refugee adjudication processes would take place in Moscow and in a new Washington Processing Center, which proved to be an excellent innovation for speed and efficiency. Family reunification cases would receive first priority for processing. Parole entries continued. The European backlog cleared up, with most going to the United States, and refugee processing began in Moscow in late 1990. The refugee ceiling stayed high in 1990 and for several years. The shift to Moscow and articulation of priority on family reunification created a massive immigration to Israel—four hundred thousand between 1989 and 1992—that had not been happening earlier.[11]

In June 1990 congressional testimony, Princeton Lyman, director of the Refugee Bureau at the State Department, addressed the changes on behalf of the administration:

> Years of steadfast insistence by the U.S. and other Western governments that the Soviet Union and other Eastern European countries meet international standards of human rights practices and eliminate their barriers to international travel and emigration are at last bearing fruit. We continue to believe that freedom to leave one's country and return to it is a basic human right. . . . Soviet Government travel and emigration practices have improved to the extent that today the sanctions against a Soviet citizen wishing to emigrate have almost disappeared. However, we are still waiting codification of these changes in the form of a new Soviet emigration law.[12]

Human rights and Soviet emigration stayed on the agenda. In December 1990, President Bush temporarily waived the 1974 Jackson-Vanik amendment (which barred access to official credit and credit guarantee programs to countries that restrict emigration) for agricultural commodities to help the Soviet authorities address food shortages. The White House fact sheet cited that three hundred sixty thousand Soviets were being allowed to emigrate in 1990, and assurances had been received that the liberalization would continue. The president kept the pressure on for human rights, however, stating at his press conference with Soviet Foreign Minister Eduard Shevardnadze, "While I've taken this step I still look forward to a passage of the Soviet emigration law codifying the generally excellent practices of the past year. And this then will permit us to make further progress toward the normalization of the U.S.-Soviet economic relationship."[13] Subsequently, in May 1991, the Soviets passed their emigration law, and later that year President Bush sent a U.S.–Soviet trade agreement to Congress for ratification, which included most-favored-nation status.

One could argue that Bush took a hard line on linking emigration to trade because of strong congressional sentiment on Jewish emigration and to remain faithful to the law. This human rights emphasis, however, had been a theme emanating sincerely from the president from the beginning of the administration (and before). The administration had dealt with the situation compassionately and practically, managing the flows while also acknowledging that fear of persecution could no longer be applied to everyone leaving the Soviet Union and thus all could not qualify as refugees.

CASE 2: VIETNAMESE REFUGEES AND REEDUCATION CAMP PRISONERS

We must, first of all, unequivocally reaffirm the practice of first asylum, thereby safeguarding the protection and humane treatment of all those who seek asylum.

—U.S. Deputy Secretary of State Lawrence S. Eagleburger[14]

Simultaneously with the Jewish refugee situation, a crisis had been brewing in Southeast Asia, where tens of thousands of Vietnamese refugees ("boat people") had been living for years in camps. They had fled Vietnam in the months and years after North Vietnam defeated South Vietnam and its ally, the United States, and united the country. The United States felt a moral obligation to the refugees, as well as a human rights interest in them and all the citizens of Vietnam, where the government was denying rights and freedoms and keeping large numbers in "reeducation camp" prisons. Since 1975, over one and a half million Vietnamese, Cambodians, and Laotians had been resettled in third countries; the United States had taken nine hundred thousand. The outflow continued.

By 1989, arrangements put in place in 1979 for the refugees proved inadequate. On top of the thousands already in the camps, over ninety-six thousand new boat people landed on the shores of the first-asylum countries of Malaysia, Thailand, Hong Kong, Indonesia, and the Philippines in the first six months of 1989. The overburdened, frustrated first-asylum countries had grown restive with the high numbers coming out of Vietnam and the "longstayers." The United Nations High Commissioner for Refugees (UNHCR) believed it was time to involuntarily repatriate the boat people from the camps to Vietnam. The United States strongly opposed this move but did realize that new rules and a new system had to be set up to save first asylum and recognized that not all the Vietnamese fleeing Vietnam were political refugees.

Working together, the asylum countries, UNHCR, resettlement countries (with strong U.S. participation), Vietnam, and NGOs constructed the Comprehensive Plan of Action (CPA). It was agreed to at the International Conference on Indochinese Refugees, held in June 1989. The CPA preserved first asylum, promised resettlement of the longstayers and all refugees, and set a cut-off date of arrival for asylum seekers to be guaranteed refugee status. All who arrived after the cut-off date would be adjudicated, and they would be returned to the country of origin if they were deemed to be migrants rather than refugees, with UNHCR monitoring their safety. Vietnam would stem mass departure and increase the speed and numbers of legal departures in the Orderly Departure Program (ODP). Involuntary repatriation would be staved off.[15]

Staving off involuntary repatriation while allowing voluntary repatriation was a major achievement. Significantly, in agreeing to the CPA, the United States concurred that not all Vietnamese were refugees fleeing persecution by a communist country, as also was the case with the Soviet emigration, but all received adjudication. The CPA protected first asylum—asylum seekers could not be turned away at sea or forcibly returned to Vietnam, though they were strongly encouraged to return. The United States believed it was a fair policy that would save lives. Indeed, asylum seekers who returned to Vietnam were assisted and closely monitored and not harassed by their government.

U.S. Deputy Secretary of State Eagleburger's statement at the CPA conference gave support and tied it all together with U.S. policy, processes, and principles. He included the statement, "And, we will continue to defend the human rights of individuals who seek asylum, whether or not they are found to be refugees."[16] In spite of the CPA, in July the situation deteriorated further, with slow resettlement and more arrivals. Malaysia had begun pushbacks. Congress, in particular, and the NGO community were vocal and concerned, with letters and hearings. At a conference in Southeast Asia, Secretary of State Baker reaffirmed the U.S. commitment to the CPA and promised higher numbers of admissions to the United States. The Asian parties recommitted to the CPA.

In the first year after the CPA was signed, 70 percent of the boat people in camps had been processed, Vietnam was cooperating in the expanded Orderly Departure Program, and the United States had doubled its Southeast Asia admissions. Overall arrivals in first asylum countries were down by 25 percent but higher in some places and lower in others, and most first asylum nations were allowing safe landing for asylum seekers.[17] For the United States, this human rights and humanitarian problem also included reeducation camp prisoners—really political prisoners—many of whom had worked with the United States during the war. The United States wanted them all released and was willing to take them all. The commitment was in Eagleburger's 1989 CPA speech; and it was helpful that the United States and Vietnam had signed an agreement on resettlement of reeducation camp prisoners. The first groups reached the United States in January 1990, and all had been released by 1992.

For the United States, these humanitarian and human rights issues were related to normalization of relations with Vietnam, which had not yet occurred. The United States had leverage and would use it over the next several years to encourage change in Vietnam. The April 1991 U.S. "roadmap" for normalization covered accounting for prisoners of war and missing in action (POW/MIA) and other humanitarian issues, which meant resettlement of prisoners and refugee matters. Progress along the way resulted in gradual lifting of sanctions for Vietnam. May 1992 saw President Bush declaring, after a breakthrough agreement on U.S. access to POW/MIA records negotiated by General Jack Vessey, Senator John Kerry, and Senator John McCain, "And today, finally, I am convinced that we can begin writing the last chapter of the Vietnam War."[18] More liberalization on trade followed, and normalization was completed in the next administration.

Again, the Bush administration had used the leverage of trade, aid, and normalization to get movement on human rights, as with Soviet Union emigration. Significantly too, the administration and international community agreed to protect first asylum and adjudicate Southeast Asian asylum seekers, recognizing that many asylum seekers were economic migrants rather than political refugees. Processes were sped up, with a plan that worked for U.S. goals and values within an international agreement.

CASE 3: WORLD SUMMIT FOR CHILDREN

We've seen children—swollen bellies—we've seen the pleading eyes of starvation, we've heard the cries of children dying of disease. So let us affirm in this historic summit that these children can be saved. They can be saved when we live up to our responsibilities, not just as an assembly of governments, but as a world community of adults, of parents. . . . Saving one child is a miracle. As world leaders, we can realize such miracles, and then we can count them in millions.

—President George H. W. Bush, September 30, 1990[19]

UNICEF's executive director, James Grant, had a vision for a UN summit of world leaders to bring attention and commitment to the needs of children globally and to enlist each country in pointed planning to better the lives of their children. Canadian prime minister Brian Mulroney and others pushed it along. It was a long shot, though, to get leaders to travel from all over the globe for such a topic, especially as commitments to actions would be required. Would they come? What would draw them?

The statistics were compelling. Forty thousand children were dying from malnutrition and disease every day. Children were suffering from danger, poverty, illiteracy, hunger, discrimination, abuse, and loss of home as refugees and displaced persons. The Convention on the Rights of the Child had passed unanimously in the UN General Assembly the previous year—a landmark human rights treaty that defined childhood (up to age eighteen) and recognized children's social, economic, political, civil, and cultural rights. This summit could further solidify commitments to children's protection and well-being.

Some in the Bush administration advocated that President Bush attend; others argued against it, saying it was not an effort worthy of the president. President Bush stepped up and demonstrated the humanity and breadth of his leadership and American leadership by committing to attend. Without him, it is likely that the gathering would have taken place with delegations led by foreign or health ministers instead of scores of world leaders with the clout to move the issues. The Swedish ambassador to the UN at the time, Jan Eliasson, said there was jubilation when Bush's planned attendance was announced: "I can't even tell you enough how important it was that the U.S. president respected the UN and the issue of children. His announced commitment to attend was a very important signal. The level was raised by his commitment. It played an important role for the whole process."[20]

The World Summit for Children convened September 29–30, 1990, as the largest gathering of world leaders to date, with seventy-one heads of state and government and eighty-eight senior (mostly ministerial level) officials. The leaders adopted a Declaration on the Survival, Protection and Development of Children[21] and a Plan of Action[22] for implementing the declaration between 1990 and 2000, which included twenty-seven goals. It was front-page news in the *New York Times*, with an additional two pages of analysis, stories, and excerpts from leaders' remarks and the declaration. It was deemed an "extraordinary" event and raised hopes for momentum on addressing children's issues,[23] which did come, though haltingly and with fewer post–Cold War resources than hoped.

At the summit, President Bush delivered heartfelt remarks about the importance and plight of children around the globe and discussed U.S. commitment to them. He singled out key elements of U.S. national goals for children in education and health. He also sent a letter addressed to the World Summit for Children that referred to the timing as an opportune moment for unity in addressing the needs of three billion children. He forwarded the formal U.S. plan of action for children (and families) to the UN in late 1992, including comprehensive national plans and goals and international children's programs.

As for the Convention on the Rights of the Child—adopted thirty years ago at the United Nations—the United States did not ratify it then as a record number of countries did, signed it only in 1995, and has not yet ratified it. The United States is the only UN member country in the world that has not ratified this human rights treaty. It sits in the Senate, along with several others, unable to go forward because of long-held Republican views that these treaties conflict with self-government and the U.S. Constitution. President Bush, though, did succeed in getting a key human rights treaty ratified in 1992, as we will see in the section on case 7 below.

As for progress in the well-being of children around the world, in 2001 the UN secretary-general summarized results as mixed. He spoke of heightened attention and real progress, such as reduction in child mortality by three million deaths a year. Over 150 nations had submitted a plan of action and followed up with progress reports. But there was "slippage" and "unfinished business" and still much to do.[24] International goals specifically for children were a significant part of the UN Millennium Development Goals adopted in 2000, and children figure prominently in the Sustainable Development Goals for 2030. This focus on children was bound to happen eventually, but it can be said that the World Summit for Children—coming as the Cold War wound down (and hotter, smaller wars caught fire) with world-leader attendance led by President Bush—demonstrated that the world needed to and could devote more attention to human need and well-being, especially for children.

SIGNPOST: PERSIAN GULF WAR

While in New York for the World Summit for Children and to deliver his UN General Assembly speech, President Bush had other compelling business with world leaders. Iraq had invaded Kuwait in an aggressive move that could not stand in the post–Cold War world; President Bush was building international participation in a coalition to turn the Iraqis back. He held formal bilateral meetings with twenty-three leaders in New York between September 29 and October 1. As history shows, Saddam Hussein's forces were turned out of Kuwait in early 1991, supported by UN Security Council resolutions and international solidarity, including the Soviet Union. But in the aftermath a further commitment of U.S. power became necessary as Kurds, terrified by the wielding of remaining Iraqi military power, fled into the northern Iraqi mountains from their towns and villages.

CASE 4: RESCUING IRAQI KURDS— OPERATION PROVIDE COMFORT

We must build on the successes of Desert Storm to give new shape and momentum to this new world order, to use force wisely and extend the hand of compassion wherever we can.

—President George H. W. Bush, April 13, 1991[25]

With four hundred thousand desperate Iraqi Kurds in the mountains in early April 1991, UN Human Rights Commissioner Ogata declared that they would be treated as refugees in their own country rather than a country of first asylum—a first for the internally displaced of the world. Since the UN and UNHCR had insufficient capability to reach them with relief, it was agreed that the U.S. military would mount a humanitarian operation under UN auspices with the necessary Chapter VII authority.[26] This precedent-setting intervention saved the Kurds and brought them down from the mountains safely. At the same time, the international community established no-fly zones to protect the Kurds.

The U.S.-led relief operation was turned over to UNHCR and UN guards on June 9, with President Bush telling Mrs. Ogata the U.S. military could not stay on the ground indefinitely: "It is not a U.S. problem—it is a world and UN problem," he said.[27] Bush also was demonstrating U.S. respect for the sovereignty of other nations versus potentially perceived hegemony if the United States remained on the ground in Iraq. Sovereignty was an important principle of the new world he wanted to see.

See Dayton Maxwell and Andrew Natsios's chapter in this book for more details.

CASE 5: ETHIOPIA—RESCUE OF ETHIOPIAN JEWS AND PEACEFUL TRANSFER OF POWER

In April [1991], as insurgent forces closed in on the capital [of Ethiopia], I called Rudy Boschwitz. I asked Senator Boschwitz to go to Addis Ababa urgently as a personal emissary of the President to seek to arrange the expedited departure of the Ethiopian Jews. Events since Senator Boschwitz and his team took their trip have unfolded with dazzling speed. . . . Arrangements were put in place between Israel and Ethiopia for one of the boldest humanitarian airlifts in history. It succeeded . . . in carrying more than 14,000 Ethiopian Jews to new lives in Israel.

—President George H. W. Bush, June 4, 1991[28]

The story goes further back for George H. W. Bush's involvement with the Ethiopian Jews. (They are also called *Falashas* by some, but it is a pejorative term. *Beta Israel* is the preferred term.) When he was vice president, Bush had been instrumental in arranging the rescue of hundreds of Ethiopian Jewish refugees from Sudan, where they had fled famine. This group had been left behind after the secret Israeli Operation Moses, which rescued almost eight thousand, was shut down suddenly in early 1985 when exposed after a short life. In March 1985, Vice President Bush met in Sudan with Sudanese leader Numeiri at the request of President Reagan (following pressure from Congress) to ask for resumption of the operation. He got the go-ahead for a one-shot U.S. operation, and worked to arrange the mission. Operation Sheba unfolded clandestinely and successfully on March 28, 1985, with U.S. C-130 aircraft flying all Ethiopian Jews who could travel—about five hundred—out of an airfield near their refugee camps in Sudan.[29] Bush and Reagan did not tout this action publicly; and, while not mentioned in Bush's Rose Garden remarks in 1991, it provides some insight into the emotion he expressed that day.

During the Bush administration, the United States had foreign policy and humanitarian interests in Ethiopia. For one thing, about seventeen thousand Ethiopian Jews were still there in 1991. Bush administration policy was to encourage free movement of people and, in this case, for Ethiopian Jews to be allowed to emigrate to Israel. The American Jewish community strongly supported this effort. Israel believed they belonged there as a "right to return" (witness Operations Moses and Sheba), and from 1989 to 1990 had been ferrying about five hundred a month out of Ethiopia. This human rights gesture by Ethiopia was a product of the Cold War coming to an end. The Soviet Union had cut its aid to Ethiopian leader Mengistu Haile Mariam after the fall of the Berlin Wall, and he had turned to Israel for arms, using the Ethiopian Jews as bargaining chips.

Mengistu had ruled Ethiopia as a bloody dictator since 1974. The situation began to unravel as his forces were losing their long civil war with the secessionist Eritrean Popular Liberation Front, Tigray People's Liberation Front, and Oromo Liberation Front armies. The Bush administration could see that the forces arrayed against Mengistu had joined together and were moving in on the Ethiopian capital of Addis Ababa, where millions of citizens and thousands of Ethiopian Jews were in dire straits and fearing the coming battle. The Ethiopian Jews, in particular, seemed vulnerable. The Bush administration did not want a bloodbath in the city.

Seeing the humanitarian disasters that could unfold in Addis Ababa, Bush asked former Senator Rudy Boschwitz to go to Ethiopia with a peace conference proposal and a personal letter to Mengistu asking that the Ethiopian Jews be permitted to leave in a massive airlift. The visit was April 26–27, 1991. The team included a White House National Security Council staff member, Robert Frasure, who had served in Addis Ababa (later tragically killed on a peace mission to Bosnia). Frasure provided a visible White House presence to make the points to the dictator. The meetings lasted several hours over two days. Mengistu resisted the peace conference, but he was more amenable to speeding up release of Ethiopian Jews, secretly and in return for generous financial assistance. Mengistu emphatically did not agree to the suggestion pressed by Frasure that he resign and go peacefully.

Barely three weeks later, on May 21, as the rebel forces closed on the capital, Mengistu fled to Zimbabwe, encouraged again by the United States through the White House. The new acting Ethiopian president, General Tesfaye, convoked the American chargé d'affaires and requested U.S. assistance in facilitating a negotiated end to the war. The chargé responded that the United States was prepared to be helpful but wanted to see "parallel momentum" on the evacuation of the Jews. Tesfaye responded positively. To seal the deal, the chargé asked for and received within hours a letter from President Bush to Tesfaye offering a peace conference, and that Ethiopia would commit to the evacuation of the Jews to Israel. Upon receipt, Tesfaye gave the green light to the Israelis to commence Operation Solomon.[30]

The United States worked with the rebels to arrange a halt to their advance on Addis during the evacuation. On May 24–25, Israeli commandos provided protection along the route as the Ethiopian Jews were moved to the airfield. Then, loaded tightly onto Israeli aircraft, they were flown out—14,310 in thirty-six hours. The rebels entered the city with little resistance, taking over the government. The peace conference took place in London, led by the United States. A bloodbath had been avoided and the Jews were home.[31]

The diplomatic and humanitarian missions and American intervention had been successful. Influence and diplomacy had come together in ways not always possible. The United States had once again used its power for humanitarian and human rights purposes. Press Secretary Marlin Fitzwater announced the operation as it was underway, and preparations got underway for a Rose Garden ceremony to acknowledge the team that had helped make it possible, lauded by the president who had actually made it possible.

CASE 6: CREATING A NEW UN HUMANITARIAN ASSISTANCE COORDINATING BODY

UNGA Resolution 46/182 had a tremendous impact. We could get active in a more effective and energetic way [in providing humanitarian assistance] because of the new mechanism and the mandate of all the countries in the General Assembly.

—Ambassador Jan Eliasson[32]

The Iraqi refugee crisis—not just the Kurds—and other humanitarian crises had shown the United Nations to have unclear lines and weak processes related to relief delivery and management. Furthermore, continuing demand in Iraq and deteriorating humanitarian situations in Somalia and the Balkans, especially Bosnia, heightened the need for a mechanism that could more effectively address complex humanitarian emergencies. It was becoming clear that the aftermath of the Cold War would see numerous ethnic conflicts that would spawn human misery, including record numbers of refugees and internally displaced persons.It also was clear that the lifting of the Cold War divisions and tensions could give rise to more concerted and coordinated attention to people, a point also made in case 3 above about children's rights.

Several UN ambassadors, led by Swedish ambassador Jan Eliasson, who was vice president of the Economic and Social Council (ECOSOC), had brainstormed about the humanitarian problem and decided that both a mandate and a new coordinating mechanism were needed. They worked on it the summer of 1991 at ECOSOC in Geneva. In July, the London Economic Summit, which President Bush attended, endorsed the notion of such a plan, with a central figure to coordinate, as part of the "need to reinforce the multilateral approach to the solution of common problems and work to strengthen the international system of which the United Nations, based on its charter, remains so central a part."[33] Negotiations for a UN General Assembly resolution began in earnest in the fall.

President Bush supported creating the new organization, and his team marched forth. Ambassador Eliasson stated, "The U.S. was on board all the time with very strong support."[34] He especially noted the role of U.S. permanent representative Tom Pickering, who was a very strong leader and voice at the United Nations. In fact, the United States was on the drafting team in the large working group of ambassadors that formed. The Soviet Union was very supportive too. The process especially required much negotiation with the G77, as some countries and probably the whole continent of Africa feared the resolution portended a rebirth of colonialism and infringement on sovereignty by potential intervention. Proponents were told the word "intervention" was to be banned during the negotiations.

Fortunately, and to great relief, agreement was reached and the UN General Assembly adopted Resolution 46/182 by consensus on December 19, 1991,[35] to establish new arrangements for humanitarian coordination led by twelve guiding principles. The head of the new organization, who would report directly to the UN secretary-general, had responsibilities for coordinating and facilitating humanitarian assistance, processing requests for same, facilitating access to emergency areas, organizing needs-assessment missions, preparing consolidated appeals and mobilizing resources, providing consolidated information including early warning on emergencies, and promoting smooth transition from relief to rehabilitation and reconstruction.

The secretary-general asked Jan Eliasson to bring life to Resolution 46/182 as the first undersecretary-general for the Department of Humanitarian Affairs. He saw his role as meeting the dual need for humanitarian diplomacy and effective coordination among the various UN agencies, governments, and nongovernmental organizations called for in the resolution. During his tenure (1992–1994), the Department of Humanitarian Affairs (DHA) engaged in the types of situations that had been foreseen. It wasn't all perfect or easy, but Ambassador Eliasson, who later served as the first deputy secretary-general of the United Nations (2012–2016), described the importance this way: "Resolution 46/182 had a tremendous impact. . . . For example, it was now possible to get active in the Horn of Africa. We got into the Sudan civil war and established the first humanitarian corridor to fly food, medicine, and supplies into war-torn areas. I went to Burma to negotiate the return of fifty thousand Rohingyas. We also used the mandate to attend to natural disasters. Now it is a natural and indispensable function of the United Nations."[36]

At this time, the department is called the Office for the Coordination of Humanitarian Affairs (OCHA), led by an undersecretary-general, and it has coordinated hundreds of relief operations helping millions of people in manmade and natural disasters. Its establishment at the end of the Cold War—by the desire and vote of nations globally, with strong U.S. and Soviet support—initiated a lasting institutional step forward in humanitarian response.

SIGNPOST: UNSC SUMMIT, AGENDA FOR PEACE, U.S. PEACEKEEPING—1992

January 1992 saw the first-ever UN Security Council summit meeting, which sought to further revitalize the United Nations and, as President Bush said to the gathering, "to advance the momentous movement toward democracy and freedom . . . and expand the circle of nations committed to human rights and the rule of law."[37] He committed the United States to these efforts and also talked about preventing proliferation of weapons of mass destruction. Only weeks before, the Soviet Union had disintegrated and Mikhail Gorbachev had been replaced by Boris Yeltsin, who attended this summit and kept up cooperation in the Security Council. The Soviet Union seat was now held by Russia.

From the summit came a request for Secretary-General Boutros-Ghali to present recommendations to ensure effective and efficient peacekeeping, peacemaking, and preventive diplomacy. To that end, he issued *An Agenda for Peace* in June, adding the concept of postconflict peacebuilding.[38] In response, President Bush's UNGA remarks in September 1992 complimented the agenda and addressed a new U.S. emphasis on peacekeeping and humanitarian relief through lift, logistics, training and exercises, communications, intelligence, and planning. He did not, however, commit U.S. forces on the ground for UN peacekeeping or agree with a standing army under UN control. This had been the president's position all along, as distinguished from emergency humanitarian operations, which had employed U.S. forces on the ground for the Kurds and in response to the 1991 Bangladesh cyclone (Operation Sea Angel).[39]

The president subsequently signed National Security Directive (NSD) 74 on Peacekeeping and Emergency Humanitarian Relief Policy in November, which provided guidance to formalize U.S. support efforts outlined in the UNGA speech.[40] Also in 1992, the United States committed in yet another way to the kind of freedoms and rights spoken of by the president for others around the world.

CASE 7: RATIFICATION OF THE INTERNATIONAL COVENANT ON CIVIL AND POLITICAL RIGHTS (ICCPR)

I am writing to urge the Senate to renew its consideration of the International Covenant on Civil and Political Rights with a view to providing advice and consent to ratification. . . . United States ratification at this moment in history would underscore our natural commitment to fostering democratic values through international law.

—President Bush letter to Senator Claiborne Pell, August 8, 1991[41]

From early in the Bush administration, there had been discussion of achieving Senate ratification of a human rights treaty as a reflection of U.S. principles and to foster respect for international human rights and the rule of law. As mentioned earlier, several major human rights treaties awaited action in the U.S. Senate, most of them for over ten years. The International Covenant on Civil and Political Rights (ICCPR),[42] which had been adopted by the UN in 1966, signed by the United States in 1977, and sent to the Senate in 1978, was selected as the logical one in light of the administration's emphasis on democracy and freedom. It also was deemed by the State Department to be the least likely to encounter Senate resistance. The Senate had acted favorably on the Genocide Convention in 1986 and the Torture Convention in 1990, and Claiborne Pell, chairman of the Senate Foreign Relations Committee, was pressing the administration to push ratification on at least one treaty. Nongovernmental organizations (NGOs) were strongly supportive as well.

The ICCPR is part of the International Bill of Human Rights along with the International Covenant on Economic, Social and Cultural Rights (still not ratified by the United States) and the iconic Universal Declaration of Human Rights. It had already been ratified by over 90 countries in 1991 (now 173), and was described by President Bush to Chairman Pell as codifying "the essential freedoms people must enjoy in a democratic society, such as the right to vote, freedom of peaceful assembly, equal protection of the law, the right to liberty and security, and freedom of opinion and expression." He also noted, "Subject to a few essential reservations and understandings, it is entirely consonant with the fundamental principles incorporated in our own Bill of Rights."[43]

Also, the United States wanted to participate in the Human Rights Committee created by the covenant, which was responsible for monitoring compliance by countries and articulating evolving human rights standards. Overall, ratifying the treaty would strengthen U.S. stature and influence on human rights in the international community through promoting U.S. concepts of civil and political rights. These points and a package of reservations, understandings, and declarations were put forth (a frequent practice by the United States and other countries in ratifying international treaties) and subsequently discussed in Senate Foreign Relations Committee hearings in November 1991. The State Department and National Security Council staff worked closely with the Senate on a bipartisan basis and also with NGOs. On April 2, 1992, the Senate voted its advice and consent. President Bush signed the instrument of ratification and announced it June 5, 1992, and it was transmitted to the United Nations.[44]

Within the State Department, the International Organizations Bureau led by John Bolton had objected, holding that the U.S. Bill of Rights already offered protection to Americans, the federal treaty power should not be used to address domestic issues, and the Human Rights Committee wasn't viewed as effective. Everyone else, including, most importantly, the president, wanted to go ahead. And in the Senate, the modifications and reservations, plus a proviso by conservative Senator Jesse Helms that the treaty not require or authorize action by the United States inconsistent with the U.S. Constitution, won the day.[45]

Ratification of the ICCPR was a significant achievement of the Bush administration by the fact of its ratification after long Senate inaction, its reaffirmation of U.S.

leadership globally on human rights, and enhanced participation on human rights at the UN. In all, it represented another step by the Bush administration to strengthen the UN as an institution. And it became another U.S. tool and demonstration in support of its themes of democracy, the rule of law, and respect for human rights in the post–Cold War period.

CASE 8: HUMANITARIAN INTERVENTION IN SOMALIA—OPERATION RESTORE HOPE

American action is often necessary as a catalyst for broader involvement of the community of nations.

—George H. W. Bush, December 4, 1992[46]

Those presidential words announced Operation Restore Hope, a highly successful, landmark U.S.-led military humanitarian intervention to feed Somalis starving to death because warlords were using famine as a weapon of war.

True to his principles and his administration's history, Bush had insisted on a UN Security Council resolution with authority under Chapter VII for the military operation, and galvanized a coalition of countries (the United States plus twenty-seven others) to participate. He had consulted extensively with Congress and world leaders. The very effective U.S. national security interagency system worked well and thoroughly, including over twenty-five Deputies Committee meetings surrounding the events of the crisis and deployment. The president clearly stated—and adhered to—the mission, limit on activities, length of stay, and respect for sovereignty. The operation was entirely humanitarian and successful in saving lives and reopening humanitarian aid channels, and it clearly demonstrated U.S. leadership and compassion. (The "Black Hawk Down" tragedy in the next administration took place after the humanitarian mission was changed, and it was not part of the Bush operation.)

See Jim Kunder's chapter in this book for more details.

CONCLUSION

During George H. W. Bush's four years as president, human rights was always a key, deeply held theme as he brought along the Soviet Union, Eastern and Central Europe, and the international community in concepts of freedom and democracy and a community of nations acting on shared standards. Humanitarian assistance, while a principle Bush believed in, evolved in detail and scope as circumstances arose that necessitated military power. President Bush never lost sight of fundamentals, including international cooperation (coalitions, UN votes), UN authority, respect for sovereignty, and the role of trustworthy U.S. leadership. He maintained his steady hand

and heart on guiding relationships and actions through uncharted waters as the Cold War dissolved and a new world emerged. His understanding of the big picture and actions to take was enhanced by his skill, caring, and, yes, vision. His own initiatives and the other actions he supported strengthened the institutions and practices by which humanity moved forward, saving lives and producing hope and new futures, and, at least for a time, the new world order he sought. He was uniquely qualified for the time and world he served as president of the United States. Here are some of the specific accomplishments:

- The United States acting as a leader and catalyst, gathering coalitions for humanitarian operations, then turning U.S.-led operations over to the United Nations or others rather than staying and being seen as a hegemon.
- Setting the humanitarian military intervention precedent internationally, though he decided case by case on U.S. participation. (For example, President Bush did not choose to participate on the ground in Bosnia humanitarian operations.)
- Strengthening the UN through using it, invigorating the UN Security Council, adding OCHA for coordinating humanitarian relief operations, and bringing the United States into a key human rights treaty.
- Preserving the principle of first asylum while working through refugee and asylum issues with empathy and practicality as circumstances changed.
- Partnership with Gorbachev, brilliantly detailed by Jon Meacham.[47] The mutual respect was a key factor in cooperation and improvement of the international system. It was Bush the human being and diplomat who built trust with Gorbachev and other key leaders to move forward.

President George H. W. Bush had a clear vision for the post–Cold War world, with human rights and humanitarian response as two major principles, or building blocks. As the case studies herein illustrate, he exercised U.S. power and leadership to build on and solidify these principles in the international system with careful thought, expertise, and devotion.

NOTES

1. Accessed August 16, 2019, https://bush41library.tamu.edu/archives/public-papers/1.
2. Ibid.
3. George H. W. Bush, Remarks to Citizens in Hamtramck, Michigan, April 17, 1989, https://bush41library.tamu.edu/archives/public-papers/326.
4. Ibid.
5. George H. W. Bush, Remarks at Texas A&M University Commencement Ceremony, May 12, 1989, https://bush41library.tamu.edu/archives/public-papers/413.
6. United Nations, *Universal Declaration of Human Rights*, December 1948, Articles 13 and 14.

7. George H. W. Bush and Brent Scowcroft, *A World Transformed* (New York: Knopf, 1998), 4.

8. Bush, Texas A&M.

9. Congress sets an overall ceiling with regional subcaps for each fiscal year for numbers of people to enter the United States as refugees.

10. George H. W. Bush, National Security Directive 27: Soviet Emigration Policy, October 2, 1989, https://bush41library.tamu.edu/files/nsd/nsd27.pdf.

11. Fred A. Lazin, "Refugee Resettlement and 'Freedom of Choice': The Case of Soviet Jewry," Center for Immigration Studies, July 1, 2005, https://cis.org/Report/Refugee-Reset-tlement-and-Freedom-Choice-Case-Soviet-Jewry.

12. *The Refugee Dilemma in Europe and Asia and the United States' Response: Hearing Before the Committee on International Operations of the Committee on Foreign Affairs*, 101st Congress (June 20, 1990) (statement of Princeton Lyman, director of the State Department Refugee Bureau).

13. George H. W. Bush, Remarks on the Waiver of the Jackson-Vanik Amendment and on Economic Assistance to the Soviet Union, December 12, 1990, https://bush41library.tamu.edu/archives/public-papers/2549.

14. Lawrence S. Eagleburger, Statement to the International Conference on Indochinese Refugees, Geneva, Switzerland. June 13, 1989.

15. Alexander Casella, *Managing the Boat People* (New York: International Peace Institute, 2016), 3–6, https://www.ipinst.org/wp-content/uploads/2016/10/1610-Managing-the-Boat-People-Crisis.pdf.

16. Eagleburger, Indochinese Refugees.

17. Lyman, Statement on Refugees.

18. George H. W. Bush, Remarks on Developments in the POW/MIA Situation, October 23, 1992, https://bush41library.tamu.edu/archives/public-papers/4984.

19. George H.W. Bush, Remarks at the Opening Ceremony of the United Nations World Summit for Children in New York City, September 30, 1990, https://bush41library.tamu.edu/archives/public-papers/2276.

20. Jan Eliasson, Nancy Bearg phone interview, September 4, 2019.

21. United Nations, Declaration on the Survival, Protection and Development of Children, New York, September 30, 1990. https://www.unicef.org/wsc/declare.htm.

22. United Nations, Plan of Action for Implementing the Declaration on the Survival, Protection and Development of Children in the 1990s, New York, September 30, 1990. https://www.unicef.org/wsc/plan.htm.

23. Paul Lewis, "World Leaders Endorse Plan to Improve Lives of Children," *New York Times*, October 1, 1990.

24. Kofi Anan, *We the Children: End-Decade Review of the Follow-Up to the World Summit for Children*. Report of the Secretary-General, A/S-27/3. New York: UNICEF, 2001. https://www.unicef.org/publications/index_4443.html.

25. Bush, Remarks at Maxwell Air Force Base War College in Montgomery, Alabama. April 13, 1991, https://bush41library.tamu.edu/archives/public-papers/2869.

26. United Nations Security Council, Resolution 688 on Iraq, http://unscr.com/en/resolutions/688.

27. Memorandum of Conversation, President Bush with Sadako Ogata, UN High Commissioner for Refugees, June 24, 1991, https://bush41library.tamu.edu/files/memcons-telcons/1991-06-24--Ogata.pdf.

28. George H.W. Bush, Remarks at the Awards Ceremony for Emigration Assistance to Ethiopian Jews, June 4, 1991, https://bush41library.tamu.edu/archives/public-papers/3059.

29. Mitchell Bard and Howard Lenoff, "Ethiopian Jewry: America's Role in the Rescue of Ethiopian Jewry." *Jewish Virtual Library*, https://www.jewishvirtuallibrary.org/america-s-role -in-the-rescue-of-ethiopian-jewry.

30. Robert Houdek (American charge d'affaires in Ethiopia in 1991), Nancy Bearg phone interview September 3, 2019.

31. The whole story is told well in: Stephen Spector, *Operation Solomon: The Daring Rescue of the Ethiopian Jews* (New York: Oxford University Press, 2005).

32. First UN Undersecretary-General for Humanitarian Affairs Jan Eliasson, Nancy Bearg phone interview September 4, 2019.

33. London Economic Summit: Strengthening the International Order, July 16, 1991, https://bush41library.tamu.edu/archives/public-papers/3193.

34. Eliasson, Bearg interview.

35. United Nations, UN General Assembly Resolution 46/182: Strengthening of the Coordination of Humanitarian Emergency Assistance of the United Nations, December 19, 1991, https://undocs.org/en/A/RES/46/182.

36. Eliasson, Bearg interview.

37. George H. W. Bush, Remarks to the United Nations Security Council in New York City. January 31, 1992, https://bush41library.tamu.edu/archives/public-papers/3897.

38. Boutros Boutros-Ghali, *An Agenda for Peace: Preventive Diplomacy, Peacemaking and Peace-Keeping: Report of the Secretary-General* (New York: United Nations, 1992), https://www .un.org/ruleoflaw/blog/document/an-agenda-for-peace-preventive-diplomacy-peacemaking-and-peace-keeping-report-of-the-secretary-general/.

39. Richard L. Berke, "U.S. Sends Troops to Aid Bangladesh in Cyclone Relief," *New York Times*, May 12, 1991, https://www.nytimes.com/1991/05/12/world/us-sends-troops-to-aid -bangladesh-in-cyclone-relief.html.

40. George H. W. Bush, National Security Directive 74: Peacekeeping and Emergency Humanitarian Relief Policy, November 24, 1992, https://bush41library.tamu.edu/files/nsd/ nsd74.pdf.

41. Bush, Letter to Senator Claiborne Pell, Chairman, Senate Foreign Relations Committee, August 8, 1991.

42. United Nations, International Covenant on Civil and Political Rights, https://treaties .un.org/doc/publication/unts/volume%20999/volume-999-i-14668-english.pdf.

43. Bush, Letter to Pell.

44. Ratification by the United States of America of the International Covenant on Civil and Political Rights. Depository Notification, https://treaties.un.org/doc/Publication/ CN/1992/CN.250.1992-Eng.pdf.

45. This proviso is not in the ratification document, by agreement between Congress and the Bush administration.

46. George H. W. Bush, Presidential Address to the Nation on the Situation in Somalia, December 4, 1992, https://bush41library.tamu.edu/archives/public-papers/5100.

47. Jon Meacham, *Destiny and Power: The American Odyssey of George Herbert Walker Bush* (New York: Random House, 2015).

15

Somalia Revisited

President Bush and Operation Restore Hope

James Kunder

On December 5, 1992, President George H. W. Bush took to the nation's airwaves to deliver a momentous speech on the famine wracking the East African country of Somalia. He said, in part:

> After consulting with my advisers, with world leaders, and the congressional leadership, I have today told [United Nations] Secretary-General Boutros-Ghali that America will answer the call. I have given the order to [Defense] Secretary Cheney to move a substantial American force into Somalia. As I speak, a Marine amphibious ready group, which we maintain at sea, is offshore Mogadishu. These troops will be joined by elements of the 1st Marine Expeditionary Force, based out of Camp Pendleton, California, and by the Army's 10th Mountain Division out of Fort Drum, New York. These and other American forces will assist in Operation Restore Hope. They are America's finest. They will perform this mission with courage and compassion, and they will succeed. The people of Somalia, especially the children of Somalia, need our help. We're able to ease their suffering. We must help them live. We must give them hope. America must act.

Within weeks following the president's address, a substantial U.S. military force was on the ground in that otherwise obscure nation assisting with the delivery of food supplies. For perhaps the first time in recorded history, a powerful nation had deployed the cream of its military force, seemingly for purely humanitarian purposes, to a nation of apparently miniscule strategic or economic interest.

BAIDOA, SOMALIA, 1992

As I prepared to write this essay on the early 1990s humanitarian crisis in Somalia and President Bush's central role in the events of that period, I had two immediate reactions to the project. First, I thought it is about time we reflect, from the perspective of more than twenty-five years, on what I believe to be one of the signal actions of George Bush's presidency. Much has been written about the president's decision to intervene dramatically in a relatively obscure nation in the throes of disaster, but most of the serious analysis is now dated. Having been personally involved in the American response to the infamous Somalia famine of 1991–1992 as director of the Office of U.S. Foreign Disaster Assistance at the U.S. Agency for International Development (USAID), I held at the time, and continue to hold, strong views on the implications of the deployment of U.S. military forces in a humanitarian crisis. So my first reaction was appreciation and eagerness to reflect, from the perspective of 2019, on the event, its meaning, and its implications for U.S. policy today.

My second reaction was more personal. I found myself recalling the last time I had the honor to speak with President Bush about Somalia, and the inconceivably peculiar circumstances of, and venue for, that discussion. The date was December 31, 1992, precisely twenty-two days after U.S. Marines and U.S. Special Forces seized the port of Mogadishu in an attempt to pave the way for humanitarian food delivery to the starving in Somalia. The location of the meeting was an orphanage for Somali children in the town of Baidoa, a midsized inland city in the southern reaches of Somalia that had the misfortune to be at the epicenter of the worst of the famine. President Bush had arrived in Somalia the day before and had been ferried by helicopter from the USS *Tripoli* to Baidoa's airport, which U.S. Marines and French Foreign Legionnaires had seized barely two weeks before the president's arrival. Traveling through a mile-long cordon of Marine gun emplacements lining the dusty Somali roads between the airport and the orphanage, President Bush became the first chief executive since Dwight Eisenhower to visit what remained a highly dangerous combat zone. Moreover, given his World War II fighter pilot experiences, he was one of the few chief executives in U.S. history to fully appreciate the risks he was taking in being choppered from an amphibious warfare ship into a region where rocket-propelled grenades and other armaments capable of downing aircraft were plentiful and in the hands of marginally disciplined fighters.

As the president strode into Baidoa's heavily guarded orphanage, he encountered more than one hundred Somali children who had been fortunate enough to survive the bloodletting and starvation that had claimed tens of thousands of lives in the previous months and earned Baidoa the shattering nickname of the "City of Death." Besides the freshly bathed, and now well-fed, children facing the president and his heavily armed escorts in the dust and heat, were a ragtag group of aid workers who had displayed extraordinary courage and endured inconceivable hardships to minister to the needs of the dying in Baidoa in the previous months. With the exception of two Irish Catholic nuns among these humanitarian workers, the orphanage staff appeared incongruously like a group of American hippies dropped into a barren purgatory.

There was a momentary pause, as the president and his escort took in the scene, and we provided a basic orientation to an obviously well-informed chief executive.

And then, without prompting, President Bush strode out of the circle of security personnel and U.S. government disaster relief officials, ignoring remonstrances to the contrary, to physically embrace the children and aid workers—those whose lives his actions had saved, and those whose pleas he had heard. As focused as I was on presenting data to the commander in chief and on the mechanics of the visit, I remember as clear as a bell thinking to myself at the time: The most powerful human being on the face of the earth is hugging the humblest of personages on the planet, and I am unlikely, as long as I live, to witness anything this stirring and important again.

How did it come to that point? How did an American president come to visit Baidoa's orphanage? How and why did he make the decision, in the fall of 1992, to take on famine in Somalia with the full power of the United States? What constellation of historical circumstances and contemporary events even led such a decision to be queued up in the first place? What were the implications for U.S. foreign policy in 1992, and are there any lessons in the president's actions than that might inform U.S. policy today, in a much different world?

Lest these seem like highly theoretical, or distant, perhaps even quaint, policy considerations, there are, of course, two additional points I must interject up front to sharpen the analysis that follows. First, the president's widely popular determination to respond to famine in Somalia in 1992 ended, in the minds of many Americans, with a dramatic and painful exclamation point: the violent and bloody killing of U.S. special forces troops in October 1993, in the "Black Hawk Down" incident. Although the bitter events of October 1993 are only tangentially related to President Bush's humanitarian decision of 1992, as I will argue later, the peaceful landing of troops in 1992 and the violent incidents of 1993 are perceptually linked and this linkage residually shapes American foreign policy to this day. Second, as readers will immediately recognize, Somalia still, twenty-seven years after the events described in this chapter, remains a partially functioning nation-state where gaps in governance and security open space for extremist organizations that can threaten U.S. and allies' interests.

In short, I believe that the drivers of the president's dramatic decision in 1992, his thinking, its immediate and long-term results, and its relevance to U.S. policy today merit a second look. Although this brief chapter is not the place for a thorough history of either Somalia or the famine of the early 1990s, a quick review of the circumstances preceding the president's momentous 1992 deployment decision serves as a useful starting point to this updated examination.

THE GREAT SOMALIA FAMINE AND ITS ANTECEDENTS

Accurate data on victims are hard to come by in the chaos of humanitarian disasters, and armed conflict makes precise data even more difficult to validate. There is, however, a broad consensus that, in the 1991–1993 period that is the focus of this chapter, approximately one-quarter of a million individuals perished in Somalia from war-related causes, starvation, or diseases that food shortages left them too weak to fight. At the time President Bush addressed the nation in December 1992, he reflected the thinking of many disaster experts when he predicted that, absent dramatic action by the international community, "in the months ahead five times that number, one and a half million people, could starve to death."

What is it about Somalia that could have led to such horrific outcomes and dire predictions? At least part of the answer lies in four factors that set the stage for state collapse and chaos in Somalia by the early 1990s: (1) the physical environment in the Somali lands; (2) the extreme individualism of Somali culture; (3) the related clan-based organization of Somali society; and (4) Somalia's historical experience with government, internal and externally managed—or, more precisely, the absence of effective governance.[1]

In terms of factor one, the physical environment of the Somali lands, since ancient times the Somali people have occupied a dry, generally barren corner of the Horn of Africa that is notable for its limited natural resources. These physical realities have engendered a traditional herding culture, a toughness during frequent hard times, and a tradition of conflict over those limited natural resources. In preparation for ratcheting up U.S. humanitarian engagement in Somalia, my colleagues and I at the Office of U.S. Foreign Disaster Assistance (OFDA) engaged a number of Somali and Somali-American academics and anthropologists to better understand how effectively to deliver relief supplies in this environment. I remember clearly the description one of these Somali experts provided to illustrate for us then novices the essence of the Somali reality. He told us: "You are a herder with twenty thirsty goats and your rifle headed to a small water hole. You see, coming from the opposite direction, another herder with twenty thirsty goats and a rifle. You both know that the hole contains water for only twenty goats." Although southern Somalia includes a number of substantial river valleys where large-scale agriculture is possible, the generally harsh environment of Somalia, with its limited ability to generate food surpluses, was a major driver of the famine.

Factor two, extreme individualism, also played into the foundation of the humanitarian disaster. The severe conditions in Somalia, the reliance on individual herds, the imperative to manage one's own fate in life, and the harsh penalties life often imposes for failure to dominate, produce individuals who are extraordinarily self-reliant, alert to opportunity, quick to seize the initiative, averse to consensus processes and, by outside standards, pitiless toward competitors. Clearly, there are generous, community-oriented souls among the Somalis, as there are in any society. But my observations during relief operations there is that extreme individualism is a dominant trait in the culture, with profound implications for how business, relief operations, or political reconciliation must be conducted in Somalia. Particularly relevant to the humanitarian crisis in Somalia, strident individualism there was, and is, often buttressed by widespread ownership of military-grade firearms, which individuals or informal groups employed with alacrity amid the chaotic and life-threatening conditions they encountered in the early 1990s.

Factor number three, the clan basis for social organization in Somali culture somewhat balances extreme individualism, but is the primary source of identity. The five major clans of Somalia are divided and subdivided into hundreds of subclans and families, membership in which serves as a primary framework for all categories of decision-making. Conflict among clans, and their subsets, was a major factor in setting the stage for the Somalia famine of the 1990s and a major impediment to resolving the famine and the conflict that undergirded the disaster. Through my work at USAID and OFDA, I have become wary of shortcut characterizations of large and complex cultures, including the Somali culture. But it is probably instructive that, in their description of their own society, Somali interlocutors frequently referred to the widely circulated proverb:

> I and Somalia against the world.
> I and my clan against Somalia.
> I and my family against the clan.
> I and my brother against the family.
> I against my brother.

Factor four, Somalia's historical experience with government systems generated internally or imposed from abroad, has particular relevance for the conditions antecedent to the crisis of the early 1990s. In briefest form, Somalia has experienced a total of nine years of elected, nonautocratic governance in its history. A lightly governed backwater of successive regional empires for most of its recorded history, Somalia suddenly fell prey in the nineteenth century to the European "scramble for Africa," with—from northwest to southeast—the French, British, and Italians establishing outposts. Sans "French Somaliland," (current Djibouti), the British and Italian colonies were patched together, with little serious preparation, in time for independence in 1960. In the nation-building drama of that era, areas with a Somali majority were awarded to other nations, including Ethiopia, Djibouti, and Kenya, setting the stage for regional rivalries that persist to this day. After Somalia's first elected president was assassinated in 1969—ending the nine years of elected, non-autocratic governance mentioned above—Somalia experienced a military coup led by Mohamed Siad Barre, who led a strongman government until fleeing the country in early 1991. During the twenty-two-year Barre dictatorship, Somalia was a participant in one of the more tortured sideshows of the global U.S.–Soviet Cold War, shifting between Soviet and American client status while simultaneously fighting, and generally losing, bloody irredentist conflicts with Ethiopia. In short, by the time of the 1990s famine, Somalia's experience with effective government has been severely limited, with a residue of distrust for outsiders and their seemingly fickle attention to sustained support of Somali interests.

By January 1991, when the U.S. Embassy in Mogadishu was evacuated by American military forces while under assault from Somali armed groups, and in the months that followed, the dynamics described above had combined to create widespread civil war and chaos in much of Somalia. President Siad Barre's sudden and forced departure from the national capital led to extensive interclan conflict for political leadership and advantage and opened space for innumerable gangs and freelancers to seize anything of value. In many parts of the country, "de-infrastructuring" took place, with water pumps, electrical generators and copper wires, underground water pipes, hospital equipment, communications gear, and other equipment required for normal public services looted, often for its scrap value. Of particular importance to the famine conditions that were soon to widely prevail, military conflict—including battles to prevent Siad Barre from regaining control of Mogadishu—raged across the southern breadbasket of Somalia between the Jubba and Shebelle River basins, destroying irrigation systems, wells, herds, and agriculture equipment and facilities, while displacing farmers from their fields.

These conflict dynamics, exacerbated by recurring drought, resulted in a humanitarian crisis of immense proportions, which would claim an estimated two hundred fifty thousand human lives within the next year and a half.

INITIAL HUMANITARIAN
RESPONSE AND ITS LIMITS

Between the time of the looting of the U.S. Embassy in Mogadishu in January 1991 and President Bush's decision in fall of 1992 to launch Operation Restore Hope, the large-scale deployment of U.S. and coalition forces to stem the famine, the humanitarian situation fluctuated widely in Somalia. The intensity of famine conditions, their severity among the regions of Somalia, the international awareness and perceptions of the situation on the ground, and response to the disaster all varied dramatically during this period. Overall, however, the bottom line stayed constant: the absence of effective government and security, widespread and intense fighting including urban combat among heavily armed factions, and resultant disruption of normal agriculture and commerce led to extraordinary levels of starvation and human suffering, with no end in sight to the conditions driving the crisis.[2]

This is not to say that external humanitarian relief efforts prior to the arrival of internationally sanctioned military forces in Somalia were inconsequential. Hundreds of international relief workers from the U.S. government, International Committee of the Red Cross (ICRC), United Nations agencies, and private relief entities (nongovernmental organizations, or NGOs) engaged in relief operations professionally and courageously, sometimes at the cost of their lives, during this period. Although quantitative measurements of the effectiveness of these efforts in 1991 and 1992 are uncertain, the U.S. Centers for Disease Control (CDC) and Refugee Policy Group suggest that they may have saved fifty thousand lives. U.S. government donations of food aid during this period, primarily through USAID's Office of Food for Peace, exceeded ninety thousand tons, and OFDA relief funding for agencies working in Somalia was over $30 million. These numbers indicate an early and aggressive response by the Bush administration to Somalia's agony, even when the scale of the crisis was relatively uncertain and long before the situation garnered widespread media attention.[3]

Not only were U.S. government and other international disaster response efforts substantial in the 1991–1992 period, they also included creative innovations to take on the special circumstances in Somalia, including the absence of a functioning government and widespread looting both by organized militias and ad hoc gangs. The International Committee of the Red Cross, for example, which conducted the single largest relief operation during this period, launched a fleet of small boats and other landing craft to remote ports and beaches in the southern famine zone. This unprecedented humanitarian "amphibious assault" was explicitly designed to avoid the congestion and looting at major ports, reach stricken areas otherwise accessible only by roads subject to armed attack, and break relief shipments into less lucrative targets for armed groups. At the direction of Andrew Natsios, subsequently appointed by President Bush as special coordinator for Somalia relief, USAID initiated a creative and promising food "monetization" program, utilizing market forces within Somalia in an attempt to reduce food prices for marginalized populations while making food less attractive to looters.

Months before President Bush's late-November decision to put U.S. troops on the ground, early attempts to get food supplies to those most in need yielded Operation Provide Relief, which President Bush announced on August 14, 1992. Operation Provide Relief took relief supplies off-loaded from ships at Mombasa, Kenya, and, employing nineteen aircraft, including fourteen U.S. military transports, airlifted supplies to targeted sites in Somalia. Although the total volume of food delivered by air was, in and of itself, not a game changer in Somalia, the results were substantial and important. Between August 1992 and January 1993, Operation Provide Relief conducted 2,486 flights, delivering twenty-eight thousand tons of emergency supplies.

Beyond these direct relief operations, the Bush administration simultaneously set in motion an important array of diplomatic initiatives with the objective of facilitating relief operations in Somalia. A number of these involved engagement with the United Nations and are of particular relevance to President Bush's subsequent decisions, as well as central to evaluating the international encounter in Somalia in historical terms. The single most important diplomatic undertaking at the United Nations in 1992 was clearly the passage of Security Council Resolution 733 in January, which called upon the secretary-general to accelerate political reconciliation, or peacemaking, initiatives among the Somali claimants to power, as well as to enhance relief efforts. UN diplomatic missions, breaking new ground in launching such efforts absent a generally recognized government in Somalia, were able in the March–April time frame to cement a temporary ceasefire between the two major Somali antagonists and broker an agreement to permit fifty unarmed international observers and five hundred armed relief protection guards to deploy to Mogadishu, as part of the UN operation dubbed UNOSOM I (for First United Nations Operation in Somalia). The dynamics set in play by these diplomatic efforts related to "humanitarian intervention," including the deployment of international forces in an environment absent authoritative government leaders, would foreshadow the difficult decisions President Bush subsequently faced at a later stage of the Somalia crisis.

This eventful period of humanitarian diplomacy, centered on the United Nations and its authorities, included several additional initiatives designed to address the causes of famine in Somalia and treat its symptoms. Secretary-General Boutros Boutros-Ghali named both a special representative to represent the United Nations in Mogadishu and lead the reconciliation effort as well as a humanitarian coordinator for Somalia. Although both had some initial successes, ultimately their efforts served primarily to emphasize the daunting impediments outsiders faced in Somalia, either in bringing factions to the peace table or in meeting the desperate needs of increasingly vulnerable crisis victims. Lack of progress by UN leadership during this period, and the concomitant sense in Washington that UN personnel and institutions would not, by themselves, solve Somalia's profound difficulties, would ultimately help shape President Bush's decision to mobilize U.S. power later in 1992.

In short, during the 1991–1992 period, both the humanitarian crisis and the underlying political crisis in Somalia remained severe, with no clear endgame visible. Although U.S. and multinational actors made several runs at fixing these problems, by July 1992, most serious observers of Somalia felt that the situation was stagnant both politically and from a security perspective, while the number of those dying from starvation, disease, and conflict continued to climb into the hundreds of thousands. A UN assessment team sent to Somalia in March 1992 estimated that a full quarter of the nation's estimated population of six million was at risk of starvation, and that more than three quarters required humanitarian aid. Beyond these depressing statistics, two further new bits of intelligence had seeped into the analysis of policymakers. First, an increasing recognition that the problem was not solely a logistics issue of getting more food and medical supplies into the country, but fundamentally a problem of looting of relief supplies. Then, second, came an increased awareness that the looted food, supplemented by the fees being paid to Somali "security" personnel by international charitable organizations, had become *the* economy of Somalia, and was the primary lubricant for the purchase of the weapons and fighters that were fueling the Somali civil war. These factors—data on death rates, a perception of diplomatic stasis and increased recognition of the looter economy—combined in mid-1992 to drive a perception within parts of the U.S. government that some dramatic game changer was required.

PRESIDENT BUSH, OPERATION RESTORE HOPE, AND ITS AFTERMATH

In this penultimate section, I want to describe President Bush's momentous decision in late 1992 to launch a major military operation, under combat conditions, for the purpose of ending starvation in Somalia, before reflecting in the closing section on how his decision might be viewed and judged today, twenty-eight years later. The Bush administration had clearly maintained a sustained interest in Somalia during that country's decomposition, as indicated by the multifaceted diplomatic and humanitarian engagement described above. What appears to have changed in mid- to late 1992 is a shift to an intensifying personal interest by the president himself and direct engagement by the president in ratcheting up U.S. action,[4] culminating in the commander in chief's November order to launch Operation Restore Hope and send 25,426 U.S. troops on a humanitarian mission to the Horn of Africa.[5]

In the two months prior to December 8, 1992, when the first contingent of Special Forces and U.S. Marines landed in Mogadishu, President Bush, according to sources close to the White House, repeatedly asked for updates on the humanitarian crisis and encouraged a "forward leaning" posture. The definitive phase of this intensified engagement came during the week before Thanksgiving. It was clear by that time that the Department of Defense, with the solid, if wary, support of Chairman of the Joint Chiefs Colin Powell, was prepared to intervene if ordered and had prepared detailed plans for a humanitarian protection operation. Top advisors presented the president with an options paper outlining three approaches to address famine conditions in Somalia. The first two were relatively cautious and indirect plans to augment the capacity of UN forces on the ground. The third option was the far-reaching outlier. In the words of the chairman of the Somali Task Force at the Department of Defense, who helped draft the decision document, option three proposed "hav[ing] the United States lead an immediate, large-scale intervention to aggressively fix the problem."[6] The president chose the boldest course, setting in motion a chain of events with profound contemporary implications that reverberate today.

By the time he left office on January 20, 1993, President Bush's triggering of Operation Restore Hope yielded dramatic, positive results in Somalia. Skillful diplomacy, led by the U.S. ambassador to Somalia, Bob Oakley, created circumstances in which the notoriously fractious Somali clan militias avoided, in almost all cases, interfering with the landing of troops. Within two months from the time the first contingent of military personnel arrived in Mogadishu, famously greeted by glaring camera lights from the numerous media teams on the beach, those forces had secured major ports and airports, initiated highly effective convoys for the delivery of relief supplies, and established themselves inland in most of the major population centers in Somalia's famine belt, with concomitant calming effects on the internecine conflict previously raging. By establishing, with OFDA, an effective Civil-Military Operations Center, U.S. and coalition forces coordinated synergistically with humanitarian groups already on the ground to speed relief operations to those most in need. Through the skillful engagement of military and State Department PSYOP and public affairs experts, media messages explaining the purpose of Operation Restore Hope and combating negative propaganda were plentiful and effective.

By the time President Bush made his highly publicized visit to the orphanage at Baidoa, described earlier, the back of the famine had been effectively broken. By the end of February 1993, mortality rates in many parts of the nation were approaching normal levels; U.S. Deputy Chief of Mission John Hirsch recalls that, in the hard-hit city of Bardera, death rates dropped from three hundred per day in November to five in February. As always, hard data on famine causalities are hard to come by in conflict situations like Somalia, and assessing how many lives were saved by Operation Restore Hope confronts the "counterfactual" conundrum: it is impossible to know how many additional human beings would have died if U.S. forces had not intervened. Estimates of the people directly saved by President Bush's decision are normally in the range of one hundred thousand. However, given the downward spiral in food production and delivery in Somalia and the likelihood of sustained civil war, my estimate is several multiples of that figure.

Effectively ending the Great Somalia Famine by late winter 1993 is certainly the apex of America's engagement in Somalia in the early 1990s, and forms one of the two key analytical pillars for revisiting and assessing Operation Restore Hope a quarter century later. The second analytical pillar—the nadir of America's engagement—requires us to fast-forward from February 1993 to October 3 of that year, and confront the "Black Hawk Down" events. On that date, U.S. Rangers and Delta Force soldiers attempting to capture the most prominent and most intractable Somali clan leader, Mohamed Farah Aidid, engaged in a sustained firefight, resulting in the deaths of eighteen U.S. servicemen and the wounding of seventy-eight more. The outcome of that vicious battle, including widely broadcast footage of a dead U.S. soldier being dragged naked through the streets of Mogadishu by Somali fighters, provoked outrage among Americans and added jet fuel to incipient congressional opposition to long-term U.S. engagement in Somalia. Given that the grim events were the topic of a best-selling book and a popular movie, in my experience, they loom larger in the collective American consciousness than the earlier, highly successful humanitarian phase of the operation. The resultant lack of enthusiasm for further assistance to Somalia is buttressed, naturally, by generally ineffective efforts by the Somalis to form a functioning national government since that time and sustained negative reporting for more than two decades on violence, extremism, and dysfunction in the country. Moreover, the October 3 incident not only dampened American enthusiasm toward Somalia, but made Western governments more wary of international interventions, especially when armed combatants are present, affecting decisions made toward Bosnia and leading to catastrophic consequences in the 1994 Rwandan genocide.

Even among those who do recall President Bush's noble and well-organized humanitarian landing and the subsequent successful relief deliveries, and who attempt to learn lessons both from Operation Restore Hope and "Black Hawk Down," I note what appears to be an acute compaction of the time line for crucial events in Somalia and a concomitant almost exclusive analytical focus on these two iconic events. It is as though America's intervention was short and limited to these two focal events when in fact the U.S. humanitarian/security engagement in post-Barre Somalia began with relief operations as early as 1991 and the withdrawal of large

U.S. troop contingents was not completed until March 31, 1994. Furthermore, an almost exclusive focus on these two events in the writings of a number of analysts produces a simple, tending to simplistic, conclusion about their meaning and their lessons for humanitarian operations, for peacemaking and peacebuilding efforts, and broadly about America's appropriate role when nation-states like Somalia fail. In the case of Operation Restore Hope, the consensus of many—although certainly not all—participants and observers runs something like this: President Bush got it right by limiting America's engagement to sharply bounded and clearly enunciated humanitarian tasks. His 1992 campaign opponent and successor, Bill Clinton, got it wrong by expanding Operation Restore Hope into a vaguely defined "nation-building" exercise, and such exercises are always doomed to failure.[7] Although there are elements of truth in this straightforward dichotomy, my view is that reading the events this way oversimplifies the situation in Somalia circa 1992, distorts useful lessons from the period and, most importantly, sells short the sophistication of what President Bush undertook in Operation Restore Hope.

In reality, what happened between the time the president addressed the nation on Somalia in December 1992 and the end of the UN peacekeeping presence there in March 1995 was a complex, nuanced, and multifaceted engagement, both by the United States and the United Nations. The bilateral and multilateral strands of international action were deeply intertwined, and the operational elements of providing humanitarian aid intersected constantly with the political and security elements, literally from beginning to end. For example, within hours of the president's decision to intervene, he had dispatched Acting Secretary of State Lawrence Eagleburger to brief the UN secretary-general on his plan and to discern how the U.S. initiative could be fitted into the appropriate UN framework. And the final withdrawal of UN peacekeeping forces in 1995 was accomplished with substantial U.S. logistics and security support. In between these two pivot points, the international actors focused primarily on ending the famine in Somalia, and the actors primarily interested in stabilizing or reconstructing the Somali state maintained a constant, if not always fully synchronized, dialogue both between Washington and New York and on the ground in Mogadishu. Critical diplomatic tools like the structure of UN Security Council resolutions, solutions to logistics issues like the supply and deployment of national peacekeeping contingents, and engagements with clan leaders in Somalia often bore the stamp of both U.S. government and UN officials. Both President Bush and his successor understood clearly that underlying conflicts within Somalia drove the famine, and that simply delivering more food would not alone end the risk of humanitarian crises in the region. Similarly, President Bush and his team, President Clinton, and UN Secretary-General Boutros-Ghali all understood that investments in reconciling the Somali antagonists, and strengthening institutions of governance—nation-building, if you will—were the only viable mid-range strategy to avoid future famines. And certainly these actors all understood, even if not always in perfect accord, that both the United States and multilateral institutions like the United Nations had essential roles to play in addressing Somalia's core dilemmas.

Is the lesson to be taken from Operation Restore Hope and its aftermath, then, that President Bush was correct to take on the short-term disaster relief phase of Somalia's agony and limit the role of U.S. forces under his command to this arduous, if relatively straightforward task, while the Clinton administration and the UN's follow-on UNOSOM II operation mistakenly undertook the more difficult nation-building phase? Hardly. To draw that lesson from the humanitarian successes of early 1993 and the bloody denouement of Black Hawk Down would be to accept the notion that America's role in shaping the world is mightily constrained, that difficult tasks in failed states are intractable tragedies to be avoided, that we will simply donate excess commodities to the next famine that takes hundreds of thousands of lives. I do not believe that was the lesson President Bush intended to leave with us his bold decision to launch Operation Restore Hope, when he broadcast, in December 1992, the words "America must act."

Rather, if there is a clear-cut distinction between the Bush administration's bounded humanitarian operation and the Clinton administration's nation-building phase, in my view it lies in three aspects of George Bush's character: (1) his expansive and sophisticated understanding of the elements of national power and how America should use that power; (2) his detailed knowledge of the capabilities and constraints of multilateral institutions; and (3) a disciplined approach to defining national objectives and a strategic approach to linking resources with effective outcomes. Operation Restore Hope, with its stunning successes on the President's watch, reflects all these elements of George Bush's character.

SOMALIA REVISITED, A QUARTER CENTURY LATER

To paraphrase an old saying, analysts have touched many parts of the "elephant" in Somalia in the period since George Bush initiated Operation Restore Hope, and reasonable individuals may draw competing conclusions. From my perspective at the Office of U.S. Foreign Disaster Assistance in the run-up to the president's decision, based on what I saw on the ground in the Horn of Africa from 1991 to 1993, and from my review of the literature on and events in Somalia since that time, I believe President Bush's bold and dramatic decisions in 1992 merit reflection in, and offer relevant insights for, the world of 2020. I would offer, with humility, the following five reflections:

1. *At multiple levels, humanitarian action matters*: The descriptor "compassionate conservative" has often been associated with George H. W. Bush, as well as with President George W. Bush. I would suggest that, regarding Somalia, President Bush was also a "compassionate realist." At one level, driven by human compassion, he understood that there existed a moral and ethical imperative to act, when our nation had the power to do so, to avoid hundreds of thousands of unnecessary deaths and inconceivable human suffering. The

natural generosity of the American people and their concern for the world's underdogs are important components of the national character. But, based on his vast international and domestic governing and policy experience, the president also understood that humanitarian action is an element of national power. Like other elements of national power, when judiciously utilized it can be an effective tool to advance national interests, and garner support for U.S. policy. At the time of the Great Somalia Famine nations of the Middle East and Islamic nations elsewhere were deeply affected by the horrific death rate of fellow Muslims in Somalia and the apparently greater investment by donor nations in the simultaneous Bosnian conflict.[8] The president's compassionate realism served both goals: on the one hand, it reflected the best instincts of America and saved lives, while also projecting an image of America that benefitted our national interest. In the world of 2020, a similar effect can be seen with the president's Emergency Plan for AIDS Relief, which has ministered to the suffering of thousands and simultaneously contributed to positive views on the United States, especially in Africa. The instinct for generosity and reputation for generosity, as President Bush understood in Somalia, are American assets to be prized.

2. *Then and now, disciplined American leadership drives the international system*: Of the Somalia policy options presented to the president just before Thanksgiving 1992, he selected the boldest choice, stating: "America must act." At the time of his determination to deploy U.S. forces, the Soviet Union had recently dissolved; theorists were touting the "end of history" with the triumph of global democracy; and the United States seemed to be the only remaining global superpower. The risk in 1992 was to overreach and either engage in prolific unilateralism or, conversely, to foment a strident multilateralism and intervene widely in those parts of the world that had "opened up" at the end of the Cold War. Recognizing by the fall of 1992 that UN action in and of itself was unlikely to end the famine in Somalia, and that inaction meant death for possibly hundreds of thousands, the president acted forcefully. But it was a highly disciplined forcefulness. President Bush and his team defined their mission carefully and resisted persistent efforts by UN leaders to glide into a full-scale nation-building effort. When provocations against American troops in Somalia occurred, the president ensured U.S. forces would respond quickly and with deadly force. But he avoided the downward slope to retribution and personification of the conflict that bedeviled the later stages of the Somalia crisis. As discussed above, the president fully understood that the underlying causes of the famine were political and that Somalia risked a return to humanitarian crises if these foundational causes were not addressed. In fact, during Operation Restore Hope initial steps were taken under President Bush's watch to reconstitute a nascent Somali police force and take other preliminary "nation-building" steps. However, as in Iraq's Operation Desert Storm, he carefully bounded the U.S. mission in Somalia during his presidency to those activities

that were ripe for solution and for which resources had been allocated.[9] In my view, this forceful but disciplined approach to American leadership in international diplomacy still resonates from Somalia a quarter century later.

3. *Both institutional and coalition-based multilateralism work*: Since the UN-OSOM II operation that followed the Bush-driven humanitarian phase in Somalia ended badly, critics have argued that multilateralism in such conflictive environments may be inherently flawed. The most extreme variant of this perspective is reflected in the words of John Bolton, then the State Department's assistant secretary for international organization affairs and subsequently national security advisor, written in 1994: "Whatever the real meaning of 'assertive multilateralism,' that policy died an early death in Somalia."[10] In fact, looking back from the perspective of 2020, multilateral resolution of complex security situations did quite well in the early 1990s. President George H. W. Bush's skillful recruitment of thirty-seven coalition partners in the First Gulf War was a major factor in hurling back Saddam Hussein's adventurism in Kuwait. That at least fourteen of Operation Desert Storm's troop contingents were from Muslim-majority countries was important to gaining acceptance for "aggressive multilateralism" in the Arab World. Moreover, in the early 1990s, UN-led peacekeeping forces played major and successful roles in managing crises from Namibia to Cambodia to El Salvador. The highly successful first phase of humanitarian operations in Somalia, skillfully launched by President Bush, was itself a UN-sanctioned multilateral coalition with twenty-seven foreign troop contingents joining U.S. forces. That is to say, looking at Operation Restore Hope twenty-eight years after the fact, there is little evidence that multilateralism, "aggressive" or not, was a root cause of mission breakdown in conflict zones. Rather, imprecision in mission definition during UNOSOM II and, especially, the pronounced mismatch between mission and resources are more likely culprits. Moreover, since Somalia, the United States has engaged in its longest-ever war, in Afghanistan. In that context, when examining lessons from Somalia, one cannot help but notice that these two are among those corners of the world that have rarely known stability and centrally organized governance throughout their respective histories. It may well be that the lesson to be learned is that significant change in such locales is possible only in rare circumstances, multilateralism notwithstanding.

4. *Somalia highlights synergy among the U.S. government's "three Ds"*: Diplomacy, defense, and development—the provinces, respectively, of the Department of State, Department of Defense, and U.S. Agency for International Development—are all part of the national "tool kit" for foreign engagement, whether twenty-eight years ago when "failed states" were the primary concern or in today's milieu of counterterrorism and countering violent extremism. As President Bush understood fully during Operation Restore Hope, all of these instruments of national power must be engaged in order to address successfully a complex humanitarian crisis like the Great Somalia Famine. As a combat

veteran himself, and as commander in chief during the First Gulf War, George Bush's actions in Somalia illustrate the centrality of using America's military power when necessary. Simultaneously, though, he ensured that a seasoned diplomat, Bob Oakley, and a highly regarded humanitarian expert, Andrew Natsios, were core members of the national team. In the intervening years between Operation Restore Hope and today, by and large this triad of "3Ds" has been strengthened through training, liaison officer exchanges, and doctrinal developments, with greater mutual understanding of what each skill set and each institution brings to the table. When interacting these days with U.S. military forces during training exercises, I frequently hear officers express the welcome, if rough-hewn, sentiment that "we know we cannot bomb our way to success"—a sustained compliment to the multifaceted, government-wide A-team President Bush assembled in 1992. Continuing investments in this complementary U.S. government team remain, in my view, crucial to addressing the complex international environment of 2020.

5. *Bipartisanship and comity count during perilous operations*: Many of the events recounted in this chapter took place, of course, during the hard-fought presidential campaign of 1992, and the actual deployment of U.S. forces in Operation Restore Hope took place after President Bush had suffered defeat in November. Election-related pressure for and against deeper engagement in Somalia (as well as for and against increased involvement in the former Yugoslavia) provided a contentious backdrop to the policy deliberations on Somalia that summer and fall. Yet, when the president made his far-reaching decision to end famine in Somalia, he reached out to President-elect Clinton and insisted on seeking his concurrence on launching Operation Restore Hope, recognizing that the work in Somalia would not be wrapped up before his departure from office. Subsequently, the president insisted on close coordination between his team and the incoming administration to give his successor as much opportunity as possible to succeed under conditions when U.S. military forces and civilian agencies, as well as American charitable organizations, were operating in perilous circumstances. Despite what must have been deepest disappointment at the electoral outcome, a profound respect for American constitutional traditions and a selfless commitment to ensuring a smooth transition of power in the U.S. polity prevailed. This characteristic of the president, and this legacy from the Somalia intervention, while they could not guarantee mission success after the handoff to the new administration, strike me as among the most important and enduring lessons from that period.

There is much more that we might consider and reflected upon given the complex and momentous events of Operation Restore Hope in Somalia and its enduring legacy in U.S. foreign policy. Considering those now long-ago events today, I am struck most by President Bush's skilled, decent, bold, and far-sighted management of virtually unmanageable circumstances. I am struck by how relevant many of the issues he faced are for policy makers today. Mostly, though, I am struck by the reality that—despite its many continuing obstacles and seemingly endless tribulations—Somalia post-1992 has never slipped fully back into the massive famine and Hobbesian warfare of that time. President Bush's bold decision somehow altered the conflict dynamic in a sweeping fashion and saved hundreds of thousands of lives into the bargain.

NOTES

1. These observations are my own, based on my work with USAID's Office of U.S. Foreign Disaster Assistance during the crisis, including three deployments to Somalia. For readers interested in a more detailed understanding of Somalia's history and socioeconomic structure and how these set the stage for the humanitarian disaster of the 1990s, I recommend I. M. Lewis, *A Modern History of the Somali* (Athens: Ohio University Press, 1992).

2. The evolution of the Somalia famine of 1991–1992 and the world's response to it have been the subject of numerous publications and are only covered briefly in this short chapter. Detailed accounts of the period are usefully found in John G. Sommer's report to the Office of U.S. Foreign Disaster Assistance titled *Hope Restored? Humanitarian Aid in Somalia 1990–1994* (Refugee Policy Group, 1994); and in John L. Hirsch and Robert B. Oakley, *Somalia and Operation Restore Hope: Reflections on Peacemaking the Peacekeeping* (New York: United States Institute of Peace, 1995). The former focuses on famine conditions and relief efforts, while the latter focuses on the diplomatic efforts to address the crisis.

3. Although it has become somewhat of an article of faith that the so-called "CNN effect" energized relief efforts in Somalia and other well-known emergency responses, the reality is more complex. In the earlier stages of the Somalia relief effort, media attention was, frankly, hard to come by. The public diplomacy efforts of government leaders like Andrew Natsios, then President Bush's USAID assistant administrator for food and humanitarian assistance, had much to do with CNN and other media outlets being mobilized. Although media coverage indisputably boosted public awareness of and support for increased U.S. engagement in Somalia in 1992, the "causal arrows" originally moved in both directions between reporters and relief proponents within and outside the U.S. government.

4. Of particular value to those wishing a more detailed explication of the U.S. government decision-making process leading to the president's decision are Hirsch and Oakley, *Somalia and Operation Restore Hope*; James L. Woods, "U.S. Government Decisionmaking Processes During Humanitarian Operations in Somalia," in *Learning from Somalia*, ed. Walter Clarke and Jeffrey Herbst (Boulder, CO: Westview Press, 1997); and an August 2019 interview with former humanitarian coordinator for Somalia, Andrew Natsios, who attended National Security Council meetings during this period, representing USAID.

5. This United Task Force, or "UNITAF" as it was universally known, would reach its maximum size in January, 1993, at 38,301 military personnel. A total of 12,875 troops from coalition nations joined the U.S. forces by that time.

6. Woods, "U.S. Government Decisionmaking Processes," 157.

7. Interestingly, a key proponent of this view at the time U.S. troops were withdrawing from Somalia in 1994, an early opponent of Operation Restore Hope, and a continuingly sharp critic of nation-building is John R. Bolton. See Bolton, "Wrong Turn in Somalia,"

Foreign Affairs 73, no. 1 (January–February 1994): 55–66, https://www.foreignaffairs.com/articles/somalia/1994-01-01/wrong-turn-somalia.

8. Secretary-General Boutros-Ghali famously noted in August 1992 that the world community seemed much more engaged in the "rich man's war" in Europe than in the larger humanitarian crisis in the Horn of Africa.

9. It is useful to recall that the United States went in "heavy" to Somalia, the president's views being buttressed by the Weinberger-Powell doctrine of overwhelming force when American troops are committed. The subsequent mismatch between military and civilian resources, on one hand, and the expanded mission undertaken by the UN in the follow-on UNOSOM II phase, on the other, bedeviled international operations in Somalia throughout the crucial 1993–1994 period.

10. Bolton, "Wrong Turn in Somalia," 66.

16

"To Make Kinder the Face of the Nation and Gentler the Face of the World"

Humanitarian Leadership during the Presidency of George H. W. Bush

Catherine Bertini

Even before his presidency began, George Bush had signaled many times his commitment to the less fortunate and his determination to provide the conditions and support necessary to help people not only survive but to thrive. In his nomination acceptance speech, the then-vice president said he would strive for a "kinder and gentler nation." From his 1989 inaugural address, he proclaimed his goal "To make kinder the face of the nation and gentler the face of the world."[1] These statements are part of the personal philosophy and legacy of George Herbert Walker Bush. As he stated in 2011, "There could be no definition of a successful life that does not include service to others."[2]

On the domestic front, the Bush administration established programs for creating training and education options for poor women receiving welfare, increased Head Start opportunities, increased funding for earned income tax credits, enhanced nutrition support for poor mothers, increased the numbers of schools providing school breakfasts, led the effort toward education performance measures, signed a Clean Air Act, played a leadership role in the development of the Americans for Disability Act, and proposed statewide implementation of electronic benefit transfer technology to replace the then paper food stamps and welfare checks with EBT cards. The major change in food stamp delivery, which exists nationwide today, was ironic considering that a 1992 video showing his surprise at new grocery store scanning technology was used to portray the president as being "distant from everyday realities."[3] The same kind of creativity and commitment to humanitarian advances was an integral part of the global policies, actions, and leadership extended by him and his administration. Whether the direction came from the White House, the State Department, U.S. Agency for International Development (USAID), the Department of Agriculture, or his nominees to lead UN agencies, a common thread was the multiplicity of efforts to improve people's lives—making "gentler the face of the world."

ORIGINS

Virtually every person interviewed for this chapter had the same perspective on why
the president directed that the United States play leadership roles in global humanitarian work. His experience as the U.S. permanent representative (ambassador) to
the United Nations (from March 1971 to January 1973), everyone said, helped
inform his decisions and his interests. His knowledge of what was needed as well as
what was possible for the international community to accomplish was a major con-
tributor to his policies and decisions. And that earlier role of ambassador was perfect
for George Herbert Walker Bush. As Jon Meacham points out in *Destiny and Power*,
"The UN job was one in which relationships mattered. Reaching out to others and
keeping them close created a personal atmosphere that sometimes translated into
tangible professional or political benefit."[4] Bush's assistant secretary for international
organizations at the State Department, John Bolton, said, "He was much more
hands-on than previous presidents because he actually knew the UN system and the
function of specific organizations in the UN."[5]

Ron Kaufman, who was Bush's director of White House personnel, said that
the president "had a global vision of where the world should go, knowing that we
wouldn't get there if the U.S. didn't take the lead. . . . He understood better than any
incoming president the importance of soft power and how to create the world into
a safer and more humane world system."[6]

The president had said this himself. In his 1990 International Women's Day message, he wrote: "Since my own service as the U.S. Ambassador to the United Nations, I have had a great deal of respect for the role of the United Nations in making
the world a better place for its inhabitants."[7]

His view of the world was famously laid out in the president's 1990 address to the
General Assembly, often called the "New World Order" speech. Among many other
things, he said: "I see a world of open borders, open trade, and most importantly, open
minds, a world that celebrates the common heritage that belongs to all the world's
people, taking pride not just in hometown or homeland but in humanity itself."[8]

According to Jan Eliasson, then Sweden's ambassador to the United Nations, "The
Bush administration had a positive view of the UN, a clear commitment to multilateralism, especially in the humanitarian sector."[9]

Bush administration officials took leadership roles in a broad range of humanitarian
activities, including the creation of UN entities, and numerous strategies for supporting
refugees, children, women, those cut off from food, and the environment. The impact
of much of this work has reached far beyond the forty-first U.S. presidency.

UN DEPARTMENT OF HUMANITARIAN AFFAIRS (DHA)

Once the Berlin Wall fell, there were multiple initiatives within the United Nations
and in the broader global community to address the anticipated additional humani-

tarian needs of people in Eastern Europe and elsewhere. Additionally, the success of independence movements and subsequent governance changes and nongovernmental disrupters throughout Africa were creating more internally displaced people and refugees. Leaders were also looking for more stability and humanitarian outreach after the Gulf War. One example is of increased UN involvement in peacekeeping. Twenty missions were authorized by the UN Security Council from 1989 to 1994; in the thirty years before only five such missions were created. There was much more discussion about how and whether to deploy military assets for humanitarian relief. In fact, there was a White House National Security Directive in 1992 that stated as a policy, "The United States should urge nations to provide military units for possible peacekeeping operations and humanitarian relief."[10]

For at least twenty years before 1991, the office of the UN Disaster Relief Coordination (UNDRO) was the chief response agency for humanitarian crises reporting to the UN Secretariat. Interestingly, it was created when George Bush was the U.S. ambassador to the UN.[11] However, it turned out to be slow moving and concentrated on "natural" disasters such as floods, earthquakes, and droughts. It did not have the authority to provide leadership within the UN context. The world was changing; the United States and others thought that the UN required the existence of an organization unlike the rest of the Secretariat—a fast moving, quick acting entity that could pull together all major humanitarian actors to provide leadership, coordination, fundraising, and quick action to save lives not only in natural disasters but also in the burgeoning number of "man-made" crises.

A small group of ambassadors from Nordic countries, led by the Swedish ambassador Jan Eliasson, began to meet in the summer of 1991 to discuss options and to outline a mandate for the future. Quickly, their informal committee expanded to include the European Union, the United States, the USSR, and other key governments.[12] This was the basis of a formal UN General Assembly working group, which Eliasson chaired.

The U.S. government was part of the effort to create a UN humanitarian coordination function, with substantive support provided primarily through USAID. Melinda Kimble, then deputy assistant secretary for international organizations at the State Department, reports that internally, there was excellent cooperation between all relevant U.S. government agencies.[13] Her department's role was to ensure that the structure was organized correctly and that the systems would keep up with the times.

The conversations about a more coordinated and effective humanitarian response mechanism were underway while the United Nations was involved in another significant event—the selection of a new secretary-general. Boutros Boutros-Ghali was elected in November and sworn in on December 3, 1991; he called on President Bush two days later in the Oval Office.[14] Reforming the Secretariat was an interest of both the new secretary-general and of the White House, with the developing humanitarian proposal high on the list. The administration had recently created its own Disaster Assistance Response Team (DART) emergency response mechanism and believed that a UN entity could enhance response capabilities and international cooperation.

The U.S. Congress was supportive of the concept in H. Con. Res 197 of September 25, 1991, sponsored by Nebraska Republican Congressman Doug Bereuter. The vote was 422 to 1 in support of his concurrent resolution that called on the "United Nations to develop plans for coordinating and expanding resources of the United Nations to respond effectively to disasters and humanitarian emergencies."[15]

So, when the UN General Assembly passed, after much deliberation among nations, its Resolution 46/182 on December 19, 1991, it did so with no opposition from member states and with the leadership of the countries who would quickly become large donors to the voluntary funds supporting much of the work of the new UN Department of Humanitarian Affairs (DHA). The existing UN Disaster Relief Organization was incorporated in DHA whose mandate was:

- Ensuring the "prompt and smooth delivery of humanitarian assistance"
- Assisting countries "in strengthening their capacity in disaster prevention and mitigation"
- Creating or expanding early warning systems
- Creating a central emergency revolving fund (CERF) to provide a more flexible funding
- Coordinating consolidated appeals for major humanitarian operations
- Creating the emergency relief coordinator (ERC) to coordinate global responses and to be the central focal point for governments, nongovernmental organizations, and the UN
- Creating an Interagency Standing Committee (IASC) made up of principals of all major operational humanitarian agencies inside and outside the UN, or their representatives, to help set policies and coordinate efforts

(Note that in Secretary-General Kofi Annan's reform proposals of 1997, he further strengthened UN humanitarian management and renamed DHA to OCHA, the Office of Coordination of Humanitarian Affairs.)

When Secretary-General Boutros-Ghali was naming his cabinet in early 1992, he appointed the Swedish ambassador Jan Eliasson, who had led the humanitarian reform effort, to be the first undersecretary-general for the Department of Humanitarian Affairs.

SOUTHERN AFRICA DROUGHT

The importance of the leadership and coordination role of DHA immediately showed its worth when the UN and its agencies took on aggressive responses to the 1992 southern Africa drought. An estimated eighteen million people in ten mostly landlocked countries were impacted by the drought. As Anthony Lewis wrote in the *New York Times*, millions of people "are living under a drought previously unknown to the region in sweep and severity. . . . All this a cruel blow to a country and a region that had reason to think that better times were coming: racial conflicts easing, regional growth a real possibility."[16]

There were limited transport lines into most of the countries. The small ports in Angola and Mozambique had few inward transport routes and both countries were in the midst of raging civil wars and themselves impacted by the drought. Four million tons of food was needed to reach the drought-stricken countries, as food and water were, obviously, scarce in the region. Many UN agencies were active, but there was no real leadership and not enough resources. USG Eliasson declared that the UN World Food Programme (WFP) would be the lead, as, aside from rain, food was the largest short-term need. WFP proposed:

- that the only viable routes were through apartheid South Africa and that it would sign agreements with the ports and the railroads, not the government, to move food through the country;
- that where the private sector transport systems were good, they would be the option of choice for shipping;
- that all plans would be discussed and coordinated with the Southern Africa Development Coordination Committee (SADDC) secretariat;
- the WFP would make its transport facilities available to any NGOs and bilateral donors who wished to move goods through the region;
- the WFP would invite the government of each impacted country to post a representative in the WFP transport office in Johannesburg, in order to track and help facilitate the food movement through South Africa to their country. This often required unloading and loading at the borders, as many country railroad track gages were of different size than those of South Africa.

In New York, USG Eliasson made sure that the UN Special Committee on Apartheid was aware of this plan before it began.[17] UNHCR facilitated the work of WFP by authorizing them to work under the UNHCR "legal umbrella," as WFP had no official status in the Republic of South Africa but UNHCR did, due to their protection of refugees in the country. The WFP plan was approved by the UN secretary-general, at the request of USG Eliasson at DHA.[18]

The *Christian Science Monitor* reported that the southern Africa drought threats sufficiently motivated the global community such that "international diplomats are redefining global security in a way that identifies as an essential element the stabilization of war- or famine-ravaged countries."[19]

The government that provided the most support to this effort—both in food and with political considerations—was the United States. Andrew Natsios wrote in 1997 that an effective humanitarian response was a top U.S. priority. The National Security Council and State, he said, "feared that massive starvation would seriously undermine the peace process pursued by the Bush administration in Mozambique and Angola, democratic and economic reforms in Zambia, and reconciliation in South Africa, fears, that, given the history of famines, were well founded."[20] Marilyn

Quayle, wife of Vice President Dan Quayle, visited the region in 1992 and wrote in the *Christian Science Monitor*, "Several of the affected countries are emerging democracies and undertaking rigorous economic reform processes. It would be a travesty to allow drought to obliterate hard-won development progress."[21] As a result, the Bush administration provided diverse and significant bilateral in-country assistance, advice and guidance on emergency aid and assistance throughout the region, political support for the transport options (even with the presidential determination against apartheid), and three-quarters of the all the food requested by the World Food Programme.

By most measures, the operations were extremely successful. Mass starvation did not occur. Governments did not topple. Positive national changes eventually followed.

OPERATION RESTORE HOPE IN SOMALIA

The same year, in the Horn of Africa, over two hundred thousand people are estimated to have starved in Somalia, due in large part to the inability of people and of aid workers to move around. The civil war, constantly an issue in this country, was at the height—or depth—of its depravity. In 1991–1992, international aid agencies struggled for access, especially into the largest city, Mogadishu. In the rural areas and smaller inland cities, aid arrived in military planes provided by the governments of Germany, Canada, and the United States. The United States often employed reservists to fly the planes delivering food. While effective, one officer said to a WFP official that the planes could not turn off their motors while they were delivering food and the propeller wind was spinning sand in the faces of the porters, because the planes were older than the pilots![22]

Once again, the United States was providing over half of the food delivered, but with many partners. For months, WFP logistics officers negotiated with various warring factions in Mogadishu to allow ships to enter and off-load at docks in the harbor. Only once was this successful; other ships had been attacked and forced to retreat.

As more people died in Somalia, various entities worked to try to improve aid deliveries. The United States began to plan, in conjunction with the UN, for a military effort to establish the basis for free flow of aid delivery to those who needed it. In fact, President Bush, in his September 1992 address to the UN General Assembly, stated that the United States would continue its "robust humanitarian assistance" to Somalia and elsewhere.[23]

The WFP executive director wrote to Secretary-General Boutros-Ghali on November 24, 1992, describing the depth of WFP's unsuccessful efforts to send adequate food into the country. In summary, she wrote: "The bottom line is, we are fully resourced and fully staffed but it has become impossible for us to reach the majority of the starving. I implore you to use this occasion to press urgently for more drastic action by the international community on behalf of the Somali people."[24] Many others weighed in, in support of military or other strong efforts to change the dynamics.

On December 3, 1992, UN Security Council resolution 794 passed, allowing "all necessary means to establish as soon as possible a secure environment for humanitarian relief operations in Somalia." The U.S. military was poised to enter the country immediately thereafter. President Bush wrote to the secretary-general the next day, thanking him for "your tremendous hard work to achieve this unprecedented outcome. A dramatic step has been taken to address the appalling suffering of the Somali people." He also said that "I want to emphasize that the mission of the coalition is limited and specific: to create security conditions which will permit the feeding of the starving Somali people and allow the transfer of this security function to the UN peacekeeping force."[25]

On December 4, 1992, U.S. Marines landed on the beaches of Mogadishu. Cameras were already set up to record their arrival. U.S. Army troops also arrived. Immediately, the International Committee of the Red Cross (ICRC), the World Food Programme (WFP), UNICEF, and many other organizations were able to feed thousands more people throughout the land. At least for a few months, with order restored, food was available, and Somali citizens could eat.

President Bush wrote to the WFP executive director on December 10, 1992, "I am pleased by the progress that has been made thus far, by our Armed Forces in facilitating the distribution of food and other vital supplies to those who are starving. It is heartening to have the cooperation of so many humanitarian relief organizations—including, of course, the World Food Programme of the United Nations—and I commend you and your staff for your commitment to help in establishing long-term stability in Somalia."[26]

As John Bolton wrote in 1994, "The Bush administration sent U.S. troops into Somalia strictly to clear the relief channels that could avert mass starvation. It resisted U.N. attempts to expand that mission . . . [Intervention in Somalia came] as an extension of the duty to preserve international security after the Gulf War."[27]

UN WORLD FOOD PROGRAMME (WFP) LEADERSHIP

In 1961, George McGovern, the head of Food for Peace in the Kennedy White House, joined European allies in advocating for the creation of a new body to accept surplus food commodities for distribution to people in countries with significant food deficits. WFP was then created as a body managed jointly by the United Nations and the Food and Agriculture Organization (FAO). It began as a development program and gradually shifted to more emergency relief. Today almost all of its $8 billion 2019 budget is considered humanitarian relief. Over time, as government surplus commodities were phased out and as more effective aid distribution funding was available, WFP was funded by cash and by in-kind food donations, mostly from governments and all voluntary contributions, no UN dues. The United States consistently gave at least one-third of WFP's resources each year, with that percentage rising to 42 percent of WFP's 2019 resources. For years, though, WFP was known as the surplus commodity program and somewhat derisively referred to by some UN colleagues as the "truck drivers." Fortunately, its governance process changed, effective January 1992, allowing the organization the independence and capability for quick decision-making in providing disaster response. To use those tools, however, the organization needed a major transformation.

In October 1990, President Bush's Secretary of Agriculture, Clayton Yeutter, raised to Secretary of State Baker the proposal that the United States should consider nominating a candidate to lead WFP. Yeutter argued that the United States was the largest donor to WFP, that there had never been an American who served a full term as head of WFP, and that having an American in the role was consistent with the president's broader interest to provide humanitarian leadership. There might be a downside, however, as there are limited numbers of senior positions in the UN that nationals of any one country could realistically hold. By tradition, not written mandate, Americans had always been appointed or elected to lead UNICEF, the UN Development Program (UNDP), and the World Bank. Therefore, the Secretary of State had to decide whether promoting an American candidate for WFP was a good idea. Ultimately, the president agreed that the United States proceed and was enthusiastic about Yeutter's proposal that Catherine Bertini be the candidate.[28] The President's talking points for discussing this topic with other leaders included: "Ms. Bertini will bring just the kind of forceful, forward-looking management needed by the WFP and even more important, needed by poor women and children of the third world being reached by WFP."[29]

There were three countries with candidates vying for the appointment by the UN secretary-general and the FAO director-general, so the State Department orchestrated a "campaign" asking countries to support the U.S. candidate. John Bolton, then assistant secretary of International Organizations, was in the lead. Because WFP is funded voluntarily, donor governments' views were highly important. With two candidates from European donor governments, Italy and Denmark, the United States could not expect European support, though Austria did provide it. Therefore, the United States had to concentrate on the other major donors—Canada, Australia, and Japan. The Canadian decision was important for the other two, and initially, the internal recommendation of its aid agency was to support their colleague, the head of the Danish aid agency. However, Prime Minister Brian Mulroney ultimately chose to endorse a different candidate, writing to his friend: "Dear George, I am pleased to inform you that Canada endorses Mrs. Bertini's candidacy and will support it fully. Yours sincerely, Brian."[30]

Why was any of this really important?

- The Berlin Wall had fallen two years before.
- The USSR collapsed at Christmas 1991.
- Wars and civil strife abounded.

- Many more people were displaced and hungry.
- WFP's decision-making authority had dramatically improved as of January 1992.
- The new executive director was to be in place in April 1992.
- WFP had the backbone of its extensive and creative logistics operation.

WFP needed a transformational leader to change the organization into a highly ef-fective global leader in humanitarian response. In all humility, the author writes that that major transformation happened over the course of her ten years at the World Food Programme, making WFP arguably the largest and most effective humanitar-ian agency. But her (my) words are not enough.

The World Food Prize Foundation chose to name Catherine Bertini its 2003 Laureate, because she "transformed the World Food Programme into the largest and most responsive food relief organization in all history" and that it was "transformed from essentially an agricultural development agency into a logistical juggernaut."[31] Alex de Waal, perhaps the eminent academic on starvation and famines, and not always a fan of WFP and its leadership, writes in his book *Mass Starvation*, "Some-thing remarkable happened over the past thirty years. The risk of dying in famine has become much, much smaller than at any time in history. . . . The fact that famines, when they do (still) occur, kill many fewer people is a laudable achievement of the public health professions and the humanitarian industry."[32]

APPOINTMENT OF THE FIRST
U.S. AMBASSADOR FOR WOMEN

A previously untold story combines the president's priority on relationship build-ing, his long-standing support for opportunities for women, and his knowledge of the UN. The president's commitment, for instance, is mentioned in his message for the 1990 International Women's Day: "We will not be satisfied until all barriers of ignorance and discrimination against women are eliminated and women and men are viewed as equals. This is a priority for us in the United States."[33]

Traditionally, since President Harry S. Truman, the president has appointed a U.S. representative to the UN Status of Women Commission (CSW). There is an "inside the Washington beltway" view that Barack Obama was the first president to promote the role to the level of ambassador, but the first president to do so was George H. W. Bush.

According to Juliette McLennan, when she was asked to be the U.S. representa-tive, she was told that the president was going to nominate her at the ambassador level because he knew, through his experience at the United Nations, that to have the influence one should have on women's issues, one needed a seat at the table that the ambassador rank would give. Ron Kaufman, director of White House personnel under Bush, said, "This wasn't a debatable appointment for the president; he wanted to do this."[34] Melinda Kimble, who was deputy assistant secretary for international organizations at State, said that "This was an important step in showing the U.S. commitment to women and to allow U.S. representatives like Judy to gain traction in the conversations."[35] This was considered revolutionary at the time as very few nations had appointed women ambassadors for any functions, and certainly not in this role.[36] Thus, she began her role as representative and then was nominated as "ambassador and representative for the United States on the Commission on the Status of Women, under the Economic and Social Council of the United Nations." On October 28, 1990, Ambassador McLennan was confirmed by the U.S. Senate. Subsequently, Presidents Clinton and George W. Bush also nominated the CSW representative at the ambassador level. President Obama expanded the role to ambassador at large for global women's issues and nominated Melanie Verveer to lead an enhanced office.

High on Ambassador McLennan's list was leading efforts to convince the United Nations to hire and promote more women, especially in leadership roles. One example is the 1991 U.S.-proposed resolution urging the secretary-general to hire more women at all levels and from all geographic areas and setting goals for this initiative. Her demeanor carried the U.S. message effectively, as described in a letter to President Bush by a delegate to the CSW conference. "Judy McLennan was an inspiration to all of us. . . . She performed with equanimity and good humor and cajoled all of us to exert our best. Certainly, all in the best 'Bush Tradition.'"[37]

OPERATION SEA ANGEL IN BANGLADESH

Another relatively untold story is that of the U.S. Navy and Marine Corps operation to save lives in Bangladesh. A huge flood ravaged the country in April 1991; in many cities, virtually every structure was underwater, all the trees had been swept away, and hundreds of thousands of people were homeless. An estimated one hundred thirty-eight thousand people perished.

President Bush sent dozens of helicopters and thousands of marines, who were generally less involved than the Army and Air Force in Operation Desert Storm. They lived aboard ships off the coast of Bangladesh and entered the country every day by small boats. They provided construction and transport advisors and health care support. One U.S. Marine officer, describing the roles of his special operations units said, "They are doing what they are trained to do—seeking out the enemy and ending the threat. The enemy in this case are malnutrition, undrinkable water, and diarrhea."[38]

"It's quite a significant contribution—in people and cost involved," said Bill Harlow, a White House spokesman. "But it is not unprecedented. We have a long history of coming to the aid of people who need it."[39]

RESCUE OF THE KURDS

In their books *The Politics of Diplomacy* and *Surrender Is Not an Option*, former secretary of state James Baker and John Bolton, respectively, recount how the United States provided leadership to save Kurds who fled their homes in Iraq as a result of the first Iraq War. Bolton writes of this experience, saying, "We arrived at a small ridge and looked out over the hilly countryside that was simply covered with people. This was one of the gathering points for tens of thousands of Kurdish refugees."[40] More recently, Bolton recollected that there were hundreds of thousands of people with no shelter, food, water, or sanitation and that he was sent to Geneva to work out a UN response, with the president especially interested in UNHCR taking the lead, even though many of the Kurds were not technically refugees, as they were still within Iraq's borders.[41] Baker pounded on the doors at every level of the U.S. government to insist on action.[42] In order to ensure that the UN agencies had the support they needed, and the cooperation of the Iraqi government, the United States proposed a Security Council Resolution (688), which was adopted in April. President Bush reviewed various drafts of the resolution to ensure it provided the wording necessary to support the displaced Kurds.[43]

AFGHANISTAN

Less than two months after President Bush took office, the NSC asked Congress to support humanitarian aid to Afghanistan. It "will be essential to the reconstruction and recovery of Afghanistan and to the establishment of a legitimate Afghan government" following the withdrawal of Soviet forces.[44]

NEW INITIATIVES FROM USAID

From the beginning of his administration, the president was determined to reform the direction of and improve the systems for effective humanitarian response. He said in his 1992 Address to the UN General Assembly: "Working with our Congress, I will propose a top-to-bottom overhaul of our institutions that plan and administer foreign assistance, drastically reducing the bureaucracy that has built up around government-based programs, streamlining our delivery systems and strengthening support for private sector development and economic reform. The Agency of International Development (AID) . . . needs to be fundamentally and radically overhauled."[45]

In the 1990 Farm Bill, the administration did make such requests of Congress, which approved significant changes in its operations. Perhaps the most impactful was the creation of the Disaster Assistance Response Team (DART) "to coordinate response in crises . . . to coordinate and manage an optimal U.S. government response, while working closely with local officials, the international community, and relief agencies."[46] A new sense of urgency was created at USAID. A 24/7 operations center was created, field officers were trained for emergency response, and a comprehensive manual was developed. The efforts were led by the director of the Office of Foreign Disaster Assistance (OFDA) who was later assistant administrator for the Bureau of Food and Humanitarian Assistance, Andrew Natsios. A recruit of the White House, he would not take "no" for an answer about why a population could not be reached. His energetic, creative, and principled style helped to implement the president's vision.

From the perspective of the World Food Programme, USAID at this time was aggressive, strategic, and creative. It was demanding but reasonable and a leading partner if not sometimes *the* lead partner in global humanitarian work. Their behind-the-scenes efforts with recalcitrant governments to open humanitarian corridors saved millions of lives. WFP's work was strengthened by its foresight. For instance, just before the Bush term was ending, Natsios recommended to WFP to create a vulnerability mapping system and sent $1.1 million for its startup. That system, called VAM, has been critical to WFP's efforts to target hungry populations to receive food assistance.

LASTING CHANGE

With the thirtieth year of UNOCHA (formerly DHA) upcoming, it has a sweeping scope of responsibilities for coordinating global humanitarian relief. All major relief organizations inside and outside the UN, and all major donors, participate in this multibillion-dollar process.

WFP's humanitarian air transport system (UNHAS) and its telecommunications capacity support entire humanitarian teams. Its VAM unit is critical to pinpointing where food insecurity exists. Millions of people are fed each year. And, since 1992, it has been led by American executive directors.

Southern Africa has been, for the most part, at peace, and postapartheid South Africa has served as the economic engine that many hoped for. Human development indicators for Bangladesh are often higher than neighboring countries, including India.

The number of women serving in the United Nations has slowly but steadily increased.

The global leadership of USAID remains crucial to the stability of populations throughout the world.

The humanitarian leadership of President Bush and his administration saved lives, supported governments, and helped economies to grow. Its work had a lasting impact on the effectiveness of global humanitarian systems.

NOTES

1. George H. W. Bush, January 20, 1989, Inauguration Speech.

2. Stated in the 2011 ceremony to honor President Reagan with the GHW Bush Award for Public Service.

3. Andrew Rosenthal, "Bush Encounters the Supermarket, Amazed," *New York Times*, February 5, 1992, https://www.nytimes.com/1992/02/05/us/bush-encounters-the-supermarket -amazed.html.

4. Jon Meacham, *Destiny and Power: The American Odyssey of George Herbert Walker Bush* (New York: Random House Publishing), 154.

5. John Bolton, personal communication, August 9, 2019.

6. Ron Kaufman, personal communication, July 2, 2019.

7. Personal message from President George H. W. Bush, Bush Library at Texas A&M, International Women's Day, March 7, 1990.

8. George H. W. Bush, "Address before the 45th Session of the United Nations General Assembly in New York, New York," October 1, 1990. Public Papers, George Bush Presidential Library and Museum, https://bush41library.tamu.edu/archives/public-papers/2280.

9. Jan Eliasson, personal communication, July 8, 2019.

10. National Security Directive 74, November 24, 1992, https://bush41library.tamu.edu/ files/nsd/nsd74.pdf.

11. Andrew Natsios, *U.S. Foreign Policy and the Four Horsemen of the Apocalypse* (Washington, DC: Published with the Center for Strategic International Studies, 1997), 86.

12. Eliasson, personal communication, July 8, 2019.

13. Melinda Kimble, personal communication, July 31, 2019.

14. Boutros Boutros-Ghali, *Unvanquished* (New York: Random House Publishing, 1999), 12–13.

15. Doug Bereuter, H. Con. Res. 197, 102nd Congress, 23 October 1991, https://www .congress.gov/bill/102nd-congress/house-concurrent-resolution/197.

16. Anthony Lewis, "At Home Abroad; Hope Turned to Dust," *New York Times*, July 10, 1992, https://www.nytimes.com/1992/07/10/opinion/at-home-abroad-hope-turned-to-dust .html.

17. Catherine Bertini, personal files.

18. Catherine Bertini, personal files.

19. John Battersby, "Aid Effort Tied to Africa-Wide Security Needs," *Christian Science Monitor*, December 16, 1992, https://www.csmonitor.com/1992/1216/16092.html.

20. Natsios, *U.S. Foreign Policy*, 49.

21. Marilyn Quayle, "South Africa's Drought Emergency," *Christian Science Monitor*, June 9, 1992, https://www.csmonitor.com/1992/0609/09191.html.

22. Catherine Bertini, personal files.

23. George H. W. Bush, "Address to the United Nations General Assembly in New York City," September 21, 1992. Public Papers, George Bush Presidential Library and Museum, bush41library.tamu.edu/archives/public-papers/4820.

24. Catherine Bertini, personal files.

25. Catherine Bertini, personal files.

26. Catherine Bertini, personal files.

27. John Bolton, "Wrong Turn in Somalia," *Foreign Affairs*, January–February 1994, https://www.foreignaffairs.com/articles/somalia/1994-01-01/wrong-turn-somalia.

28. R. Kaufman, personal communication, July 2, 2019.

29. Catherine Bertini, personal files.

30. Catherine Bertini, personal files.

31. "2003: Bertini," World Food Prize, https://www.worldfoodprize.org/en/laureates/20002009_laureates/2003_bertini/.

32. Alex De Waal, *Mass Starvation: The History and Future of Famine*. Medford, MA: Polity Press, 2018), 5, 11.

33. Personal message from President George H. W. Bush, Bush Library at Texas A&M, International Women's Day, March 7, 1990.

34. R. Kaufman, personal communication, July 2, 2019.

35. M. Kimble, Personal Communication, July 31, 2019.

36. J. McLennan, Personal Communication, July 1, 2019.

37. Elsie Vartanian, Bush Library 1990.

38. Catherine Bertini, personal files.

39. Richard L. Berke, "U.S. Sends Troops to Aid Bangladesh in Cyclone Relief," *New York Times*, May 12, 1991, https://www.nytimes.com/1991/05/12/world/us-sends-troops-to-aid-bangladesh-in-cyclone-relief.html.

40. John Bolton, *Surrender Is Not an Option: Defending America at the United Nations* (New York: Threshold Editions, 2008), 40.

41. John Bolton, personal communication, August 9, 2019.

42. James A. Baker III and Thomas DeFrank, *The Politics of Diplomacy; Revolution, War and Peace* (New York: G.P. Putnam, 1995).

43. Ibid.

44. National Security Directive 5, March 18, 1989, https://fas.org/irp/offdocs/nsd/nsd5.pdf.

45. George H. W. Bush, "Address to the United Nations General Assembly in New York City," September 21, 1992.

46. Patrick J. Leahy, S.2830—Food, Agriculture, Conservation, and Trade Act of 1990. 101st Congress, November 28, 1990, https://www.congress.gov/bill/101st-congress/senate-bill/2830.

17

The Morning After

Jean Becker

Despite all his foreign policy successes as president—and a considerable number of domestic ones as well—the American people chose to deny George H. W. Bush a second term as president.

The argument continues as to why a president whose popularity was higher than 90 percent after Desert Storm could possibly lose, with the third-party candidacy of Ross Perot, late-breaking Iran-Contra indictments, and the fact that Republicans had held the White House for twelve years among the most frequently cited reasons.

The loss was, of course, a huge blow to President Bush, who felt his work neither at home nor abroad was done. But ever the gentleman and team player, he kept his disappointment largely to himself and prepared to leave the world stage.

He left this handwritten note for his successor, William Jefferson Clinton, in the top drawer of his desk in the Oval Office:

January 20, 1993

Dear Bill,
    When I walked into this office just now I felt the same sense of wonder and respect that I felt four years ago. I know you will feel that, too.
    I wish you great happiness here. I never felt the loneliness some Presidents have described.
    There will be very tough times, made even more difficult by criticism you may not think is fair. I'm not a very good one to give advice; but just don't let the critics discourage you or push you off course.
    You will be our President when you read this note. I wish you well. I wish your family well. Your success now is our country's success. I am rooting hard for you.
    Good luck—
    George

With that, President Bush returned to his hometown Houston, Texas, and to private life.

Of course, it was not meant to be. It really was not possible for the man who oversaw the end of the Cold War, masterminded the reunification of Germany, and permanently healed the deep wounds of Vietnam with the successful leadership of Desert Storm to really retire.

The world simply was not ready for him to do so. Nor was his country.

That's not to say President Bush did not keep his word to President Clinton and the presidents who followed, including his own son. He never spoke out against a sitting president's policy; if he had advice to give, he did so privately.

But the world sought him out, time and again.

Three quick stories illustrate the influence and respect President Bush maintained around the world until he died:

- In December 1994, while visiting Japan, he mentioned he would love to visit with Emperor Akihito. His traveling aide, Michael Dannenhauer, remembers the moment well: "On a trip to Japan, President Bush mentioned to one of his Japanese 'minders' that he wondered if the emperor was in town and if he might drop by to see him. Well, you would have thought he had asked to go to the moon and back in one afternoon. We were basically told, in a giggling kind of way, 'No one sees the emperor. His schedule is set months and months in advance.' They sort of giggled that they'd check into it. Well, a couple hours or even less later, the 'minder' sheepishly came back to me to say the emperor would LOVE to see President Bush, so off to the Imperial Palace we went!"
- When Israeli Prime Minister Yitzhak Rabin was assassinated in November 1995, President Clinton asked the former presidents to accompany him to the funeral, which President Bush and President Carter did. President Bush confessed to me when he returned that he was almost embarrassed by how many heads of state attending the funeral asked to meet with him, adding that he felt like he was holding rogue bilateral meetings. He wrote his good friend Hugh Sidey "At the funeral I had a chance to greet many heads of state with whom I had dealt. It was a wonderful reunion for me even though the occasion was very sad. Helmut Kohl sought me out. . . . John Major gave me the warmest of greetings. . . . I sat next to Turkey's charming Prime Minister Ciller. . . . [Hosni] Mubarak renewed his invitation to visit Egypt. . . . I had a very nice visit with the King Hussein of Jordan."[1]
- At the very end of 2004, after a horrific Christmas Day tsunami devastated parts of South Asia, the president of the United States, George W. Bush, asked his father and former president Clinton to work together to help raise money in the private sector for the affected countries. They both readily said yes, and as part of their mission, the two presidents traveled to Thailand, Indonesia, Sri Lanka, and the Maldives in February 2005. (That trip was indeed the beginning of their friendship, dubbed the Odd Couple by Barbara Bush.) The State

Department appointed a career ambassador to travel with the two of them, to be both their briefer and to take notes in their meetings with the head of state in each country. On the plane trip home, the ambassador came and sat next to me and simply said, "I am going through all my notes and I just want to say one thing: President Clinton talked the most; President Bush said the most." Then he got up and quietly went back to his seat.

There are many such stories of heads of state seeking President Bush's counsel. They knew him. They trusted him. They respected him.

After leaving office, President Bush became a member of the paid speaking circuit, which resulted in extensive travel overseas. As his aide Dannenhauer remembers the immediate aftermath of the 1992 election, "President Bush was treated as if he was still a head of state. No matter where we went, the world leaders still wanted to meet with him while he was in their particular county. Presidents, prime ministers, kings and queens—even dictators. I think the world honestly couldn't believe he had lost the election."

His popularity was such that numerous countries awarded him their highest honor—their equivalent of the United States' Medal of Freedom: Germany, Kuwait, Albania, Bahrain, Qatar, United Arab Emirates, Hungary, Poland, Saudi Arabia, Italy, Kazakhstan, Dominican Republic, the Czech Republic, and Nicaragua—who gave him their highest honor twice, by two different presidents.

Queen Elizabeth bestowed upon him the Most Honourable Order of the Bath-Knight Grand Cross, which made President Bush a knight. (Mrs. Bush was only mildly amused when he asked her to call him "Sir George.")

Of course, not everyone loved, respected, and honored him. While visiting Kuwait shortly after leaving office, American and Kuwaiti intelligence uncovered a plot by Saddam Hussein to assassinate President Bush. President Clinton later ordered a bombing raid in Iraq to retaliate, targeting the Iraqi Intelligence Service headquarters where the plot had been hatched.

And then there was President Bush's rather harrowing journey from Damascus, Syria, to Beirut, Lebanon, during a tour of the Middle East in Spring 1996. During the journey, intelligence sources warned the Secret Service that they had intelligence that President Bush's plane might be targeted by ground-to-air missiles when he flew into Lebanese air space. The Secret Service, of course, urged President Bush to cancel the Lebanese portion of his journey. But President Bush did not want to disappoint Lebanon's prime minister, Rafic Hariri, as he was to be the highest-ranking visitor to that country in decades. President Bush mentioned his dilemma while meeting with President Hafez al-Assad, who offered to give him his own security forces to protect him while driving, not flying, to Beirut—an eighty-five-mile drive through the mountains inhabited by terrorists. Dannenhauer remembers the journey well:

So off we went by car, through the most mountainous road. Like cloak and dagger. I was in a separate car and had no idea what car President Bush was in. At the front and back of our little motorcade were two SUVs with turret like machine guns mounted on their roofs. At the top of this mountain range we stopped and had to switch to a different set of cars! During the transition, President Bush of course agreed to take photos with Assad's security detail. The Secret Service was not particularly thrilled.

President Bush wrote Sidey after the visit: "It would have been a real setback for Lebanon if I had had to cancel out on the dinner—particularly on such short notice. Nothing could have made the cancellation anything other than a terrible slap in the face of Lebanon." (Ironically, Hariri was assassinated by a suicide bomber with presumed ties to Syria in 2005.)

So what happened in all these meetings with heads of state? Having witnessed one or two and having read all of President Bush's letters to Sidey, most of them followed a similar pattern: Exchange of pleasantries, an update on the family, sometimes a little gossip, and always a long discussion of current events. Often advice and opinions were sought and given.

President Bush was discreet then, and we will be discreet now.

Before and after his trips, President Bush often briefed his friends and former teammates—former secretary of state James Baker and former national security advisor Brent Scowcroft. And sometimes the current president and current secretary of state, especially if that president was also a son. But except for this small group, and his friend Sidey, perhaps the only other people to whom President Bush entrusted the details of these meetings were his former associates at the CIA. Like all former presidents, President Bush was offered—and he accepted—daily intelligence briefings. But his relationship with the agency he once headed was a special one. After all, the name of CIA headquarters is the George Bush Center for Intelligence.

So perhaps former aide Gian-Carlo Peressutti should not have been surprised by this incident during a visit with Russian President Boris Yeltsin in 1998:

President Bush was received by President Yeltsin in their equivalent of the Oval Office, and there was a massive amount of media covering the meeting. I remember standing in a room off the one where they were meeting when one of our agents came running in and told me I needed to go into the meeting room and sit behind President Bush. I told him he was crazy. Actually, I said something else. Seconds later a huge Russian came running in and started yelling at me. That's when, with legs of Jell-O, I crept into the formal meeting room and took a seat behind Forty-one, hoping the seat cushion would swallow me up and I'd vanish inconspicuously.

When we were in the car with the doors closed, President Bush turned to me and said, "When you get back to your room, I want you to immediately write down every single thing you remember about that meeting. From what was said, to how Boris acted and your thoughts on his state of mind." What a guy, I thought. My boss knew how historic what I just experienced was and he wanted me to have my own record of the encounter for posterity. Well, not quite. Later on, having done what President Bush asked, he came into my room with his own handwritten series of pages and handed them to me. "You know why I asked you to do this, right?" He could tell by the look on my face that I was now not quite sure. He continued, "Our briefers back at home will be very interested in every detail of that meeting, no matter how small or inconsequential they may seem." Ah. Now I got it. And just like that, I had become a spy for the United States of America.

Although most of President Bush's international travel was private, he also represented the United States numerous times at official events, including:

- The reopening of the U.S. Embassy in Berlin in 2008.
- Several inaugurations: President Zedillo of Mexico in 1994; President Calderon of Mexico in 2006; and President Silva of Portugal in 2006;
- President and Mrs. Bush headed the U.S. delegation for the Opening of the Summer Olympics to Athens, Greece, in 2004.[2]
- In January 2006, he traveled to Pakistan, as part of his role as UN special envoy for the Southeast Asian earthquake, which had struck the region the previous October. The United Nations, when they asked him to take on this task, assured him all he had to do was write a few letters asking for disaster relief funds. President Bush's response was "nonsense." He insisted on visiting the region and learning firsthand what needed to be done.

And although President Bush did not attend enough funerals to re-earn the mantra "You die, I fly"—given to him by his good friend James Baker when, as vice president, George Bush became famous for the number of funerals he attended—he did attend a number of them on behalf of the United States during his post-presidency:

- As previously mentioned, Prime Minister Rabin of Israel in 1995.
- King Hussein of Jordan in 1999, accompanying President Clinton and former presidents Ford and Carter.
- Pope John Paul II in 2005, part of the delegation headed by President George W. Bush and First Lady Laura Bush, along with former president Clinton.
- President Yeltsin in 2007, accompanied by former president Clinton.

President Bush very much enjoyed the camaraderie of these funerals, seeing old friends and making new ones.

Former aide Jim Appleby remembers the surreal experience of marching in the funeral procession with Presidents Bush and Clinton at Yeltsin's funeral:

The procession itself was something I'll never forget—completely and quintessentially Russian, the casket was pulled at the head, and the road that we walked on was a sunken road with the berms on either side lined with Russians, all crying and/or paying respects. Due to the fact that we had to walk to the gravesite, I was actually in the procession right behind President Bush and President Clinton. With them were the heads of all the former East Bloc countries. The service at the cemetery was relatively brief, with a military procession, the movement of the casket to the gravesite, some words by various people, and then, at the end, a bit of milling about as people mingled and seemed to catch up with others. President Bush was in his element—these were many of the people he'd known, it seemed, while he was president and vice president. He was happy to see them, and they seemed even happier to see him.

President Bush wrote this letter to his five children after King Hussein's funeral:

It was name-dropper's paradise. . . . I saw many friends and met some of the leaders who have come onto the scene since I left. Almost everyone I talked to asked what the Governor of Texas is going to do, just as they all inquired "What's it like to have two of your sons as governor?"[3]

I did not meet the Iraqi or Iranian delegations. In fact I never saw them or if I did, I didn't identify them.

I talked to P.M. Netanyahu, President Weizman, Challenger [Ehud] Barak and Shimo Peres—all from Israel. [Yitzhak] Mordechai was there but I did not meet him. Netanyahu was pleased to have brought those who are running against him on the fifteen-minute helicopter flight from Israel.

George, President Weizman and PM Netanyahu volunteered that you had made a very favorable impression in Israel. President Mubarak of Egypt said essentially the same thing. All with whom I spoke hoped that you will run—amazing breadth to this sentiment. It was more than being nice to an old father—me.

I saw Yeltsin sitting on a couch. His aides pulled him to his feet. His face truly lit up as he asked about your Mom and greeted me with a huge bear hug. He looked very badly, but in our brief and extraordinarily friendly conversation he seemed to be totally lucid.

I visited with all the Gulf leaders—all friends of mine. Among them Crown Prince Abdullah of Saudi Arabia, Bahrain's Emir Isa bin Salman Al Khalifa, Sultan Qaboos of Oman, Prince Mohammed of the Emirates, the Crown Prince of Kuwait. I even had a long chat with Yemen's President Saleh whom I know quite well, a man who I had visited in Sana'a but with whom I got cross-threaded when Yemen sided with Saddam Hussein.

I even had a nice chat with President Assad of Syria, the Crown Prince and Prime Minister of Japan. Also President Chirac of France, my old friends Queen Beatrix of the Netherlands, King Juan Carlos of Spain, and the Aga Khan. Demirel, President Turkey, Crown Prince of Morocco, Sweden and Norway's royalty, you name it—they were all there.

I met Tony Blair for the first time—a most attractive young man. I also had a long talk with Prince Charles who remembered most pleasantly his visits to Washington and Camp David when I was President. I did not ask about Camilla . . . after all, I was a diplomat.

Have I now re-established my own name-dropping credentials? I could go on and on. The truth is I really enjoyed seeing all these people, but it did make me realize that I still do miss the part of my job that had me interacting with all of these folks.

It is oh so different for me now. No agenda, no authority have I. It was simply a chance to greet friends.

Perhaps the best story to illustrate the reality of "it is so different for me now," was an incident that occurred at the funeral of Pope John Paul II. Former aide Tom Frechette remembers:

When we landed in Rome, although it was after midnight, the delegation went straight from the airport to the Vatican, to pay their respects to the pope, who was lying in state. The president invited his dad and President Clinton to ride in the presidential limo with him to the Vatican. When we came out of St. Peter's, POTUS and the First Lady were headed to our ambassador's residence, where they would spend the night; we were headed to a hotel. The president asked his dad and President Clinton if they needed a ride. They assured him they did not; their own motorcade was nearby. POTUS seemed hesitant to leave his dad and a former president standing in St. Peter's Square at such a late hour. But they insisted again, so the huge presidential motorcade sped away. And when they were gone, there wasn't a car in sight. The square was empty. The Secret Service, [President Clinton's aide] Doug Band, and I panicked and started running about looking for our motorcade. The two presidents just continued chatting, seemingly unconcerned they were without transportation in a strange country at such a late hour. As it turns out, our cars had been left out on the street, outside the Vatican gates, since the president's motorcade had filled the square. I guess the presidents were right not to panic.

In addition to President Bush's own travels, many current and former heads of state came to Houston, to Kennebunkport, or to his presidential library in College Station, Texas, to pay their respects. Lech Walesa, John Major, Brian Mulroney, Toshiki Kaifu of Japan, Ruud Lubbers of the Netherlands, and John Swan of Bermuda all attended the opening of the George Bush Library Center at Texas A&M in 1997. Tony Blair and Jiang Zemin both gave major addresses at the library center when they were in office. Mikhail Gorbachev, Helmut Kohl, Brian Mulroney, and John Major all visited the library and Kennebunkport. Brian and Mila Mulroney came to Maine almost every summer, and John and Norma Major likewise were frequent visitors. President Bush hosted numerous high-level Middle Eastern visitors in Maine and Texas and hosted a lunch for Crown Prince Mohammed bin Salman of Saudi Arabia at his Houston home, along with the forty-third president and Secretary Baker, just a few months before he died.

President Karzai of Afghanistan made a secret journey to Kennebunkport to seek President Bush's advice, where President Nazarbayev of Kazakhstan also came to pay his respects. PLO leader Yasser Arafat visited President Bush's home in Houston.

Perhaps one of the more unusual visitors President Bush had was Saif Gaddafi, one of the sons of Libyan dictator Muammar Gaddafi. Saif came in November 2008. (This time I was the notetaker.) At the time, he was considered someone "the United States could deal with," which is why Secretary of State Condoleezza Rice asked President Bush if he would meet with him on his tour of the country. Among the questions the son asked President Bush was: "Did the United States orchestrate Iraq's invasion of Kuwait in 1990 so the Americans could go in and kill Saddam Hussein?" President Bush assured him the United States did not do such things.

One of many recurring visitors was the emir of Qatar, Sheikh Hamad bin Khalifa al-Thani, who felt very close to President Bush. The emir once left a planeload of his senior advisers and family members sitting on the tarmac in Houston so he could have dinner with President and Mrs. Bush at their home. Chase Untermeyer, who served as ambassador to Qatar under President George W. Bush, made these observations on this friendship:

> President Bush's two visits to Qatar while I was serving as ambassador were extraordinarily helpful in maintaining a relationship essential to the United States at a time we were prosecuting the wars in Iraq and Afghanistan. The national security apparatus in Washington disliked the coverage of both wars by Al Jazeera, the Arabic-language network owned by and located in Qatar, and treated Qatar as almost a hostile power. This was despite the Qataris' giving the U.S. and its coalition partners complete and cost-free access to the huge Al Udeid Air Base.
>
> Because of the Al Jazeera issue, neither the president, vice president, secretary of state, secretary of defense, nor the national security advisor visited Qatar during my three years there. Into the void stepped George H. W. Bush. The high regard in which the Qataris held him and the great hospitality they showed him showed that, despite tensions with Washington just then, the relationship with the U.S. would abide. For this the senior officers of the Central Command were deeply grateful to the former president.

It would not be incorrect to say that President Bush served as an informal special envoy from the United States to the rest of the world—not just Qatar—very quietly spreading goodwill while listening carefully to what others around the world were thinking.

He would not approve of that assessment. He would worry that it was "Carteresque." Despite his friendship with President Carter, President Bush had been disappointed when he learned President Carter had lobbied members of the United Nations Security Council against supporting Desert Storm. President Bush was determined to stay out of the way and out of the business of the sitting president and not have his own foreign policy agenda.

Nevertheless, the stories of President Bush's interaction with foreign visitors and friends during the twenty-five years of his post-presidency are truly endless. He hunted with King Juan Carlos of Spain, fished with Russian president Vladimir Putin, and played golf with Argentinian president Carlos Menem.

He may have left the world stage, but he never lost interest in what was happening in the world. As he wrote Sidey in 1994, on his way to a visit to Albania: "Why are you going to Albania? That's what our friends asked me, that's what Portugal's wonderful Prime Minister Anibal Cavaco Silva asked me—why Albania? I went because I wanted to see what happens to a country when it moves out of the darkest of the dark totalitarian ages into freedom."

President Bush also never lost interest in the future. When he chose Texas A&M University as the home of his presidential library, part of the deal he made with the university was that they would establish a master's degree program that would help train future public servants. The George Bush School of Government and Public Service already has earned the reputation of graduating some of the best career foreign service officers, city managers, policy experts, nonprofit leaders, and more than a few CIA operatives. He hated the word *legacy* but admitted the Bush School was just that.

The respect given President Bush around the world was perhaps best characterized by Brian Mulroney, in his eulogy given at President Bush's state funeral at the National Cathedral in Washington, D.C.:

> [In] fifty or one hundred years from now, as historians review the accomplishments and context of all who have served as president, I believe it will be said that, in the life of this country—which is in my judgement, the greatest democratic republic that God has ever placed on the face of this earth—no occupant of the Oval Office was more courageous, more principled and more honorable than George Herbert Walker Bush. . . . There is a word for this: it is called "leadership"—and let me tell you that when George Bush was president of the United States of America, every single head of government in the world knew they were dealing with a true gentlemen, a genuine leader—one who was distinguished, resolute, and brave.

NOTES

1. President Bush and Hugh Sidey, a former *Time* magazine correspondent and a presidential historian, corresponded frequently after President Bush left the White House in 1993 up until Hugh died in 2005.

2. President Bush also attended the opening ceremonies of the 2008 Summer Olympics in Beijing, but he did so as Honorary Captain of the U.S. Olympic Team. President George W. Bush and First Lady Laura Bush headed the American delegation to Beijing.

3. George W. Bush was governor of Texas and Jeb Bush was governor of Florida at this time.

Index

Middle East policy: Arab-Israeli conflict
relation to, 122–26, 132, 141; under
Carter, 102, 106, 138; after Gulf War,
14, 15, 26, 133,141; Haass role in and
approach to, 103–10; legacy from, 134;
Madrid Peace Conference and, 14,
18, 26, 117, 123, 126, 133, 137, 141;
NSD and, 103–4; realism in approach
to, 20, 122, 141; relationships with
regional leaders and, 5, 121–22, 240,
241. *See also* Gulf Crisis and War; *specific
countries*
military: Baker on, threat without action, 4;
strong and actionable, belief in, 4, 13,
17; transparency, Open Skies Agreement
on, 71–72; UNITAF forces, 218n5
military interventions: doctrine of
overwhelming force with, 219n9; in
Panama, 9, 48, 103, 146, 179; personal
responsibility for, 135n13; successful
initiations of, 4,. *See also* Gulf Crisis and
War; humanitarian assistance; Kurds;
Somalia
military service: combat injury during, 2, 3;
worldview and philosophies influenced
by, 2, 6, 13, 17, 101; World War II, 2,
3, 6, 11–12, 13, 17, 44, 62, 204
Mitterrand, François: on conventional arms
and forces negotiations, 73; Germany
reunification and, 78; Germany support
under, 82; Kurdish crisis relief work by
wife of, 174; Reagan relationship with,
79; relationship and meetings with, 14,
72–73, 79, 87, 106, 111
Mubarak, Hosni, 5, 111, 121, 127–28, 138,
236, 240
Mullins, Janet, 37
Mulroney, Brian: on Bertini as WFP lead,
228; Eastern Europe policy meeting
with, 61, 62; funeral eulogy for Bush, G.
H. W., 243; relationship and meetings
with, 61, 62, 106, 161–62, 241, 243;
World Summit for Children support of,
190
multilateralism, 12, 17, 25, 194–95, 213–
14, 216, 222
Muskie, Edmund S., 42–43

NAFTA. *See* North American Free Trade
Agreement
Namibia, 177–78, 216
Nandan, Satya, 179
National Security Act of 1947, 18, 43
National Security Council (NSC): Blackwill
role at, 65, 67, 70-1, 74, 76–77; Clinton
administration transition of, 41–42,
53n3; crises during presidency for, 48;
Deputies Committee members and
meetings, 46, 47, 50, 54n24, 64, 104–5,
108–9, 119, 144, 146, 198; Gates role
at, 19–20, 46–47, 49, 64–65, 76, 91,
103, 108, 146; Germany reunification
advice from, 49, 76–77, 79; Iran-
Contra affair handling by, 42, 48; Iraq
policy reviews by, 103;Kurdish crisis
response and, 143, 144, 156; pressures
and work schedule for staff of, 48,
49; under Reagan, 44; reforms, 6, 8,
41–51,; reforms, process for, 46–48;
Scowcroft leadership of, 6, 19–20,
41–51, 54n26, 64; staffing of, 49–50,
54n26, 54n31, 55n34, 64; staff legacies,
39, 50, 55nn35–36; Tower Commission
investigation and recommendations
for, 6, 19, 42–44, 64; vice presidency
experience with, 12, 35
National Security Directives (NSD), 103–4,
186, 196, 223
NATO. *See* North Atlantic Treaty
Organization
Natsios, Andrew: Kurdish crisis intervention
role of, 118, 145–46, 153; Somalia relief
role of, 209, 217; on South African
drought relief, 225
natural disasters. *See* Disaster Assistance
Response Team; disasters, natural
Navy, U.S. *See* military service
Negroponte, John, 37
Nesen, Robert, 40n4
Neustadt, Richard, 39
Nicaragua, 13, 37, 42, 61, 237. *See also*
Iran-Contra affair
Nixon, Richard, 20, 32, 59; China relations
under, 23, 89; Scowcroft position and
experience under, 42, 43, 45, 46

UN High Commissioner for Refugees (UNHCR), 148, 188, 192, 225, 231
UNITAF. *See* United Task Force
United Kingdom: Germany divide with, 73; knighting by, 237; relations with, 14; on SNF debates, 67, 76; in UNSC presidency, 100. *See also* Major, John and Thatcher, Margaret
United Nations (UN), 39n1; ambassadorship at, 3, 12, 17, 31, 32, 44, 102, 140, 167, 183, 222; Cold War end role of, 178; CSW ambassadorship, 229–30; El Salvador peace agreement negotiation under, 176–77; humanitarian assistance agency historically for, 223; humanitarian assistance coordination, 194–95, 199, 222–24, 232; Hussein, S., met with, 171; ICCPR adoption by, 196–98; Iraqi embargo resolution meeting at, 107–8; Law of the Sea Treaty and, 179–80; Namibia independence role of, 177–78; reforms, 180; Responsibility to Protect report of, 149; Soviet Union collapse response from, 178; states recognition by and admission to, 49; Taiwan in, failure to keep, 32, 89; Universal Declaration of Human Rights, 185, 197; World Summit for Children, 189–91; "Zionism is Racism" resolution repeal by, 126, 175–76. *See also* World Food Programme
United Nations Security Council (UNSC): Britain assuming presidency of, 100; Cheney on awaiting resolution on Kuwait from, 110, 130; China resistance/support for Gulf War resolution of, 98-99, 110, 111, 112, 169, 170; design and purpose of, 167, 168; diplomacy focus and approach with, 4–5, 13, 138, 171; Gulf War humanitarian relief of, 170, 171; Gulf War military force approval from and role of, 5, 13, 25, 98–99, 105–12, 129, 130–31, 138, 167–75, 191,; Gulf War resolutions details, 169-74; Gulf War termination and, 171–72; Kurdish crisis

response from, 144, 148, 174, 231; meeting logistics, 168, 178; nonaligned members of, 168, 169, 175–76, 179; Operation Restore Hope approval from, 198, 227; Panama conflict resolution under, 179; peacekeeping summit in 1992, 196; Russia role on, 178; Shevardnadze at meeting on Kuwait at, 107–8; Somalia crisis response role of, 175, 198, 209–10, 213; UNSCOM disarmament mission, 174; vetoes on Gulf War resolutions, 168, 169, 170, 171
United Nations Transition Assistance Group (UNTAG), 177-78
United States. *See specific topics*
United Task Force (UNITAF), 218n5
Universal Declaration of Human Rights, 185, 197
UN Office for the Coordination of Humanitarian Affairs (UNOCHA): creation of, 194-5, 199, 222–24; global impact of, 232; mandates for, 224; South African drought relief and, 224–26
UNSC. *See* United Nations Security Council
UNTAG. *See* United Nations Transition Assistance Group
Untermeyer, Chase, 36, 38, 242
"Uruguay Round" global trade talks, 74, 160–61, 164
U.S., Mexico, Canada Agreement (USMCA), 165–66
U.S. Agency for International Development (USAID): funding increase for, 7, 143, 146–47, 156,; global leadership of, 232; Natsios leadership of, 155; reform efforts for, 231–32; Somalia relief efforts role of, 204, 208, 209, 211, 216–17, 218n1; State Department coordination with, 145; UN humanitarian assistance coordination support from, 223. *See also* Disaster Assistance Response Team
U.S. government and policy. *See specific topics*
USMCA. *See* U.S., Mexico, Canada Agreement

About the Contributors

James A. Baker III served in senior government positions under three U.S. presidents. He served as the nation's sixty-first secretary of state from January 1989 through August 1992 under President George H. W. Bush. During his tenure at the State Department, Baker traveled to ninety foreign countries as the United States confronted the unprecedented challenges and opportunities of the post–Cold War era. Baker's reflections on those years of revolution, war, and peace—*The Politics of Diplomacy*—was published in 1995. Baker served as the sixty-seventh secretary of the treasury from 1985 to 1988 under President Ronald Reagan. From 1981 to 1985, he served as White House chief of staff to President Reagan. Baker's record of public service began in 1975 as undersecretary of commerce to President Gerald Ford. It concluded with his service as White House chief of staff and senior counselor to President Bush from August 1992 to January 1993. Baker is presently a senior partner in the law firm of Baker Botts. He is the honorary chairman of the James A. Baker III Institute for Public Policy at Rice University and serves on the board of the Howard Hughes Medical Institute.

Nancy Bearg served as national security advisor to Vice President Bush during the Reagan administration, and was national security council director for international programs and public diplomacy during the Bush presidency, where her portfolio included U.S. policy on refugees and immigration, humanitarian assistance, peace-keeping, foreign assistance, human rights, and public diplomacy. She has also served as staff member on the Senate Armed Services Committee; director of policy analysis for the Near East, Africa, and South Asia at the Department of Defense; deputy assistant secretary of the Air Force; founder and director of the Aspen Institute's International Peace, Security, and Prosperity program; and president/CEO of an international development NGO.

Jean Becker was President Bush's chief of staff from 1994 until his death. Along the way, she oversaw the opening of the George H. W. Bush Library in 1997; edited his book of letters, published in 1999; and helped organize the commissioning of the aircraft carrier USS *George H. W. Bush* in 2009.

Catherine Bertini was the first American executive director of the UN World Food Programme and the third woman to run a UN agency, having been recommended by President George H. W. Bush to the United Nations. She is credited with leading a transformational change of WFP for which she was awarded the 2003 World Food Prize. Since leaving the UN, Ms. Bertini has taught at the Maxwell School of Citizenship and Public Affairs at Syracuse University and served as a fellow at the Bill & Melinda Gates Foundation and the Rockefeller Foundation. Currently, she is a distinguished fellow at the Chicago Council on Global Affairs, where she has chaired multiple reports on agricultural development policies, development programming for rural girls, and international organization leadership.

Andrew H. Card Jr. was named Interim CEO of the George & Barbara Bush Foundation in June 2020. He continues to serve as Chairman of the National Endowment for Democracy (NED), a nonprofit organization dedicated to the growth and strengthening of democratic institutions around the world, a position he assumed in January 2018. Card has also held numerous positions at senior levels of government under three U.S. presidents throughout the years, including Chief of Staff to President George W. Bush, where Card became the second longest tenured White House Chief of Staff. Card served as Deputy Chief of Staff to President George H. W. Bush, as well as U.S. Secretary of Transportation, and served President Ronald Reagan as a Deputy Assistant to the President for Intergovernmental Affairs. He also served eight years in the Massachusetts House of Representatives.

The Honorable **Edward P. Djerejian**'s Foreign Service career spanned eight presidential administrations, from Kennedy to Clinton. During the George H. W. Bush administration, he served as ambassador to Syria and assistant secretary of state for Near Eastern affairs, before going on to become ambassador to Israel during the Clinton administration. Following his retirement from government service, he became the first director of Rice University's Baker Institute for Public Policy. He is the author of *Danger and Opportunity: An American Ambassador's Journey through the Middle East.*

Richard Haass is president of the Council on Foreign Relations. From 1989 to 1993 he was special assistant to the president and senior director for the Near East and South Asia on the National Security Council. He worked previously in the Pentagon during the Carter administration and in the State Department under Ronald Reagan, and subsequently in the State Department (as director of policy planning) under George W. Bush. The author or editor of fourteen books on U.S. foreign policy or international relations, he holds a BA degree from Oberlin College and the MPhil and DPhil degrees from Oxford University.

Ambassador **Carla A. Hills** served as United States trade representative from 1989 to 1993. She led the U.S. negotiations in the Uruguay Round of multilateral trade talks, concluded the North American Free Trade Agreement, and entered into a substantial number of trade and investment agreements with countries around the world. Earlier, she served as secretary of the Department of Housing and Urban Development and as assistant attorney general in the Civil Division of the U.S. Department of Justice. Currently, Ambassador Hills is chairman and chief executive officer of Hills & Company, International Consultants, which provides advice to U.S. businesses on investment, trade, and risk assessment issues in emerging market economies globally.

Robert Kimmitt served as undersecretary of state for political affairs from 1989 to 1991, advising the president and secretary of state during the Gulf Crisis and War. His service in this capacity led George H. W. Bush to award him the Presidential Citizens Medal, the country's second-highest civilian award. From 1991 to 1993, he served as U.S. ambassador to Germany, and later during the Bush 43 administration as deputy secretary of the U.S. Treasury, where he led U.S. negotiations for the International Compact with Iraq. He is an honor graduate of West Point and a combat veteran of the Vietnam War.

During the George H. W. Bush administration, **James Kunder** served as director of USAID's Office of U.S. Foreign Disaster Assistance, where he played a major role in delivering U.S. humanitarian aid to Somalia and deployed there to prepare for the president's 1992 humanitarian intervention using U.S. troops. He has served in several other USAID posts, including deputy administrator, assistant administrator for Asia and the Near East, and director for relief and reconstruction in Afghanistan. Kunder has authored numerous publications on international humanitarian issues, reconstruction, peacekeeping, and crisis management.

Jane Holl Lute served as the last director for European and Soviet Affairs on the National Security Council Staff from 1991 to 1994. Ms. Lute began her professional career as an officer in the U.S. Army, with service in Europe, the United States, and in the Middle East during the 1991 Gulf War. She served in various capacities in the United Nations and as deputy secretary of the U.S. Department of Homeland Security. Ms. Lute holds a PhD in political science from Stanford University and a JD from Georgetown University Law Center.

Dayton Maxwell led the Disaster Assistance Response Team during Operation Provide Comfort in 1991. He has worked in development assistance and crisis response management since 1959, serving in diverse posts with the U.S. Agency for International Development with work in Laos, Chad, Niger, Bosnia, and Iraq. He also served as the head of the Coalition Provisional Authority's office of policy planning and analysis in Baghdad in 2003.

Andrew S. Natsios served as director of USAID's Office of U.S. Foreign Disaster Assistance during the George H. W. Bush administration, where he oversaw the U.S. relief effort in several humanitarian emergencies. Currently, he is an executive professor at the Bush School of Government and Public Service at Texas A&M University and director of the Scowcroft Institute of International Affairs. Natsios was formerly a distinguished professor in the practice of diplomacy at the Walsh School of Foreign Service at Georgetown University and former administrator of the U.S. Agency for International Development under George W. Bush. He is the author of three books, including *Sudan, South Sudan and Darfur: What Everyone Needs to Know* (2012).

Douglas H. Paal is a distinguished fellow at the Carnegie Endowment for International Peace. He previously served as vice chairman of JPMorgan Chase International (2006–2008) and was an unofficial U.S. representative to Taiwan as director of the American Institute in Taiwan (2002–2006). He was on the National Security Council staffs of Presidents Reagan and George H. W. Bush between 1986 and 1993 as director of Asian Affairs and then as senior director and special assistant to the president. Paal held positions in the policy planning staff at the State Department, as a senior analyst for the CIA, and at U.S. embassies in Singapore and Beijing. He has spoken and published frequently on Asian affairs and national security issues.

Ambassador **Thomas R. Pickering** served as ambassador to the United Nations during the George H. W. Bush administration. His four-decade career in the State Department's Foreign Service also included ambassadorships in Russia, India, Israel, El Salvador, Nigeria, and Jordan. After his retirement, the State Department's Foreign Affairs Fellowship Program was renamed the Thomas R. Pickering Foreign Affairs Fellowship Program to honor his service.

In the George H. W. Bush administration, **Condoleezza Rice** served on the National Security Council as Soviet and Eastern European affairs advisor during the dissolution of the Soviet Union and reunification of Germany. Later, she served as the sixty-sixth U.S. secretary of state in the administration of George W. Bush, a role in which she worked to expand the number of well-governed, democratic states able to meet the needs of their citizens. She currently teaches at Stanford University.

Dennis Ross was the director of policy planning in the State Department for much of the Bush 41 presidency. Asked to stay on for an interim period by the Clinton administration, he became the administration's envoy to Middle East peace, serving until January 2001. He served three years in the Obama administration, first in the State Department and then in the White House as special assistant to the president and senior director of the central region. Currently, he is counselor at the Washington Institute for Near East Policy and distinguished professor in the practice of diplomacy at Georgetown. He is the author of several books, including *The Missing Peace, Statecraft,* and *Doomed to Succeed.*

Horst Teltschik was the national security advisor to Chancellor Helmut Kohl, who led Germany through the end of the Cold War and reunification. During this time, Mr. Teltschik communicated almost daily with U.S. national security advisor Brent Scowcroft. As such, he has intimate knowledge of the diplomacy that occurred behind the scenes to bring about the reunification of Germany.

Ambassador **Chase Untermeyer** served as assistant to President George H. W. Bush, a role he filled until 1991 when he became the director of Voice of America. Following a decade in the private sector, he returned to public service in 2004 as U.S. ambassador to Qatar, a post he held until 2007. Ambassador Untermeyer currently serves as chairman of Humanities Texas, the state humanities council.

Philip Zelikow served the George H. W. Bush administration on the National Security Council, where he was deeply involved in the process of German reunification at the end of the Cold War. His work in the public sphere also includes extensive service with the U.S. Navy and the State Department. Currently, he is a professor of history at the University of Virginia, and previously served as the director of the university's Miller Center, the preeminent institute for studies of American presidential history. He has published several books on presidential history and American foreign policy, including *Germany Unified and Europe Transformed: A Study in Statecraft* (with Condoleezza Rice).